Human Error Prevention

BW (Ben) Marguglio

Bookinars™, Inc.
Cold Spring, NY, USA

ISBN 978-0-9817100-1-3
LCCN 2008903207

First printing 2008

Introduction

In addition to discovery, invention and improvement in human health, human error prevention can be the greatest contributor to higher productivity, safety and quality. Thus, the subject is meritorious.

This book is unique in its format. This book is written as a seminar using a PowerPoint presentation in "Notes Page" format. It's better than a seminar, better than a webinar; it's a Bookinar™!

One may read this Bookinar™ as if attending a seminar, with the presenter displaying a slide and speaking the words that appear in the notes block below the slide. In this format, this Bookinar™ is a relatively easy read, especially considering the scope and complexity of the subject. Also, it enables self-paced learning.

The information in this Bookinar™ is substantially original. For example, there are taxonomies, models and templates that never before have been published and only seen earlier in this presenter's public and in-house seminars.

Obviously, for the sake of continuity and logical development of a theme, this Bookinar™ covers some information that may be similar to that which has been published previously. However, even for this information, this Bookinar™ provides substantial originality—improvements in and different ways by which to understand and implement the information.

Given the intent to provide information that is of value and unique and original, this Bookinar™ does not present information that is already available in many other books. For example, the subject of *human factors analysis*, as a tool used in the design of administrative and technical processes and equipment, is merely noted here and there.

Within its scope and intent, this Bookinar™ is complete and presented with a high degree of specificity. The completeness and specificity are such that the "take-aways"—the principles and practices—can be directly implemented.

Throughout the Bookinar™, in the notes, certain words, terms and ideas are printed in italics. This convention is to alert the reader that the words, terms or ideas have a specific management or technical meaning or significance.

Also, immediately following the use of such words, terms or ideas, there may be a cross reference to other pages in which the definitions of these words or terms are provided or in which the same or related ideas are addressed. This convention is intended save the reader's time. The reader may go to the cross-referenced page(s) directly, without having to search an Index. Otherwise, the reader may disregard the cross-reference.

Obviously, the implementation of the foregoing conventions took additional time. Hopefully, these conventions are well worth the benefits to the reader.

On some pages, a question (or two) is asked, just as might be asked in a live seminar to encourage participation. The answer(s) is given immediately below or on the next page.

BW (Ben) Marguglio

Acknowledgement

With fifty-three years of experience, working with high technology enterprises, there is no reasonable way by which to thank my professional predecessors, and organizational supervisors, peers and subordinates who have taught me so much and who have given me the foundation with which to create this Bookinar™. They have my sincerest appreciation. They've done one of the kindest things that can be done. They shared knowledge. This Bookinar™ is intended to do the same.

Thanks also to the staff at About Books, Inc. for their expertise and assistance in the publishing of this Bookinar™, and especially to Cathy Bowman who worked with me on the cover design and page layout.

BW (Ben) Marguglio

Purchasing and Licensing:

To purchase this Bookinar™, please visit www.Bookinars.biz

or

To purchase this Bookinar™, please send to the address below a check or US Postal Service money order made payable to **Bookinars™, Inc.** and made payable in **US dollars**. Only checks and money orders in US dollars will be accepted. All sales are final. Please allow six weeks for delivery.

Bookinars™, Inc.
P. O. Box 100
Cold Spring, NY, 10516
USA

The purchase price per book is as follows:

Quantity Of *Human Error Prevention* Bookinars™ to Be Purchased	Price Per Bookinar™ (U.S. Dollars) (Price Includes Shipping Within the U.S.A.)	
1–9.	$129.00	
10–29.	$119.00	Add $10.00 USD per Bookinar™ for a shipment outside of the U.S.A.
30–49.	$109.00	
50–99.	$99.00	
100–299.	$89.00	
300–499.	$79.00	
500 and greater.	$69.00	

or

This Bookinar™ is available in the electronic PowerPoint version, along with the right to use this material at your facility for in-house courses, seminars or workshops. For licensing information, please send an e-mail to **licensing@bookinars.biz.**

or

To attend a public presentation of the "Human Error Prevention" Seminar, please visit **www. HighTechnologySeminars.com.**

or

To arrange for BW (Ben) Marguglio's presentation of the "Human Error Prevention" Seminar, in whole or in part, at your facility, please send an e-mail requesting in-house presentation information to **ben@ hightechnologyseminars.com.**

Human Error Prevention Bookinar™
Learning Objectives

- The four fields of focus for human error prevention;
- Human error prevention, problem reporting, root cause analysis, and corrective action terminology;
- The relationships among culture, beliefs, values, attitude and behavior;
- The seven causal factors of human error;
- The four levels of human error;
- The three levels of barriers to human error;
- The four types of barriers within each barrier level;
- Techniques by which to make barriers effective;
- Error-inducing conditions and behaviors by which to counteract these conditions;
- Non-conservative versus conservative decision thought processes and behaviors;
- Coaching to reduce the recurrence of human error;
- Root cause analysis using any of the techniques listed in the Outline, below;
- Human error root causes;
- Corrective actions;
- Defense in depth;
- Design and management of a program for problem prevention, problem reporting, root cause analysis, and corrective action.

Human Error Prevention Bookinar™
Outline

- Terminology and definitions
- Behavior model
- Classifications of human error
- The seven human error causal factors
- Model of event prevention—four levels of error and the three levels of barriers to error and hazards
- Total quality and safety matrix-relationship of barriers to the total quality / safety function.
- Process design criteria
- Techniques for strengthening barriers
- Poka yoke
- Sources of error-inducing conditions and error-likely situations
- Types of error-inducing conditions and error-likely situations
- Behaviors to counteract error-inducing conditions and error-likely situations
- Thought processes and behaviors leading to non-conservative decision-making
- Thought processes and behaviors for conservative decision-making
- Coaching to reduce human error recurrence
- Problem reporting, root cause analysis, and corrective action system objectives
- System participant responsibilities
- System capabilities
- Problem data collection criteria
- Standard data tables
- Data to be collected and why
- Fact versus conclusion
- Analysis for extent of problem
- Operating experience
- Risk-based initial screening of problem reports

- Risk, urgency and significance
- Root, contributing and direct causes
- Criteria for action
- Administration of root cause analysis
- Data collection
- Interviewing
- Root cause analysis
    —Change analysis
    —Failure mode and effects analysis
    —Hazard-barrier-effects analysis
    —Cause and effects analysis / Fishbone diagram
    —Time-line analysis
    —Probabilistic risk or safety analysis, with event and fault trees
    —Management and oversight risk tree analysis
    —Process flow diagrams
    —Value stream diagrams
    —Other
- Hardware failure modes
- Hardware failure causes
- Human performance root causes
- Analysis for extent of preventive corrective action
- Types of corrective actions
- Corrective action verification
- Leading and lagging performance indicators
- Performance and status indicator reports
- Defense in depth
- Review of Marguglio's theorems and principles

Examples, exercises and case studies throughout

Words and Terms Used

The following words and terms are used in this Bookinar™ and have specific management or technical meanings. In this and the next few pages, the explanation following each word or term is intended only to provide an indication of the meaning of the word or term. These pages do *not* constitute a glossary; these pages are *not* intended to provide definitions of the words or terms. The words and terms are defined upon first use in the Bookinar™.

80/20 rule—a generalization of the Pareto principle

Accelerated life testing—a technique for design assessment and corrective action verification

Active error—as an category of error based on the timing of its undesired effect

Adequacy—no more and no less than is necessary to do the job

Administrative process barrier—the 1st type of barrier

Alert—a type of Level 1 Barrier

Ameliorate / amelioration—the Level 3 Barrier

Ameliorative corrective action—the 2nd type of corrective action

AND gate—in a fault tree, all conditions needed for the next higher condition

Apparent root cause analysis—a technique for root cause analysis

As is / as found—the configuration of a hardware item or the existing condition of a document

Attitude—an influence on behavior

Attribute—a defining element of a hardware item, process or human

Audit—an independent assessment of an item or process

Availability—a function of reliability and maintainability

Bar chart—a tool for data analysis

Barrier—the three levels of barriers to prevent, detect and mitigate / ameliorate error

Barrier Level 1—for the prevention of error

Barrier Level 2—for the detection of error or of the hazard activated by error

Barrier Level 3—for the mitigation / amelioration of the undesired effect of error or the hazard

Behavior—an action that yields a result

Belief—a contributor to one's value(s)

Binning—combining end states in an event tree

Blame spiral—resulting in an ever worsening loss of communication and trust

Boolean logic—used in the construction of fault trees

Causal factor—the three types of causal factors

Cause and effects analysis—a technique for root cause analysis

Caution—a type of Level 1 Barrier

Certification—an independent attestation of qualification

Change analysis—a technique for root cause analysis

Characteristic—a defining element of an item, process or human

Classification of defects—a method of indicating the level of significance of a defect

Classification of design characteristics—to indicate the level of significance of an attribute

Close-in-time bias—a type of bias leading to non-conservative decisions

Coaching—a method of preventing error recurrence

Cognition-based error—the 2nd human error causal factor

Common mode failure—a failure resulting in the total loss of the benefit of redundancy

Compensatory corrective action—the 4th type of corrective action

Condition reporting and corrective action tracking—a method of preventing error recurrence

Confirmation bias—a type of bias leading to non-conservative decisions

Conservative decision-making—the 3rd field of focus

Constructability—a consideration for the design of a hardware item

Containment—a type of Level 3 Barrier

Contributing cause—the 2nd causal factor

Co-piloting—a type of operational loafing leading to non-conservative decisions

Corrective action—the four types of corrective action

Corrective maintenance—a type of maintenance

Counteracting behavior—a behavior to overcome error-inducing conditions

Critical—a classification of significance of a defect, design characteristic or undesired effect

Culture—a pattern of thought and behavior

Data element—a category of data

Defect—a non-conformance to a requirement for a hardware or process design characteristic

Defective—an item of hardware or a process that contains a defect

Defense in depth—the six levels of defense in depth or the six levels of opportunity

Degradation influence—a contributor to a failure mechanism

Design attribute or characteristic—a defining element of a hardware item or process

Design margin—a spread between a characteristic's requirement and its maximum load

Designated challenge(r)—a behavior by which to counteract an error-inducing condition

Detect / detection—Barrier Level 2

Detection barrier failure—Error Level 3

Direct cause—the 1st causal factor

Disposability—a consideration for the design of a hardware item

Document corrective action—the 1st type of corrective action

Dropping guard—a type of operational loafing leading to non-conservative decisions

Effectiveness—adequacy and efficiency

Efficiency—adequacy at the least cost

EHS&Q—environmental (protection), (employee and public) health and safety, and quality

EHS&Q culture—a type of culture appropriately considerate of EHS&Q

EHS&Q-conscious work environment—an element of an EHS&Q culture

Employee empowerment—a counter to risky-shifting; a non-participative management style

End state—in an event tree

Environmental (protection), (employee and public) health and safety, and quality—EHS&Q

Environmental qualification—a consideration for the design of a hardware item

Equipment barrier—the 3rd type of barrier

Error—a behavior with an undesired result or effect

Error categorization—by type of behavior, timing of effect, significance, and causal factor

Error—the four levels of error

Error Level 1—when necessary, the failure to prevent error

Error Level 2—an initiating error

Error Level 3—the failure to detect error or the hazard activated by error

Error Level 4—when necessary, failure to mitigate the undesired effect of an error or hazard

Error of commission—an error category by type of behavior

Error of omission—an error category by type of behavior

Error recurrence prevention—the 4th field of focus

Error-inducing condition—anything that increases the probability of error

Error-inducing condition-based error—the 4th human error causal factor

Error-inducing conditions and counteracting behaviors—the 2nd field of focus

Error-likely situation—anything that increases the probability of error

Escape—a type of 3rd level barrier

Event—a classification of significance of an undesired effect

Event tree—a tool for design quality assessment and root cause analysis

Extent of cause analysis—a technique to find all locations of a given or similar cause

Extent of problem analysis—a technique to find all locations of a given or similar problem

Fail-safe—the most undesired kind of failure

Failure mechanism—a contributor to failure mode

Failure mode—the way by which a design characteristic or attribute fails

Failure mode and effects analysis—a technique for design assessment and root cause analysis

Failure rate—a measure of reliability

Fault tree—a tool for design quality assessment and root cause analysis

Field of focus—the four fields of focus for human error prevention

Fitness for duty—a human responsibility

Fitness for use—a term indicating quality

Five Ds—deterrents to preventive corrective action

Five-part communication—a behavior by which to counteract an error-inducing condition

Flinch—the inspection acceptance of a marginal defect

Focus—an element of situational awareness

Free-riding—a type of operational loafing leading to non-conservative decisions

Frequency and similarity bias—a type of bias leading to non-conservative decisions

Functionability—a consideration for the design of a hardware item

Good practice—a method providing an exceptional technical or economic benefit

Groupthink—behavior of individuals in a group leading to a non-conservative decision

Hazard—anything that can impart an undesired effect

Hazard-barrier-effects analysis—a technique for design assessment and root cause analysis

Hazards and barriers—the 1st field of focus

Human barrier—the 4th type of barrier

Human corrective action—preventive corrective action for non-conforming behavior

Human error—behavior leading to an undesired result or effect

Human error causal factor—the seven universally applicable reasons for error

Human error clock—a tool to provide a training opportunity

Human error prevention—the subject of this Bookinar™

Human factors—an element of human error prevention

Human performance—behavior yielding results

Independence—a contributor to objectivity

Initiating action—a direct cause of an occurrence yielding an undesired effect

Initiating error—Error Level 2

Initiating occurrence / initiating event—in an event tree

In-service inspection—a method of maintaining the quality and safety of a hardware item

Inspectability—a consideration for the design of a hardware item

Inspection—a method of determining the acceptability of a item or process characteristic

Inspection hold point—a step in a process at which an inspection is required

Institutionalizing corrective action—a means of precluding the return to an undesired state

Interpretation—different understandings from the language in a procedure

Intervention—taking the opportunity to correct an undesired effect

Investigation—data collection as a prerequisite to root cause analysis

Job analysis—a means for identifying gaps between needed and available training

Knowledge-based error—the 1st human error causal factor

Lagging PI—a performance measure that does not enable timely intervention

Lapse-based error—the 7th human error causal factor

Latent defect—a defect that cannot be identified upon initial inspection or test

Latent error—a category of error based on the timing of its undesired effect

Leading PI—a performance measure that provides the opportunity for timely intervention

Level of opportunity / level of defense—the six levels of opportunity or defense

Level of cognition—the six levels of cognition

Life—a measure of reliability

M—the six Ms

Maintainability—a consideration for the design of a hardware item

Major—classification of significance for a defect, design characteristic, or undesired effect

Malicious behavior—sabotage in contrast to error

Malicious compliance—conformance knowing that an undesired effect will result

Management oversight and risk tree analysis—a technique for root cause analysis

Manufacturability—a consideration for the design of a hardware item

Mean time to restore—a measure of maintainability

Minor—a classification of significance of a defect, design characteristic or undesired effect

Mitigate / mitigation—Barrier Level 3

Mitigation barrier failure—Error Level 4

Near miss—a classification of significance of an undesired effect

Node—in an event tree

Non-conformance—a departure from a requirement

Operability—a consideration for the design of a hardware item

Operating experience program—a means of learning from conditions existing elsewhere

OR gate—in a fault tree, any one condition needed for the next higher condition

Order bias—a type of bias leading to non-conservative decisions

Outward neutralizing—a type of operational loafing leading to non-conservative decisions

Overload bias—a type of bias leading to non-conservative decisions

Over-simplification bias—a type of bias leading to non-conservative decisions

Pareto principle—of the distribution of wealth as described by Professor Wilfredo Pareto

Pareto chart / Pareto diagram—a tool for data analysis

Part corrective action—the 1st type of corrective action

Peer inspection—a type of inspection

Peer review—a type of document review

Performance indicator / performance measure—a presentation of quantitative grouped data

Phonetic alphabet—a behavior by which to counteract an error-inducing condition

Place-keeping—a behavior by which to counteract an error-inducing condition

Poka yoke—a technique for error prevention and detection

Post-job assessment—a behavior by which to counteract an error-inducing condition

Precautionary principle—a fundamental approach to employee and public safety

Precursor—a classification of significance of an undesired effect

Pre-job briefing—a behavior by which to counteract an error-inducing condition

Pre-production item—a thing used to assess design and manufacturing process quality

Prevention—Barrier Level 1

Prevention barrier failure—Error Level 1

Preventive corrective action—the 3rd type of corrective action

Preventive maintenance—a type of maintenance

Probabilistic risk analysis—a technique for design assessment or root cause analysis

Probabilistic risk assessment—same as *probabilistic risk analysis*

Probabilistic safety analysis—same as *probabilistic risk analysis*

Probabilistic safety assessments—same as *probabilistic risk analysis*

Problem—an error, anomaly or departure from logic

Problem thing—the three things in which a problem may exist

Problem statement—the various data elements necessary to adequately describe the problem

Process flow diagram / process flow chart—a tool for design analysis and root cause analysis

Process qualification—an action to help to assure the quality of a process

Protection—a type of 3rd level barrier

Prototype item—a thing used to assess design quality

Qualification—the ability to perform a specific task

Quality of design—an element of the scope of the total quality and safety function

Questioning attitude—an element of a EHS&Q-conscious work environment

QVV—question, verify and validate

Recovery—a type of 3rd level barrier

Reflexive-based or reactive-based error—the 5th human error causal factor

Reliability—a consideration for the design of a hardware item

Reliability centered maintenance—a type of preventive maintenance

Risk—an element of significance; effect times probability of recurrence of effect

Risky-shifting—a type of operational loafing leading to non-conservative decisions

Root cause—the 3rd type of causal factor

Root cause analysis—techniques to ID things to be corrected to prevent problem recurrence

Run to failure—a decision to not replace a hardware item prior to its failure

Sampling plan—an economically and technically beneficial scheme for inspection and test

Satisficing—a type of non-conservative decision-making

Self-assessment—an evaluation of one's own hardware, processes and performance

Self-revealing problem—a problem for which the undesired effect has been experienced

Sentinel event—an occurrence with a physical adverse effect on a patient in a hospital

Significance—of a design characteristic, of a defect, of an undesired effect

Significance classification—for a defect, design characteristic or undesired effect

Significance level—same as significance classification

Single failure analysis—a technique to avoid a single item's failure from causing an event

Situational awareness—a behavior by which to counteract an error-inducing condition

Six levels of opportunity / six levels of defense—to avoid error from escaping the enterprise

Skill-based error—the 6th human error causal factor

Spatial diagram—a tool for data analysis

Specificity—the level of detail needed to retain technical and economic benefits of a method

Standard data table—to enable the grouping of data for performance and status measurement

STAR—a behavior by which to counteract an error-inducing condition

Statistical process control chart—a tool for data analysis

Statistical "t" test—to determine if there is a significant difference between sets of data

Statistically significant difference—for verifying the effectiveness of corrective action

Stop work order—an external behavior by which to counteract an error-inducing condition

Surveillance—a process assessment technique

Systematic approach to training—an approach to improve the effectiveness of training

Task analysis—a means for identifying gaps between needed and available training

Taxonomy of human error causal factors—the universally applicable reasons for human error

Technical process barrier—the 2ⁿᵈ type of barrier

Testability—a consideration for the design of a hardware item

Three-part communication—a behavior by which to counteract an error-inducing condition

Time-line analysis—a techniques for root cause analysis

Time-out—a behavior by which to counteract an error-inducing condition

Top response / top event—in an event tree, a system responding to a undesired challenge

Track and trend—for problems of lesser significance

Truncation—of an analysis

Turn-over meeting—a behavior by which to counteract an error-inducing condition

Ultimate event—in an event tree

Undesired effect—a result of an error or hazard activated by an error

Unsharing—a type of operational loafing leading to non-conservative decisions

Urgency—an element of significance

Value chain diagram / value chain table / value stream—a tool for analysis of a process

Value-based error—the 3ʳᵈ human error causal factor

Values—contributors to attitude

Verbalization—a behavior by which to counteract an error-inducing condition

Vital few—the causes for which preventive corrective action resources should be applied

Walk-down—a behavior by which to counteract an error-inducing condition

Warning—as a 1ˢᵗ level barrier

Workability—a consideration for the design of a hardware item

Working instrument—a measurement device at the lowest level in the hierarchy of accuracy

Working calibration standard—a measurement device used to calibrate a working instrument

The reader is referred to the *Glossary of Terms* published by the *American Society for Quality.*

Human Error Prevention

BW (Ben) Marguglio
BW (Ben) Marguglio, LLC
Management and Technical Consulting
High Technology Seminars
P.O. Box 8
Cold Spring, NY 10516, USA

ben@hightechnologyseminars.com
www.HighTechnologySeminars.com

- Leaders in enterprises with strong *culture* of *environmental protection, employee health, safety,* and *quality (EHS&Q)* demonstrate the *culture* by addressing, as a first or early order of business, an item of interest regarding environmental protection, employee health, safety, and quality. The live seminar leader should do the same.

- A few words and terms should to be addressed at this point. Others will be addressed in the *Terminology Section* of this Bookinar™.

- The term *human error* is used consistently in government, industry and commerce. However, the word *human* is unnecessary because *error* is human. Recognizing this, often in this Bookinar™, the word *error* may be used in lieu of the term *human error*.

- The title of this Bookinar™, *Human Error Prevention*, is shorthand for *Human Error Prevention and Mitigation and Amelioration of Human Error Effects*. To *mitigate* means to make mild. To *ameliorate* means to lessen. The reader is urged to keep in mind that the shorthand term has the longhand meaning.

- The word *barrier* is used in a positive context, not as a hindrance to a worthy objective but, rather, as means by which to *prevent error, detect* it, or *mitigate* and *ameliorate* its *undesired effects*.

- There are types of *error* that cannot be *prevented* by *barriers*, regardless of the rigor with which the *barrier* is designed and implemented.

- If the *undesired effects* of an *error* are intolerable, *barriers* must be such as to try to *prevent* the *error*, to *detect* the *error* or the *hazard* activated by the *error* and then to *mitigate* and *ameliorate* the *undesired effects* of the *hazard*. The absence of any such *barrier*, itself, constitutes *error*.

- Given that some types of *error* cannot be *prevented*, the reader may question the use of the term *human error prevention*, instead of…*reduction. Prevention* is used because it's consistent with common usage, because less that 100 percent *prevention* is still, to some extent *prevention*, and because *error* can be *prevented* from *recurring*.

- This presenter's corporate experiences were mainly in activities related to design, construction, operations and maintenance of nuclear powered electricity generating facilities and nuclear research facilities, and in activities related to aerospace manufacturing. As a consultant and seminar presenter, added experiences were gained in a wide variety of industries. This Bookinar™ is presented from the perspective of these experiences.

- The principles and practices of *error prevention* are universally applicable, regardless of the type of governmental, industrial or commercial enterprise and regardless of the function performed within the enterprise. However, the reader is responsible to transition these universally applicable principles and practices to his or her enterprise and function.

- In a live setting, the seminar attendees are provided with a handout consisting of a copy of each slide without the notes. The presenter's copy of the slides has the notes.

- In the notes for some slides, the final entry is a question or two. Each question pertains to a subject covered on the slide or on the next slide in sequence. The question is intended to facilitate attendee's participation, as well as to gain information about their perspective and level of understanding of the subject. (In a live setting, participation is always a major objective.)

- The attendees are asked to *not* turn to a slide in the handout beyond the slide that is projected on the screen. In this way, attendees do not see the presenter's answer to the question and are given the opportunity to answer from their perspective.

- In addition to facilitating participation, this sometimes enlightens the presenter as well.

- From this point on, first read the slide at the top of the page and then read the notes in the box below. The notes will elaborate on selected points in the slide.

- Important principles and practices may be repeated from place to place in this Bookinar™. The repetition is by intent.

Major Learning Objectives

- Terminology
- The seven human error causal factors
- **Hazards and Barriers**
  - Techniques for identifying hazards and their potential effects
  - The four levels of error
  - The three levels of barriers
  - The four types of barriers to error and hazards
  - Techniques for establishing effective barriers

- Upon completion of this Bookinar™, the reader should be able to understand, and use with precision, the management-specific and technique-specific language applicable to the principles and practices of *error prevention*.

- For the advanced professional, the *Terminology Section* may be somewhat of a review. Regardless, it's recommended that this section be read. The reader may get a different perspective on some terms, this presenter's perspective, and, therefore, the reader also may be better able to understand the subsequent sections in which these terms are used.

- *Hazards and Barriers* is the first of *four fields of focus* or major areas of interest in *error prevention, detection* and *mitigation* and *amelioration* of the *undesired effects* of *hazards* activated by *error*.

- The word *hazard* has the broadest possibly meaning—anything that can cause or contribute to an outcome that is undesired. In addition to safety hazards, there are many other types of hazards that will be described later.

- Upon completion, the reader should understand and be able to use or facilitate the use of techniques by which to identify hazards in administrative processes, technical processes, and hardware or equipment. Although others will be covered in this Bookinar™, the three best techniques by which to identify hazards are:

1. *Failure mode and effects analysis;*

2. *Hazard-barrier-effects analysis;*

3. *Probabilistic risk analysis* using *event trees* and *fault trees*.

- Upon completion, the reader should understand the *four levels of error*:

  1. Level 1—Failure to prevent initiating error;

  2. Level 2—Initiating error;

  3. Level 3—Failure to detect initiating error or the hazard activated by the error;

  4. Level 4—Failure to mitigate and ameliorate the effect of the hazard.

  This will be demonstrated.

- Upon completion the reader should understand the *three levels of barriers*. Whenever there is an intolerable *undesired effect* from a *hazard* actuated by *error*, *barriers* are needed to:

  1. Level 1—Prevent the error;

  2. Level 2—Detect it or the hazard that was activated by the error;

  3. Level 3—Mitigate and ameliorate the effects of the hazard.

  The absence or ineffectiveness of such *barriers* constitutes *error*, in itself. This will be demonstrated.

- Upon completion, the reader should understand the *four type of barriers—administrative process, technical process, equipment,* and *human*. However, the focus in this Bookinar™ is on *administrative* and *technical process barriers*—their design and the written procedures which communicate the their design. Aside from these, other types of *barriers* are not addressed in depth. For example, supervision is an important *administrative process barrier*, but only a few select supervisory skills are addressed in depth in this Bookinar™. *Coaching* is one such skill.

- Upon completion, the reader should be able to recognize voids and other inadequacies in administrative and *technical process barriers*, and understand and use principles and practices by which to *prevent* voids and inadequacies in these *barriers*—principles and practices by which to improve the effectiveness of these *barriers*.

Major Learning Objectives

- **Error-Inducing Conditions and Counteracting Behaviors**
  - Sources of error-inducing conditions and error-likely situations
    - Task
    - Environment
    - Human
  - Types of error-inducing conditions and error-likely situations
  - Types of behaviors to counteract error-inducing conditions and error-likely situations
    - Group behaviors
    - Individual behaviors

- *Error-Inducing Conditions and Error-Likely Situations* is the second of the four fields of focus or major areas of interest in *error prevention*.

- An example of an *error-inducing condition* or *error-likely situation* in a task is a requirement to perform the task within a tight time constraint.

- Upon completion of this Bookinar™, the reader should understand and be able to easily recognize the various types of *error-inducing conditions* and *error-likely situations* that exist in the work task, in the work environment, and in the inherent and acquired traits of humans.

- Upon completion, the reader should understand and be able to use dozens of different types of *counteracting behaviors—behaviors* by which to *counteract error-inducing conditions* and *error-likely situations* such as to reduce the likelihood of *error* because of the condition or situation.

- Persons working alone or working as a group can use these *counteracting behaviors*. Persons at all levels—managers, supervisors and individual contributors—can use these *behaviors*.

- These *counteracting behaviors* can only help to *prevent error*, but such *behaviors* cannot *mitigate* or *ameliorate undesired effects*, as can *barriers*. Subsequent to the occurrence of an *undesired effect*, these *counteracting behaviors* can help to *prevent* further *error*, which might exacerbate the *undesired effect*.

Major Learning Objectives (Con't)

- **Non-Conservative and Conservative Decision-Making**
  - Types of non-conservative decisions
  - Thought processes and behaviors leading to non-conservative decisions
    - Biases
    - Operational loafing
    - "Satisficing"
  - Thought processes and behaviors leading to conservative decisions
    - Situational awareness
    - Other behaviors to avoid non-conservative decisions

- *Conservative Decision-making* is the *third field of focus* in *error prevention.*

- *Conservative decisions prevent error,* and may also help to *mitigate* and *ameliorate* the *undesired effects* of *hazards* activated by *error.* To the contrary, non-conservative decisions result in *error.*

- Upon completion of this Bookinar™, the reader should understand the significant differences between field decisions and analytical decisions.

- Upon completion, the reader should understand the various types of thought processes and *behaviors,* such as *biases, operational loafing* and *satisficing,* that can contribute to *non-conservative decisions*—each of which, of course, to be explained. Being conscious of them, the reader should be in a better position to avoid the thought processes and *behaviors* that can lead to non-conservative decisions.

- Upon completion, the reader should understand thought processes and *behaviors* that lead to *conservative decisions.* Again, being conscious of these thought processes and *behaviors,* the reader should be in a better position to apply them consistently.

Major Learning Objectives (Con't)

- **Error Recurrence Prevention**
  - Field observations and coaching
  - Management system for condition reporting, root cause analysis, corrective action and performance and status measurement
    - Participants and their responsibilities
    - Criteria for design of a condition report and corrective action tracking system
    - Criteria for a problem statement
    - Operating experience
    - Problem impact on operability and reportability
    - Criteria for establishing problem significance

- *Error Recurrence Prevention* is the *fourth field of focus* in *error prevention.*
- Upon completion of this Bookinar™, the reader should understand all of the processes that make up the *management system for condition reporting, root cause analysis, corrective action, and performance and status measurement.*
- The things listed at the third level of indentation in the slide must be addressed in the management system.

Major Learning Objectives (Con't)

- **Error Recurrence Prevention** (Cont'd)
  - Management system for condition reporting, root cause analysis, corrective action and performance and status measurement (Cont'd)
    - Extent of problem analysis
    - Data collection techniques, including interviewing
    - Root cause analysis techniques or processes
      - Change analysis
      - Failure mode and effect analysis
      - Hazard-barrier-effects analysis
      - Time-line analysis
      - Cause and effects analysis / fishbone diagram
      - Process flow diagram

- Upon completion, the reader should understand and be able to use good interviewing techniques in the context of safety, quality and environmental *problem investigation*. However, expertise in interviewing comes with practice.

- Upon completion, the reader should understand and be able to perform or facilitate the performance of the *root cause analysis* techniques listed in the slide.

- Unfortunately, the names for some of these *root cause analysis* techniques are not consistent among, or even within industries. For example, *failure mode and effects analysis* is often referred to as *failure modes and effects analysis*. *Hazard-barrier-effects analysis* goes by many names. There is no right or wrong in this, only individual preference.

Major Learning Objectives (Con't)

- **Error Recurrence Prevention** (Cont'd)
  - Management system for condition reporting, root cause analysis, corrective action and performance and status measurement (Cont'd)
    - Extent of causal factor analysis
    - Types of corrective action
    - Criteria for the corrective action statement
    - Evaluation of the effectiveness of preventive corrective action
    - Reports to management
  - Review of theorems and principles
  - Defense in depth

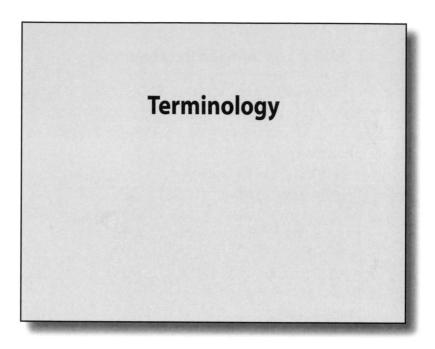

Terminology

- This is the *Terminology Section* of the Bookinar™.
- The words and terms covered in this section are of fundamental importance for the understanding the of the principles and practices of human *error prevention*.
- In the absence of a consistent understanding of these words and terms, there will be confusion and a loss of learning.
- The reader is encouraged to use these words and terms with accuracy and precision.

Questions: What is meant by *culture*? What are its *attributes*?

Culture

The beliefs, values, attitudes, and other thought patterns
that are
fostered at all levels of an organization
and that form the basis for the behavior patterns,
including the decision patterns,
that exist in the enterprise

- Sometimes the definition of a word or term is provided in the slide with a separate phrase on each line. Such is the case in this slide. Each phrase constitutes an important *attribute* of the definition.

- *Beliefs*, *values* and *attitudes* are thoughts. Thoughts cannot be observed.

- One's *beliefs* lead to one's *values*, which lead to one's *attitude*, which contribute significantly to one's *behavior*.

- *Behavior* can be observed.

- When many individuals in an enterprise, at all levels in the enterprise, have the same or a similar thought pattern, that pattern results in a corresponding *behavior* pattern throughout the enterprise.

- Basically, the *behavior* patterns define the *culture* of the enterprise.

- *Culture* may be that which is desired or that which is undesired.

- *Culture* may differ from stratum to stratum within the enterprise or from department to department within the enterprise.

- *Culture* is learned over time from earlier *behaviors* in all strata and in all functions of the enterprise. For better or worse, every *behavior* contributes to *culture*. The contribution is favorable when a desired *behavior* is upheld by higher management or when an undesired *behavior* is overturned by higher management. The contribution is unfavorable when a desired *behavior* is overturned by higher management or when an undesired *behavior* is upheld by higher management.

11

Environmental, Health, Safety and Quality Culture

The existence of a culture

in which,

as an overriding priority,

environmental, health, safety and quality considerations

receive the attention warranted by their significance.

- Having previously defined the word *culture*, it can be used in this definition.

- Philip Crosby (1926–2001), an Honorary Member of the American Society for Quality, wrote that *quality is first among equals*. The phrase *first among equals* is similar to the phrase *as an overriding priority*. Basically, these phrases convey the same thought.

- In some enterprises, the principles and practices for the assurance of *environmental protection, employee and public health and safety, and product and process quality, EHS&Q*, are being integrated into a single business management system.

- Of course, in the definition, *significance* is based on the criteria established for it—which will be addressed later in this section. If the criteria for *EHS&Q* significance are weak, then, certainly, the *EHS&Q culture* will be weak. For example, if, among the criteria for the highest level of *significance*, environmental protection considerations are omitted, by logical extension, the *culture* is weak.

Questions: What is an *EHS&Q-conscious work environment*? What are its *attributes*?

EHS&Q-Conscious Work Environment

An environment in which all employees
maintain a questioning attitude and are required
and encouraged to identify and report EHS&Q problems
without fear of retaliation,
and
in which problems are promptly reviewed,
given the proper priority based on their significance,
and
appropriately resolved with
timely feedback

- An *EHSQ-conscious work environment* is a subset of an *EHS&Q culture*.

- *All employees* means just that. An enterprise in which the reporting of *EHS&Q problems* is limited to workers at lower organizational echelons is an enterprise that lacks an *EHS&Q-conscious work environment*. In such an enterprise, *problems* of higher *significance*, the kind more often found by employees of higher rank, when not entered into the official *condition report and corrective action tracking tool*, are addressed in less formal ways, resulting in less effective *preventive corrective action*.

- In maintaining a *questioning attitude*, it's important to maintain politeness and respect as well. A *questioning attitude* coupled with crassness can hurt interpersonal relationships and cause loss of communication.

- Requiring employees to report is only half the story; encouraging them to report is the other half—the half that truly yields success.

- Dr. W. Edwards Deming (1900–1993), who was an Honorary Member of the American Society for Quality, and who was largely credited with revitalizing the Japanese economy following World War II, wrote a book entitled *Out of the Crisis* in which he described fourteen points by which US industry could compete with the revitalized Japanese industry. One of his points was to eliminate fear. It may be Deming's most important point and the most difficult challenge for leadership.

- The final four phrases in the last five lines of the slide are addressed in detail in the *Error Recurrence Prevention Section* of this Bookinar™.

- Employees must have on-going evidence that the *problems* they report are acted upon.

Question: What must leaders do to create and maintain an *EHS&Q-conscious work environment?*

13

Leaders Create Culture

- Leadership responsibilities:
  - Reasonable goals, objectives and expectations
  - Effective design and communication of policies and procedures
  - Consistent implementation of policies and procedures
  - Adequate resources
  - Removal of inappropriate constraints and impediments
  - Employee recognition and celebration
  - Timely and certain preventive corrective action
  - Performance measurement
  - Honest and fair management-employee relationship
  - Listen to learn

- An *EHS&Q-conscious work environment* must exist and be demonstrated in the policies and procedures of the enterprise.

- The design of *policy* and *procedure barriers* must be such as to effectively *prevent errors* that activate *hazards, detect such errors,* and *effectively mitigate and ameliorate the their undesired effects.* For example, if the design of engineering *administrative and technical procedure barriers* is weak—if analytical tools are not provided by which to assure the quality of equipment design—there is a high likelihood that the *equipment barriers,* themselves, will be weak. The effectiveness of the engineering *administrative and technical procedure barriers* bears heavily on the effectiveness of the *equipment barriers,* themselves.

- Leaders are responsible for the effectiveness of the design of *policy* and *procedure barriers* and for the communication of this design in written documents.

- Given good design, *policy* and *procedure barriers* must be consistently implemented. Leaders are responsible for assuring this.

- In the absence of effective *policy* and *procedure barriers* and in the absence of effective *equipment barriers,* claims of an *EHS&Q culture* and *EHS&Q-conscious work environment* are empty words—merely *talking the talk,* not *walking the walk,* and not *acting the act,* as is said.

- The *EHS&Q culture* and *EHS&Q-conscious work environment* can be demonstrated further by recognizing employees for the identification of *EHS&Q problems,* particularly when it is the result of extraordinary effort. In some enterprises, *good catches* are celebrated.

- In an *EHS&Q culture* and *EHS&Q-conscious work environment,* leaders are responsible for assuring that *preventive corrective action* is timely and certain (and effective)—a concept drawn from our system of justice.

- Leaders should have the information needed to identify threats to the *culture* and work environment. Therefore, leaders are responsible for assuring the existence of *quantitative performance and status indicators* of the types described later in this Bookinar™. In the absence of such indicators, leaders are significantly disadvantaged. Such indicators can be available only with data from a robust *condition report and corrective action tracking tool.*

- Leaders are responsible for maintaining relationship that support *EHS&Q*. A few *behaviors* by which to maintain this relationship are as follows: *empowering* employees; sharing information with employees; feeding back the results of actions taken in response to *problems* reported by employees.

Question: What is the definition of *human performance?*

Human Performance

- Behavior: What a person does. It's observable.
- Result: Outcome of behavior.
- Performance = Behavior + Result
- Performance measure = [# of behaviors for which results were acceptable ÷ total # of behaviors] [100%]

- What one thinks is not observable. What one does is observable. What one does is called *behavior.*
- *Behavior* is to accomplish a task. In the broadest sense, even when one speaks, it's to accomplish a task.
- *Behavior* is intended to achieve a *result* in accordance with one's desire or standard. For better or worse, one's standard need not necessarily be aligned with the standard of the enterprise.
- The outcome of *behavior* is a result that may be acceptable or unacceptable to the enterprise.
- *Human performance* is the combination of *behavior* and its *result.*
- The measure of *performance* given in the slide may be somewhat impractical if it is difficult to count the large number of *behaviors* needed to complete any given process

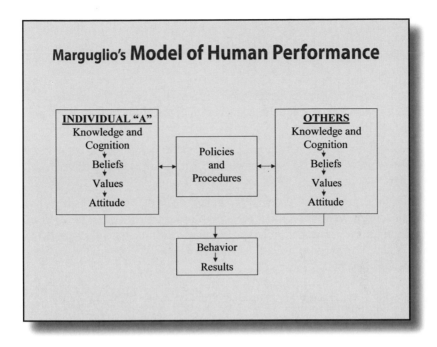

- Initially, visualize the upper left-hand (LH) block of the slide as being applicable to individual *A*, who is to perform a process.

- The information provided to this individual, the way in which the information is provided, and the way in which the individual's *cognitive abilities* act upon the information and its provisioning, will lead to the establishment of the individual's *beliefs*.

- The individual's *beliefs* will contribute to the individual's *values*, which, in turn, contribute to his or her *attitude*.

- Cognition processes, *beliefs*, *values* and *attitude*, in and of themselves, are not observable.

- The individual's *attitude* significantly impact the individual's *behavior* from which there are *results*.

- *Behavior* and *results* yield *performance*.

- The concepts from the LH block of the slide are that:

  - The *daisy chain* impacts *behavior*.

  - The information one receives and how one receives it starts the chain. Therefore, it's imperative that supervisors provide appropriate information in the appropriate way. Information that is inappropriately withheld or that is provided in an inappropriate way can adversely impact one's *beliefs* and, ultimately, *behavior* and *results—performance*.

- Now visualize the upper right-hand (RH) block of the slide as being applicable to others, who, along with individual *A* have contributed to the design of the policies and processes and to the written documents for these policies and processes (i.e., written policies and procedures).

- The same daisy chain applies to these other persons. Their *knowledge, cognition, beliefs, values* and *attitude* will be reflected in the design of the process and in the written policies and procedures for the process.

- The concept here is that individual *A* is not only influenced by his or her own *daisy chain* but also by the written policies and procedures that, in turn, were influenced by *daisy chains* of others.

- The further concept here is that *error* occurs not only at the point at which the process was last touched (by individual *A*) but occurs also upstream (by others) in the design of the process and in the preparation of the written policies and procedures that govern the process. The validity of this concept will be demonstrated time and time again in the exercises and case studies used in this Bookinar™.

Question: What is *human error?*

Human Error

Behavior

that is

wholly expected to achieve a desired result

(in accordance with the standard)

but that does not

- Remember, the standards held by an individual may not necessarily be aligned with the standards desired by the enterprise.
- The undesired result of an *error* may not be obvious or immediately discernable. The result may be delayed. The result may be lurking, awaiting some later *initiating action*. This will be expanded upon and demonstrated as the discussion of terminology progresses.
- Either the person who made the *error* or some other person or persons (or their operations) may be directly affected by the undesired result. Usually, when there is a delayed result, the direct impact is on another person or persons (or their operations). This, too, will be expanded upon and demonstrated as the discussion of terminology progresses.

Question: What types of *behavior* yield undesired results for the enterprise, but are not *error*?

NOT Human Error

- Malicious compliance
- Malicious behavior
- Good decision with a partially or wholly undesired effect

- *Malicious compliance* is *behavior* that is in accordance with a written or oral authoritative directive, while knowing that the result of the *behavior* will be undesired by the enterprise. For example, it's following a procedure while knowing that a *defect* will result.

- *Malicious compliance* occurs in the absence of an *EHS&Q-conscious work environment* in which there is little or no encouragement to identify and report *problems*.

- *Malicious compliance* occurs when one believes that the problems he or she reported in the past have not been addressed. Therefore, the individual sees no benefit in questioning or reporting the *problem* with the current situation; it's simply best to follow the directive and let the consequences be what they will - *no skin off my nose*.

- *Malicious compliance* is not an *error* because the result is in accordance with one's expectation – e.g., the *defect*.

- *Malicious behavior* (not to be confused with *malicious compliance*) is, basically, sabotage. This, too, is not *error* because the *behavior* is in accordance with the saboteur's standard and the result of the *behavior* is in accordance with the saboteur's expectation – e.g., disruption of the process. Of course, if the saboteur's *behavior* does not result in disruption of the process, the saboteur made an *error*.

- A *good decision with a partially undesired effect*, is not an *error*. For example, if a lightening strike would occur on average once every two years and would result in a loss of $200,000, an annual *risk* of $100,000, and if the cost for the design and installation of a lightening arrester system would be $2,000,000, the decision to accept the *risk* would be valid. When, thereafter, lightening strikes, and causes the loss, there is no *error*. The overall effect is still cost beneficial.

- A *good decision with a wholly undesired effect* is not an *error*. For example, if a lightening strike would occur on average once every twenty years and would cost $4,000,000 per occurrence, an annual *risk* of $200,000, and if the cost for the design and installation of a lightening arrester system would be $2,000,000, the decision to accept the *risk* would be valid. If, in the next year, lightening strikes, and causes the $4,000,000 loss ($2M net), there is no *error*.

- Here's another example. If it's technically and economically appropriate to operate an installed component to failure, rather than to meter its operating hours and replace it prior to the end of its expected life, when it fails, there is no *error*. The decision to *run to failure* was technically and economically valid.

- *Malicious compliance, malicious behavior,* and *good decisions with partially or wholly undesired outcomes* are beyond the scope of *human error* and, therefore, beyond the scope of this Bookinar™.

Human Error Classification
Classified by Type of Behavior

- Error of commission-action
- Error of omission-inaction

- *Error* can be classified in many ways.
- One way of classifying *error* is by *commission* versus *omission*.
- For an *error of commission*, a *behavior* or action was taken, with the result being undesired.
- For an *error of omission* a required or expected *behavior* or action was not taken, with the result being undesired.
- Acting and not acting when required or expected to do so, are both *behaviors* of different kinds. Action may be observed. Inaction when required or expected can be observed.

Human Error
Classified by the Timing of the Result / Effect

Active error:
Initiating action: Immediate undesired effect

Latent error:
Initiating action: ⎯⎯⎯⎯⎯⎯▶ Delayed undesired effect
Passage of time

- Another way of classifying *error* is in terms of the timing of its *undesired effect*.

- An *active error* is one for which the *undesired effect* immediately follows the *initiating error* or action (or inaction).

- A *latent error* is one for which the *undesired effect* is delayed by the passage of time.

- The *initiating action or initiating behavior* may not, necessarily, be erroneous.

- For example, if an operator, in accordance with an approved operating procedure, repositions a valve from closed to open, resulting in an *undesired effect*, the operator's *initiating action* did not constitute the initiating *error*. The operator followed operating procedure. The *initiating error* was in the preparation, review and approval of the procedure. However, the operator's action was the *direct cause*. (See page 39.)

- On the other hand, for example, if the operator repositioned the valve in violation of the approved operating procedure, resulting in an *undesired effect*, the operator's *initiating action* was the *initiating error*. Again, the operator's action was the *direct cause*.

- For every *undesired effect*, there is always an *initiating error* (except for *malicious compliance*, *malicious behavior* and *good decisions with bad outcomes*). Sometimes the *initiating behavior* is not the *initiating error*; sometimes it is.

- Notice that the terms *active error* and *latent error* are misnomers because it's not the *error* that's *active* or *latent*. It's the effect of the error that's immediate or delayed.

- This is similar to a *latent defect* which does not become evident until the passage of time (or until a certain type of operating or environmental condition exists which is not the initial operating or environmental condition).

Exercise—Active or Latent?

- A driver steers his car into on-coming traffic.
- A parent leaves matches on a table.
- Engineers design a car such that its gas tank can be breached with a 35 mph rear-end impact.
- A clerk types an incorrect valve number into a plant operating procedure.
- A designer mis-draws the circuit in a schematic used for tag-out.
- A technician does not test to verify the electrical isolation of a component immediately prior to performing maintenance on the component.

- The first and last bullets are *active errors*—for the last, assuming that the technician will immediately start the to work on the physical equipment.
- The third, fourth and fifth bullets are *latent errors*. The car, procedure and schematic will not be used until long after their creation.
- The second bullet could go either way, depending on the child's immediate or delayed presence in the vicinity of the table, as well as the child's immediate or delayed curiosity.

Human Error—Classified by Level of Significance of the Undesired Effect

Undesired Effect:

An adverse impact on human safety and health;

the environment;

the quality of the product (item or service);

compliance with the law;

relationship with a stakeholder,

accomplishment of a mission or function;

or economic status for any reason

- *Error*, or the occurrence resulting from *error*, is classified also in terms of the *significance* of its *undesired effect*.
- The level of the *significance* of an *undesired effect* may be identified by the terms *event*, *near miss*, *precursor*, or *minor*, or by some scheme of alpha, numeric or alpha-numeric *significance levels* such as *SL1*, *SL2*, *SL3*, or *SL4*, for example.
- This will be described in detail on pages 26–36.

Human Error
Classified by Significance of Effects

- Event
- Near Miss
- Precursor
- Minor

- In this Bookinar™, the terms *event, near miss, precursor* and *minor* are used. In some industries, other terms may be used. For example, in hospitals in the United States, any serious adverse effect to a patient is referred to as a *sentinel event*.

- The purpose of this classification is to determine the amount of resources that are to be spent for:

  - *Investigation* and analysis of the occurrence to identify its *root* and *contributing causes;*

  - *Preventive corrective actions.*

- For a *classification of design characteristics system*, a *consequence analysis system*, or a *failure mode and effects analysis*, the terms *critical, major* and *minor* may be used to define the importance of a *design characteristic* of an item rather than to define the *significance* of the *undesired effect* of the occurrence.

- For example, a *critical design characteristic* is one that, were it to be *non-conforming*, would cause an *event*—the highest level of *undesired effect*. The *non-conformance* of a *major characteristic* would cause an *undesired effect* below the level of an *event* but, nevertheless, of some consequence. The *non-conformance* of a *minor characteristic* would cause a trivial *undesired effect*—unless the frequency of its occurrence were intolerable.

- There's a substantial difference between classifying the *significance* of a *design characteristic* and classifying the *significance* of an *undesired effect*.

- Classifying *design characteristics* is not as easy as it would appear from the discussion above. For a given *characteristic*, among other factors to be considered are the degree of *non-conformance* and the ability to *detect* the *non-conformance*.

- Also, for a *classification of defects system*, the terms *critical, major* and *minor* may be used to define the *significance* of the *defect* within the *characteristic*, rather than to define the *significance* of the *characteristic* as a whole or the *significance* of the *undesired effect*.

Question: What *undesired effects* warrant the occurrence to be classified as an *event*?

Event

- Undesired effect of high significance—e.g.:
  - Fatality
  - Hospitalization
  - Non-compliance with a law
  - Reportable to a stakeholder
  - Discomfort in a relationship with a stakeholder
  - Loss of pre-designated types of missions
  - Loss of pre-designated $X or more—directly or indirectly
- Failure of all barriers
- One or more root causes

- An *event* is an occurrence for which the *undesired effect* is of high *significance*. This definition is from the perspective of this Bookinar™—from an *EHS&Q* perspective. From a lay perspective, an *event* is a happening, an occurrence, either adverse or not, especially of some importance, but not necessarily of importance.

- The enterprise establishes the criteria for that which constitutes high *significance*.

- In the developed world, an occurrence that results in a human fatality (an obviously *undesired effect* of high *significance*) is always classified as an *event*.

- Continuing from the perspective of the developed world, almost always, an occurrence that results in a person's overnight hospitalization (another obviously *undesired effect* of high *significance*) will be classified as an *event*.

- Many enterprises will classify an occurrence as an *event* if the *undesired effect* is a *non-compliance* with a law or if the occurrence is *reportable* to a regulatory agency, insurer, client or customer—or even to stockholders or a community interest group.

- For example, if an accident results in an injury that is *reportable* in accordance with OSHA rules and regulations, the accident is classified as an *event*.

- Here's another example. If an accident results in an oil spill that is above *deminimus* and that is *reportable* in accordance with US EPA or state environmental regulatory agency rules and regulations, the accident is classified as an *event*.

- The classification of an occurrence based on the degree of *discomfort in a relationship with a* stakeholder may be considered on a case-by-case basis. Often, for political reasons, occurrences that yield discomfort with a stakeholder are classified at a higher level of *significance* than would be the case if a stakeholder were not affected.

- Another criterion for an occurrence to be classified as an *event* is the *loss of a pre-identified type of mission or function* that is of such high importance that there is no need to estimate its dollar loss for the purpose of classification.

- For example, at a power plant, if the *undesired effect* is the unintended stoppage of electricity generation, a forced outage, the occurrence would be classified as an *event*.

- Notice that the first six criteria are not quantified. The final criterion for the classification of an occurrence as an *event* is loss of a *pre-established amount of money or more*.

- An *event* is the result of:

    1. *The failure of all barriers which should have prevented the error which activated the hazard;* or

    2. *The failure of all barriers that should have detected the error or the hazard activated by the error;*

    3. *The failure of all barriers that should have mitigated and ameliorated the undesired effects of the occurrence.*

- A non-existent but needed *barrier* constitutes a *failed barrier*. An existing *barrier* that is poorly designed or that is poorly implemented constitutes a *failed barrier*.

- An *investigation* and formal *root cause analysis* should be performed for an *event* if there is a the same *level of significance* or the same *risk* going forward.

- With proper *investigation* and *root cause analysis*, almost always, more than a single *root cause* will be identified for the *event*.

Question: What is a *near miss*?

Near Miss

- Undesired physical effect of moderate or minor adverse significance or no undesired physical effect
- Sometimes, a highly significant political effect
- Unacceptably high likelihood of becoming an "event"
- Failure of one or more barriers, with only one or relatively few barriers not failing
- One or more root causes

- A *near miss* is an occurrence for which the physical *undesired effect* may be moderate or *minor* or non-existent.

- From time to time, a *near miss* is reported by the public news media, particularly a *near miss* in the airline industry that has high public visibility. For example, it's reported that airplanes have narrowly averted a collision on a runway. In such cases, the *undesired effect* from a political perspective is *significant*.

- Unfortunately, for other industries for which there is not high public visibility, but for which there is relatively high public and employee *risk*, *near misses* are not reported by the public news media—e.g., in the petrochemical industry.

- For a *near miss*, there is a high likelihood of a future, similar occurrence becoming an *event*.

- For a *near miss*, although one or more *barriers* failed, at least one or, possibly, a relatively few *barriers* did not fail.

- The success of the one or relatively few *barriers* is what distinguishes a *near miss* from an *event* in which all *barriers* have failed.

- Almost always there are multiple *root causes* for a *near miss*, just as there are multiple *root causes* for an *event*.

- *Investigation* and formal *root cause analysis* should be performed for a *near miss*.

Question: What is a *precursor*?

Precursor

- Undesired effect of low significance
- Failure of a single barrier or relatively few barriers, with most barriers not failing
- Single root cause or relatively few root causes

- A *precursor* is an occurrence for which the *undesired effect* is of relatively low *significance*.

- The differences between a *precursor* and a *near miss* are that:

  1. For the former, there is a relatively small monetary loss and no political *undesired effect*, whereas for the latter, there can be monetary loss can be zero to moderate, but there can be a *significant* political *undesired effect*.

  2. For the former, there are fewer *barrier* failures than for the latter. From the *barrier* failure perspective, the difference between the former and latter is a matter of the relative number of *barrier* failures.

  3. Similarly, for the former, there are fewer *root causes* than for latter. Again, the difference is a matter of the relative number.

- *Apparent root cause analysis* should be performed for *precursors*. (See page 271.)

- The frequency of *events* will be reduced if good *apparent root cause analyses* are performed for *precursors*.

Minor

- Trivial undesired effect
- "Track and trend"

- An *error*, or the occurrence caused by the *error* that is classified as *minor* has trivial *undesired effects*.

- A *minor* occurrence is barely above the threshold for reporting into the official *condition report and corrective action tracking tool*.

- For a single *minor* occurrence, the only *corrective action* may be to fix the *thing that has the problem*. There is no analysis as to the *problem* cause. It's not worth it.

- However, with a robust *condition report and corrective action tracking tool*, the frequency of each type of *minor* occurrence is accounted.

- Therefore, the action for this type of occurrence is sometimes referred to as *track and trend*.

- If the frequency of *minor* occurrences rises to a level at which the cost of the occurrences in the aggregate becomes significant, of course, additional action should be taken.

Exercise-Event? Near Miss? Precursor?

- A young, agile employee descending a flight of stairs, holding the handrail, slips on a patch of ice on a step, does not fall, and does not incur any injury.

- A young, agile employee descending a flight of stairs, not holding the handrail, slips on a patch of ice on a step, falls, latently grasps the handrail to stop the fall, and incurs a slightly pulled muscle.

- An older, less agile and less physically fit employee descending a flight of stairs, not holding the handrail, slips on a patch of ice on a step, tries to but fails to grasp the handrail, falls, and breaks his hip.

- The first bullet is a *precursor*, the second is a *near miss*, and the third is an *event*.
- For the *precursor*:
  - First, there was a procedure *barrier* failure. The procedure for removing ice from the stairwell failed. It's not known whether the procedure failed due to its poor design or due to its poor implementation. It's not known whether there was an administrative procedure *barrier* failure, or a technical procedure *barrier* failure, or both.
  - Second, there was an equipment *barrier* failure. The slip prevention tread on the stairwell failed because it was covered with ice which, in turn, was due to the procedure *barrier* failure. Frequently, procedure *barrier* failures yield equipment *barrier* failures.
  - Also, there may have been a human *barrier* failure of inattention.
  - The *barriers* that held are:
    - The administrative training procedure *barrier* through which the employee had been trained to hold the handrail;
    - The human *barrier* of the employee's compliance with his or her training;
    - The human *barrier* of physical agility;
    - The human *barrier* of muscle tonus.
  - This is a *precursor* because there was minimal or no *undesired effect* and because multiple *barriers* held. However, to be conservative, this *precursor* could be upgraded to a *near miss*, given the fact that human *barriers* constituted the large majority of the *barriers* that held, and given the large amount of variation in the effectiveness of human *barriers*. Unfortunately, this type of upgrade doesn't happen as often as it should.

- For the *near miss*, the *human barriers* of agility and reflexes, enabling the handrail to be grasped, are the only *barriers* that held.
- Of course, for the *event*, none of the *barriers* held.

Question: Given that *errors* or occurrences resulting from *error* are classified based on their *significance*, what is meant by *significance?*

Significance

Significance = Risk + Urgency
where:

- **Risk** = (Severity of the undesired effect) X (Probability of recurrence)

- **Urgency** = Extent of the **window of opportunity** in which to fix the root and contributing causes of the barrier failures

- Usually, *significance* is categorized as a *significance level* using a number or alphabetic character. For example, an *event* would be categorized as *Significance Level 1 (SL1)*; a *near miss* as *SL2*; a *precursor* as *SL3*; a *minor* as *SL4*.

- Referring back to page 28, if any one of the first six criteria is met, the occurrence is classified as an *event, SL1*. In this case there is no need to apply the formula on this slide.

- However, unlike the others, the seventh criterion, dollars, is quantifiable.

- The dollar loss is the *severity of the undesired effect of the occurrence*. It can be multiplied by the *probability of the recurrence*. The product is the *risk*.

- Recognize that this probability has a time period associated with it.

- For example, if the loss is $1,000,000 and the *probability of the recurrence* in the next twelve months is 0.25, the risk for the next twelve months is $250,000.

- If $250,000 exceeds the pre-established threshold for classification as an *event*, the occurrence would be classified as an *event, SL1*. Conversely, if $250,000 is less than the pre-established threshold for *SL1* but more than the threshold for *SL2*, the occurrence would be classified as *SL2*, and so on.

- The SL classification is made so as to indicate the level of effort to be expended for *investigation* and *root cause analysis*.

- For any *SL1* involving any of the first six criteria on page 28, certainly there would be the highest level of effort—*investigation* and formal *root cause analysis* leading to the cost effective elimination or correction of the *root* and *contributing causes* of the *barrier* failures.

- For any *SL1* that involves only a dollar loss, it's conceivable that the *risk* could be transferred by the acquisition of insurance. It's further conceivable that the enterprise would combine *investigation* and *root cause analysis* with the acquisition of insurance.

- For any *SL2*, especially for a *near miss*, the highest-level effort also should be used to determine the *root* and *contributing causes* of the *barrier* failures—again, *investigation* and formal *root cause analysis*.

- For *SL3*, *apparent root cause analysis* should be used.

- For *SL4*, there is no need for analysis because the *risk* is tolerated.

- In addition to: (a) eliminating *risk* by the correction of *root* and *contributing causes*, (b) transferring *risk* by the acquisition of insurance; and (c) tolerating *risk*-(d) *risk* can be compensated for—e.g., a fire watch can be established during welding activities.

- The other element of *significance* is *urgency*—the window of opportunity within which to identify and eliminate or correct the *root* and *contributing causes*.

- For example, assume that occurrences in Processes A and B each have a *risk* of $1,000,000. Further assume that Process A is scheduled to be performed again within a week and that Process B is scheduled to be performed again not sooner than six months from now. Addressing the *root* and *contributing causes* for Process A is far more urgent than addressing them for Process B.

- The added *urgency* for the occurrence in Process A increases the *significance* of the occurrence in Process A compared to the *significance* of the occurrence in Process B.

- Of course, this *urgency* must be taken into consideration when establishing the schedule for the *investigation, root cause analysis*, and *preventive corrective actions*.

Human Error—Classified as to Type of Cause Based on Root Cause Analysis

Root Cause Analysis:
Data acquired by investigation
subjected to established analytical techniques,
to identify the things and behaviors
that need to be changed
such as to prevent or
minimize the probability of
recurrence of the error and its effects

- *Investigation* and *root cause analysis* are separate processes.

- *Investigation* involves the following types of data collection: (a) document review (e.g., review of design documents, procedures, records); (b) *interview*; (c) *on-line, real-time observation* of the process; (d) *inspection, testing* and laboratory analysis; and (e) specialized techniques [e.g., *statistical design of experiments*, engineering calculations, modeling, finite element analysis].

- The effectiveness of the analysis is limited to the effectiveness of the *investigation*—the extent to which the *investigative* data is meaningful, complete and accurate.

- The *established analytical techniques* may be any of those described in this Bookinar™ (e.g., starting on page 281, *change analysis, failure mode and effects analysis, hazard-barrier-effects analysis, time-line analysis, cause and effects analysis,* among others).

- For *SL1* or *SL2*, very often, multiple *root cause analysis techniques* are used. For example, a *time-line analysis* or a *cause and effects analysis* (a *fishbone* or *Ishikawa diagram*) may need to be supplemented by a *failure mode and effects analysis* and / or a *hazards-barrier-effects analysis*. But more on this starting on page 281.

- There are two elements of the established *root cause analysis technique* (a) a logical and disciplined arrangement and display of the data; (b) a logical and disciplined analytical thought process applied to the data.

- The *root causes* are those, which if eliminated or corrected, will *prevent recurrence* or *reduce the probability recurrence* of error. Other causes may be identified, but unless their correction *prevents* or *reduces the probability of recurrence,* they are not *root causes.*

- **Absent the identification of causes of *human error*, the analysis is missing the *root*.**
- There are *four levels of human error*:
  - *The first level of error is the failure to establish a barrier(s) to prevent an initiating error, when such a barrier is warranted.* Sometimes, *prevention* cannot be accomplished, or cannot be accomplished economically, or sometimes the consequence of *error* is negligible. In such cases, the absence of the *barrier* would not constitute an *error*. Sometimes a *barrier* can only partially effective, less than 100 percent effective, either because of technical limitations or cost benefit considerations. Again, in such cases, to the extent that the *barrier* achieves its expected effectiveness, there is no *error*.
  - *The second level of error is the initiating error*—i.e., the *error* that may directly actuate the *hazard* or the *error* that may lying in wait for an *initiating action* to actuate the *hazard*.
  - *The third level of error is the failure to establish a barrier(s) to detect the initiating error or to detect the hazard actuated by the error.*
  - *The fourth level of error is the failure to establish a barrier(s) to mitigate and ameliorate the effects of the hazard.*

Direct Cause

Any initiating error

or

any initiating action
that immediately precedes the occurrence
that yields the undesired effect

- The *direct cause* can be either of two types:

  1. An *initiating error* – i.e., a *behavior* that constitutes a *human error*.

     For example, if the operator repositions a valve in violation of the approved procedure, and if this *initiating error* immediately results in an occurrence for which there is an undesired effect, this *initiating error* constitutes the *direct cause*.

  2. An *initiating action* – i.e., a *behavior* that does not constitute a *human error*.

     For example, if the operator repositions the valve in accordance with the approved procedure, and if this *initiating action* immediately results in the occurrence, this *initiating action* constitutes the *direct cause*. In this case the *initiating error* is in the procedure preparation, review and approval process.

     Also, for example, if a component fails in operation, and if this failure immediately results in the occurrence, this failure constitutes the *direct cause*. In this case, if there was an appropriate decision to *run to failure*, there was no *initiating error*. Otherwise, the *initiating error* is either (a) a *quality of design problem* [an inadequate design of the item, including considerations for its application, transport, storage, and maintenance], or (b) a *quality of conformance problem* [a *non-conformance* to design].

- (See page 23.)

39

Contributing Cause

Any deficiency or error that
increases the likelihood of the occurrence
that yields the undesired effect
but that, by itself,
cannot cause the occurrence,
or any deficiency or error that
exacerbates the level of significance of the undesired effect

- A deficiency in a hardware item or in a document may result in an occurrence. A *human error* may result in an occurrence. Sometimes, however, the *human error* is not the result of a deficiency in the human—e.g., *skill-based* and *lapse-based error* need not be the result of human deficiency. (See pages 44–52.)

- A *contributing cause* can be either of two types:

  1. It can increase the likelihood of the occurrence.

  2. It can exacerbate the level of *significance* of the *undesired effect*.

- In performing *root cause analysis*, it's important to also identify *contributing causes*.

- The *contributing causes* for one occurrence (e.g., an *event*) may be a *root cause* for a different occurrence (e.g., another subsequent *event*).

Root Cause

Any deficiency or error,
which when eliminated or corrected,
prevents
or
reduces the probability of
a repetition of the occurrence
that yields the undesired effect

- Only a human deficiency can be the *root cause* of any *near miss* or *event*. By definition, a *near miss* or *event* occurs in the absence or ineffectiveness of appropriate *barriers*, and *human error* caused by human deficiencies are at the *root* of such absence or ineffectiveness. A lot, lot more on this later.

- The *root cause* is identified by asking and getting answers to the question *why?* in accordance with criteria listed on page 266.

- An intermediate cause (as contrasted to an ultimate cause) of a *error* is not a *root cause*.

- The *thing that has the problem* is not a *root cause*. For example, an inadequacy in a procedure is not a *root cause*, such as step for which the required action is incompatible with human capability. However, this inadequacy is not a *root cause*. *What caused the inadequacy? Why? Why?* It's a *human error* of one of the types described starting on page 44. And then *Why?*, *Why?* some more to find the *root causes*.

- Sometimes, *prevention* cannot be accomplished or cannot be accomplished economically. Sometimes, a reduction in the *probability of recurrence* of the *error* or a reduction in the *significance* of its *undesired effect* is the best that can be done.

Human Error
Classified by Type of Behavior /
Human Error Causal Factor

Causal Factor:

Anything that

yields an occurrence that results in an undesired effect

or

that exacerbates of the level of severity of an undesired effect

- A *causal factor* can be at any level in the hierarchy of types of causes—from *direct cause* to *root cause*.

- At the lowest level of *causal factors*, there can be a *root cause* of *human error*—an ultimate cause of a specific type of *human error*. "Ultimate" in this context means after *why?* has been asked repeatedly and the answers have been received to exhaustion. (See page 251.)

- At the next lowest level, a *contributing cause* may increase the probability of the occurrence or exacerbate its *undesired effects*.

- At a higher level, a *causal factor* may be (a) inadequate design of a process, (b) inadequate communication of the process design [i.e., the procedure], (c) inadequate design of an equipment, or (d) a *non-conformance* to a design.

- At the highest, a *causal factor* may be the *direct cause*—either the *initiating cause* or the *initiating action*.

Rasmussen's Taxonomy
Human Error Causal Factors

- Rule-based
- Knowledge-based
- Skill-based

- A *taxonomy* is a scheme of classification of things within a given field of interest.
- This taxonomy was created by Dr. Norman Rasmussen (1927–2003) of MIT and discussed in a book entitled *Human Error*, written by Dr. James Reason of Manchester University—renown for their contributions to nuclear and airline safety, respectively.
- A *rule-based error* is an *error* based on *behavior* that does not conform to an existing good rule or *behavior* that conforms to a bad rule.
- *Rule* in this context means any sort of authoritative directive—e.g., a written policy or procedure or a management expectation, even if undocumented.
- Not stopping one's vehicle at a traffic stop sign is an example of a *rule-based error*.
- A *knowledge-based error* is an *error* based on a *behavior* for which a rule does not exist.
- An erroneous response to a circumstance that is not addressed in the operating procedure, is an example of a *knowledge-based error*. There was no rule covering the circumstance and the response to the circumstance was erroneous.
- To try to avoid *knowledge-based errors*, procedures should be specific. It's best to identify the circumstance, determine the response to the circumstance and incorporate that response into the procedure when it is being prepared, rather than to allow the circumstance to come upon the operator unexpectedly and to hope that the operator makes a correct response in the field. (See pages 79–82.)
- A *skill-based error* is an *error* based on a *behavior* lacking manual dexterity.
- Certainly, this is an acceptable set of classifications or taxonomy. However, the alternative taxonomy on the next page may help to guide one closer to the identification of the *root causes* of *human error*.

Marguglio's **Taxonomy of Human Error Casual Factors**

Knowledge-based – **Error based on behavior:**	**Lacking receipt of the knowledge of the requirement, expectation or need**
Cognition-based – **Error based on behavior:**	**Lacking ability to process the knowledge (memorize, understand, apply, analyze, synthesize or evaluate the requirement, expectation or need)**
Value-based or Belief-based – **Error based on behavior:**	Lacking acceptance of the requirement, expectation or need
Error-Inducing Condition / **Error-Likely Situation-based –** **Error based on behavior:**	Lacking recognition of the error-inducing condition / error-likely situation or lacking appropriate behavior to counteract the condition / situation
Reflexive-based / Reactive-based – **Error based on behavior:**	Lacking conservative judgment in making an immediate response to a stimulus
Skill based – **Error based on behavior:**	Lacking manual dexterity
Lapse-based – **Error based on behavior:**	Lacking attention

- This *Taxonomy of Human Error Causal Factors* was devised from this presenter's review of literally many hundreds, if not a few thousand *problem, incident, non-conformance* and *condition reports* and the like, as well as this presenter's extensive participation in the *root cause analyses* and reviews of *root cause analyses* emanating from such reports.

- A *knowledge-based error* may occur when one has not received the information, either because it wasn't transmitted or got lost or garbled in the transmission or in its receipt.

- A *cognition-based error* may occur when one does not properly process the information that one has received—does not properly memorize it, understand it, apply it, or in jobs requiring higher cognitive abilities, does not properly analyze it, synthesize it or evaluate it.

- A *cognition-based error* is derived from the work of Benjamin Bloom (1913–1999), an educational psychologist who, in 1956 published a taxonomy describing the *six levels of cognition* that apply to learning (*Taxonomy of Educational Objectives: The Classification of Educational Goals*)

- These six levels are described in the next two pages.

- There's a significant difference between not having the information (*knowledge-based*) and not having the ability to process the information (*cognition-based*).

Bloom's Taxonomy—Six Levels of Cognition

- Knowledge
- Comprehension
- Application
- Analysis or diagnosis
- Synthesis
- Evaluation

- *Knowledge*—the most basic, *first cognitive level*. The ability to remember or recognize terminology, definitions, facts, ideas, materials, patterns, sequences, methodologies, principles, etc.

- *Comprehension*—the *second cognitive level*. The ability to understand the things listed in the knowledge *level of cognition*, including tables, diagrams and other forms of communication that combine words and graphics.

- *Application*—the *third cognitive level*. In job-related situations, the ability to use the information and understandings acquired at the knowledge and comprehension levels.

- *Analysis* or *Diagnosis*—the *fourth cognitive level*. The ability to:
  - Break-down information into its constituent parts;
  - Recognize the organizational and systemic relationships of the parts; and
  - Identify actual and potential part *non-conformances*, anomalies and improvement opportunities.

- *Synthesis*—the *fifth cognitive level*. The ability to:
  - Put parts together such as to show a pattern or structure that was not evident previously;
  - From a complex set of data, identify the data that support conclusions; and
  - From a complex set of data, identify data that are appropriate to examine further in order to form new solutions or methods.

- *Evaluation*—the highest and *sixth cognitive level*. The ability to make judgments regarding *significance*, value or worth, usually by using appropriate criteria or standards to estimate accuracy, effectiveness, economic benefits, etc.

- Higher *levels of cognition* are needed to *prevent problems*. Higher *levels of cognition* also are needed to identify the existence and nature of *problems*.

- There are two exceptions:

  1. The existence and nature of a *problem* may be so obvious as to be regarded as *low hanging fruit*, so to speak.

  2. A *problem* may be *self-revealing*—i.e., the *problem* may be one that already has resulted in an occurrence for which the *undesired effect* has been seen.

- For example, a component that is required to provide an output of 120 volts ± 5%, during functional test may provide an output of only 100 volts. The existence of the *problem* has revealed itself. However, much higher *levels of cognition* are required to determine the nature of the *problem*. Is it a design deficiency and, if so, specifically what kind of design deficiency, and why did it exist? Is it a manufacturing *non-conformance* and, if so, what kind of a manufacturing *non-conformance*, and why did it exist?

- In designing: (a) the administrative processes used to govern how business is to be conducted, including how product is to be designed, (b) the product, either a hardware or a service or a combination of both, and (c) the technical or conversion processes used to convert computerized design and hard copy design documents into the physical hardware—in designing these things, tools should be used to enhance cognitive abilities for *preventing problems* and for *detecting* them, and *correcting* them and their causes in the draft stage of design. These tools include *failure mode and effects analysis, hazard-barrier-effects analysis,* and *probabilistic risk or safety analysis,* among others.

- No, this is not a misprint. *Failure mode and effects analysis* and *hazard-barrier-effects analysis* can and should be used in the design of administrative and technical / conversion processes, as well as in the design of hardware—to discover *problems* and correct their causes before the occurrence of an *event* or *near miss*.

Marguglio's Taxonomy of
Human Error Causal Factors

Knowledge-based – Error based on behavior:	Lacking receipt of the knowledge of the requirement, expectation or need
Cognition-based – Error based on behavior:	Lacking ability to process the knowledge (memorize, understand, apply, analyze, synthesize or evaluate the requirement, expectation or need)
Value-based or Belief-based – Error based on behavior:	**Lacking acceptance of the requirement, expectation or need**
Error-Inducing Condition / Error-Likely Situation-based – Error based on behavior:	**Lacking recognition of the error-inducing condition / error-likely situation or lacking appropriate behavior to counteract the condition / situation**
Reflexive-based / Reactive-based – Error based on behavior:	Lacking conservative judgment in making an immediate response to a stimulus
Skill based – Error based on behavior:	Lacking manual dexterity
Lapse-based – Error based on behavior:	Lacking attention

- Continuing with the taxonomy:

- A *value-*or *belief-based error* may occur when one does not respect a known requirement, expectation or need, thinking it to be wrong or unnecessary in a given situation.

- In large part, procedure *non-compliance* is due to *value-*or *belief-based error*. Sometimes the procedure is, in fact, wrong. Sometimes there should be an alternative option for a given situation. However, one would make an additional *reflexive-based error* by acting in *non-compliance* with the procedure, rather than stopping to get the procedure changed as addressed on pages 151–152.

- An *error-inducing condition-based error* may occur when an *error-inducing condition* exists that has not or cannot be eliminated and when one has not used the appropriate *behavior(s) to counteract the condition.* These *conditions and counteracting behaviors* are covered in detail in the second major section of this Bookinar™ starting on page 122.

- Following is an exercise to demonstrate *error-inducing condition-based error*

Exercise—"F"s Sentence

Assignment

In the sentence in next slide, in ten seconds, count the number of "F"s.

- This simple exercise can be used to demonstrate *error-inducing condition-based error*
- Ask the seminar attendees to hold-off reading the sentence on the following slide until the time count is started.
- When the next slide is projected onto the screen, immediately start counting the seconds out loud.
- Count with increasing volume.
- Count with increasing speed, giving the attendees only seven seconds before removing the slide from the screen.

Exercise—"F"s Sentence (Cont'd)

FINISHED FILES ARE
THE RESULTS OF YEARS
OF SCIENTIFIC STUDY
COMBINED WITH THE
EXPERIENCE OF YEARS.

Exercise—"F"s Sentence (Cont'd)
How many did you count?

Errors made in this case would be classified as either:
- Error-inducing condition-based / Error-likely situation-based; or
- Lapse-based.

- Ask the seminar attendees how many *F*s they counted.
- Three is the most frequently counted number. Very few attendees will count more than three. Rarely will one count all six of the *F*s.
- *Error-inducing conditions* in this case are:
  - Time pressure—ten seconds;
  - Too little time—only seven seconds;
  - Three of the six *F*s in small words, *OF*, that are skimmed over in reading;
  - Poor background, poor contrast;
  - Distraction, counting out loud, conflicting with the reader's count.
  - Distraction, lack of syntax—"Finished files are the results of years of scientific study combined with *the experience of years*" instead of "Finished files are the results of years of scientific study combined with *years of experience*".
- A *pre-job brief* could have helped to *alert* the reader to the possibilities of *F*s in small words, poor background, and distraction.
- Even under ideal conditions, of one hundred readers, probably two or three would count less than six *F*s due to *lapse-based error*.
- *Inspection* is not 100% effective.

Marguglio's **Taxonomy of Human Error Causal Factors**

Knowledge-based – Error based on behavior:	Lacking receipt of the knowledge of the requirement, expectation or need
Cognition-based – Error based on behavior:	Lacking ability to process the knowledge (memorize, understand, apply, analyze, synthesize or evaluate the requirement, expectation or need)
Value-based or Belief-based – Error based on behavior:	Lacking acceptance of the requirement, expectation or need
Error-Inducing Condition / Error-Likely Situation-based – Error based on behavior:	Lacking recognition of the error-inducing condition / error-likely situation or lacking appropriate behavior to counteract the condition / situation
Reflexive-based / Reactive-based – Error based on behavior:	**Lacking conservative judgment in making an immediate response to a stimulus**
Skill based – Error based on behavior:	**Lacking manual dexterity**
Lapse-based – Error based on behavior:	**Lacking attention**

- A *reflexive-based error* may occur when one is presented with a condition or situation to which an immediate response or reaction is required. Sometimes, in addition to the immediacy of the required response, the newness or infrequency of the condition may contribute to the *error*.

- For example, a submarine captain performed a periscope sweep in a little over one minute, whereas it normally takes about three minutes. A collision resulted. Although there were *error-inducing conditions* (VIPs on board whom the captain wanted to impress, and a hazy sky forming a backdrop that made it difficult to see the white-hulled ship with which the submarine collided), the quick-sweep was a reflexive-based non-conservative decision for which captain, with an otherwise stellar reputation, the victims, and all others affected paid dearly. (See the case study on pages 196–205.)

- Here's a little more controversial example, for which the situation was approximately as follows: The NY Yankees were winning a game with the Boston Red Sox, a game which had no bearing on the division standings because the Yankees had already won their division. A Red Sox batter hit a pop fly into foul territory near the third base box seats. The fly drifted dangerously close the seats. Derek Jeter, the Yankee shortstop, made a heroic, running catch of the ball but his speed and forward momentum carried him into the box seats, head first. It could have been a catastrophe for both Mr. Jeter and the Yankees. Fortunately, Mr. Jeter emerged from the seats with only a moderate laceration on his face. From the perspective of the post-season play, this was a reflexive, non-conservative decision. What makes this perspective controversial is that the drive behind Mr. Jeter's action is what make him the best ever shortstop (of course, coming from an avid Yankee fan) and it would be unwise to discourage this drive. That's a satisfactory conclusion. What's important is that the human behavior be understood.

- No matter how practiced a worker, *skill-based errors* also will exist until the time that they are avoided by automation. For example, in manual welding, even with the utmost attention, slag occurs.
- Humans are fallible. Therefore, *lapse-based errors* will exist until they are avoided by automation.

Exercise—Driving in Kansas

Assignment

In this scenario:

- Identify the causes of the accident.
- Using the *Taxonomy of Human Error Causal Factors*, categorize each cause as to its type of causal factor.

Exercise—Driving in Kansas (Cont'd)

- A driver of a car is approaching an intersection in farm country.
- The terrain is flat. The wheat has yet to grow.
- It's a clear day. Visibility is exceptionally good.
- The driver looks carefully and repeatedly in all directions.
- There are no structures to obscure the driver's view.
- There are no other vehicles or pedestrians in sight.
- The driver sees a conventional, octagonal "STOP" sign.
- The driver drives past the sign without reducing the speed of the car.
- The car hits a bump in the intersection.
- The driver loses control of the car.

Assignment Completion

- Driver:

  - *Value-based / belief-based error* because in the absence of other vehicles and pedestrians, the driver didn't accept the need to stop.

  - *Knowledge-based error* because in not seeing a *BUMP* sign, the driver didn't now that a bump existed, other than the crown in road for drainage. A red and white octagonal *STOP* sign is wrong sign for a bump.

  - Possibly a *reflexive-based error*. The driver made a non-conservative snap judgment.

  - There is no lapse here. The driver saw the *STOP* sign and remained aware of it.

- When doing this exercise in a seminar, almost always, the immediate and sole focus of the seminar attendees is on the driver, the last person to touch the process. It's often the same in real life in government, industry and commerce—*Operator error, operator cautioned*.

- Think of what's happened (or hasn't happened) in the process upstream.

- Traffic Manager:

  - *Knowledge-based error* because the manager didn't know of the existence of the bump.

  - Or *value-based error* because the manager knew of the bump but decided that the red and white octagonal *STOP* sign was sufficient—no added value in the *BUMP* sign.

  Sometimes, there's controversy regarding the conclusion of the manager's *value-based error*, the rationale being that one should operate to the highest level of the requirement. Regardless of the absence of the *BUMP* sign, the driver should have adhered to the *STOP* sign, the highest level of the requirement.

That's an acceptable position to take in a controlled environment, such as in a plant. However, in a non-controlled environment, such as an intersection in Kansas, where there is the potential for knowledge-based and *value-based error* in combination, the appropriate *BUMP* sign is preferred. Agree to disagree; it's not really the main point of the exercise.

- Road Maintainer / Constructor:

  - What about the bumpy condition of the road? Why should it have been in that condition in the first place? Did the road maintainer / constructor or the traffic manager know about the bumpy road condition? If they didn't know about it, was it possible that the road was recently reconstructed or repaired and that a bump materializing shortly thereafter was not expected? Was the reconstruction / repair done properly?

  - The road maintainer / constructor could have made *errors* of the type described in the *Taxonomy of Human Error Causal Factors*.

Points Demonstrated by this Exercise:

- *Errors* fall into the categories given in the *Taxonomy of Human Error Causal Factors*. For example, *knowledge-based error, cognition-based error, value-based error*, and *reflexive-based error* all having had the potential in this exercise.

- For a given *player*, so to speak, multiple categories of *causal factors* may apply simultaneously. For example, three potentially applied for the driver—*knowledge-based, value-based* and *reflexive-based*. Although the definitions of each *causal factor* are mutually exclusive each other, the *causal factors* may exist simultaneously.

- *Errors* occur in processes upstream of the process in which the last *error* was made. *Errors* occur by others than the last person to touch the process. For example, in this case, *errors* were made in the signage process and, possibly, in the road maintenance or construction process.

- -

- The following case study will demonstrate the foregoing even more clearly and dramatically.

Case Study—Therac-25

Assignment

From the following scenario:

- Identify the causes of the accident.

- Using the **Human Error Causal Factor Taxonomy**, categorize each cause as to its type of causal factor.

Case Study—*Therac-25*
Scenario:

Therac-25 was a million dollar radiation machine designed to precisely aim a beam of radiation at a patient in order to treat tumors or cancerous growths. Patients recovering from operations that had removed the bulk of a tumor often underwent these radiation treatments to remove what was left.

The *Therac-25* was high-energy radiation machine, but radiation treatment usually involved many low-energy dosages across successive treatment sessions. The machine and the operator were located in different rooms, as with most radiation therapy, in order to protect the operator from unnecessary exposure. The machine was controlled through a computer (a terminal hooked up to an old Vax mainframe).

There were two basic modes in which the *Therac-25* could function.

The first was the electron mode, the low-energy mode in which an electron beam of about 200 rads was aimed at the patient and sent off in a short burst.

The second was the x-ray mode, which used the full 25 million electron volt capacity of the machine. When the machine was switched into this mode, a thick metal plate would get inserted between the beam source and the patient, and as the beam passed through the plate, it was transformed into an x-ray, which would radiate tumors and the like.

To switch to electron mode, the operator typed "e" at the computer terminal. To switch to x-ray mode, the operator typed "**x**" at the computer terminal.

Case Study—*Therac-25* (Cont'd)
Scenario (Cont'd):

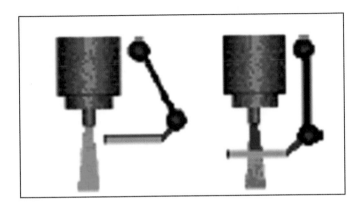

Immediately above, the left-hand side of the sketch shows the electron mode and the right-hand side shows the x-ray mode.

Well, Ray Cox, a Texas oil-worker, went in for his usual radiation treatment for a tumor he had removed from his left shoulder. He had received this treatment eight times before, so this was business as usual. While he was on the table, the operator went down the hall to start the treatment. The operator sat down at the terminal, and typed "x" to start the process. She immediately realized she made a mistake, since she needed to treat Ray with the electron beam, not the x-ray beam. She pressed the "up" arrow, selected the "Edit" command, typed "e" for electron beam, and pressed "Enter", thinking she was done re-configuring the system and was ready to start treatment.

The total time for these key strokes was a few seconds.

It turns out that this particular sequence of actions within this timeframe had never occurred in all of the testing and evaluation of the *Therac-25*. If it had occurred, it would have pointed out a dangerous bug in the system. The system presented the operator with a "Beam Ready" prompt, indicating it was ready to proceed; she typed "b" to turn the beam therapy on. She was surprised when the system gave her an error message.

She wasn't familiar with this particular message, but these particular errors usually meant the treatment hadn't proceeded. She cleared the error to reset the *Therac-25* so she could do it again. She got the "Beam Ready" prompt and again pressed "b" to initiate the treatment. Same outcome—an error message and the system stopped. She tried it a third time.

Meanwhile, back in the treatment room, Ray was feeling repeated burning, stabbing pains on his back. None of the previous treatments had been like this. Although he cried out several times, asking (first jokingly) whether the system was right, no one came to check on him. Finally, after the third painful burst, he pulled himself off the table, and went to the nurse's station.

Case Study—*Therac-25* (Cont'd)
Scenario (Cont'd):

The *problem* was that when this particular sequence of commands was executed in a short time, the arm correctly withdrew as it should be in electron beam mode, but the beam was not switched to low power. Although the machine told the operator it was in electron beam mode, it was actually in a hybrid proton beam mode. As a result, the system was delivering a radiation blast of 25,000 rads with 25 million electron volts, more than 125 times the normal dose. The particular sequence of steps executed by the operator had moved the metal plate from the beam's path, but left the power setting on maximum!

Ray Cox's health deteriorated rapidly from radiation burns and other complications from the treatment overdose. He died four months later.

It is worth noting that the *problem* wasn't actually diagnosed until 3 weeks later, when it happened again to another patient. At this point, the senior operator realized that something about the sequence of steps taken must have triggered this flaw. Subsequently, he found and reported condition it to the manufacturer. Subsequently, it was also found that there had been similar overdoses elsewhere.

Assignment Completion

Operator:

- Striking a wrong key on the keyboard was either a lapse-based or *skill-based error*. One can't distinguish between the two with the information provided.

- Not understanding the meaning of the error message is a *knowledge-based error*.

- Proceeding with process in the absence of the understanding of the meaning of the error message is a *non-conservative, reflexive-based error*.

Case Study—*Therac-25* (Cont'd)
Assignment Completion (Cont'd)

- Patient:
  - Following the initial painful reaction, remaining on the treatment table was either a *cognition-based* or *reflexive-based error*. One can't distinguish between the two with the information provided. Certainly, he should have known what to expect, having had the treatment earlier. That rules out a *knowledge-based error*.
  - He could have also made a *value-based error* from the perspective of never accepting the possibility that he could be hurt by hospital operations.

- Radiology / Hospital Administrator:
  - Not providing a means of voice and visual communication between the operator and the patient was either a *cognition-based* or *value-based error—cognition-based* if the need was not recognized and *value-based* if the need was recognized but not satisfied due to a fiscal concern.
  - Not assuring the patient's full awareness and understanding of the *risks* was probably either a cognition-based or *lapse-based error*. Was there a form that should have been completed to indicate that the patient had been informed fully of the expectations of the treatment?

- Radiology / Hospital Administrator or *Therac-25* Manufacturing Company Project Engineering Team or Both:
  - Not assuring that the operator was trained to understand the error message was probably a *cognition-based error*.
  - Not correcting the *problem* in a timely way was a *cognition-based* or *value-based error*.

    This speaks for itself in indicating that the *condition reporting, root cause analysis, corrective action, and performance & status measurement system* failed. From the information already available, it's hard to determine whether the failure was in the design of the system or in the *non-compliance* with an adequately designed system. If it was the former, it's probably a *cognition-based error*. If the manufacturer did not believe the reports, as is indicated in some studies of these accidents, the *error* is *value-based*.
  - Preventing the hospital's use of a Vax terminal instead of assuring the use of equipment with which the *Therac-25* was designed to work was probably a *cognition-based error*.

- *Therac-25* Manufacturing Company Project Engineering Team:
  - Not designing *Therac-25* to *fail-safe*, such as with an interlock, is a *cognition-based error*. The logic for this conclusion follows.

    IF adequate Engineering Administrative Procedures existed requiring *fail-safe* design, requiring the performance of *fail-safe analysis*, and providing the specifics of the analytical techniques by which to assure *fail-safe design*,

    THEN the entire design team simply *failed by lapse* to conform to these adequate procedures (not likely) or failed by *value-based error* to bypass the required analysis to save time and money (also not likely).

Case Study—*Therac-25* (Cont'd)
Assignment Completion (Cont'd)

- *Therac-25* Manufacturing Company Project Engineering Team (Cont'd):

  - Not designing *Therac-25* to *fail-safe*, such as with an interlock, is a *cognition-based error*. The logic for this conclusion follows (Cont'd).

    Given the unlikelihood of each of these alternatives, it's more likely that adequate Engineering Administrative Procedures did not exist.

    In the absence of adequate Procedures, the team needed, but lacked the cognitive ability to create and analyze for *fail-safe* design.

  - In an article by entitled *An Investigation of the Therac-25 Accidents* by Nancy Leveson, University of Washington, and Clark S. Turner, University of California, Irvine, published in *IEEE Computer*, Vol. 26, No. 7, July 1993, pp. 18–41, it was written that "In March 1983, (one of the manufacturers) performed a safety analysis on the *Therac-25*. This analysis was in the form of a fault tree and apparently excluded the software". This is a *cognition-based error*. The same logic for this conclusion applies as given in the bullet immediately above.

- *Therac-25* Manufacturing Company Engineering Administration:

  - The absence of adequate Engineering Administrative Procedures for *fail-safe design* and *fault tree analysis* (e.g., not requiring the *fault tree* to take into consideration the hardware interface with the software) is a *cognition-based error*.

- The reader need not necessarily agree with each of the foregoing judgments with regard to *causal factor* category. That would be okay because that's not the point. The point is that whatever *causal factor* categories are chosen by the reader, hopefully, they will be consistent with the *Taxonomy of Human Error Causal Factors*.

- Also, of course, it must be emphasized that the foregoing is not a formal *root cause analysis*. The opportunity does not now exist to determine why these *human error causal factors* existed and the analyses performed by others, as good as they were, did not address the *human error causal factors* and why they existed.

- -

Points Demonstrated by this Case Study:

- The *Taxonomy of Human Error Causal Factors* is applicable.

- *Errors* occur in processes upstream of the process in which the last *error* occurred (in this case, the last *error* having been the operator's decision to proceed).

- *Errors* occur in the design of administrative processes that govern the design of the product, as well as in the design of the product, and in the technical processes that convert the design to actual hardware. Almost always, when there are serious *errors* in the design of the hardware, there are serious *errors* in the design engineering administrative procedures that govern the design of the hardware, to begin with.

Case Study—*Therac-25* (Cont'd)

Points Demonstrated by this Case Study (Cont'd):

- *Errors* result in *barrier* failures—in this case:
  - *Administrative and technical procedure barrier failures;*
  - *Equipment barrier failures* (e.g., the machine, itself, and the absence of communication equipment in the hospital);
  - *Human barrier failure* in that the operator lacked sensitivity or intuition given that she proceeded without an understanding of the error message.
- *Events* occur only when one errs in failing to create and implement *barrier(s)* to:
  - *Prevent initiating error;*
  - *Detect initiating error or the hazard activated by the error;*
  - *Mitigate and ameliorate the hazard activated by an error.*
- The *undesired effect(s)* of an occurrence can be exacerbated by an *error* (failure to *mitigate* and *ameliorate*).

Hazards and Barriers

- This is the *Hazards and Barriers Section* of the Bookinar™.

- *Hazards* and *barriers* is the *first field of focus* and major area of interest for *preventing human error* and, when it can't be *prevented*, for *detecting* it, and *mitigating* and *ameliorating* its *undesired effects*—the *effects* of the *hazard* activated by *human error*.

- The following are addressed in this section:
  - The scope and objectives of *barriers*;
  - Models of the occurrence of *events*;
  - The *four levels of error*;
  - The *three levels of barriers*;
  - The *four types of barriers* at each level;
  - Criteria for effective *administrative* and *technical process barriers*.

- Additional terms will be defined in this section.

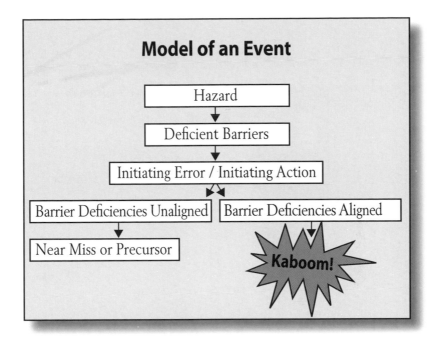

- This standard model was modified by this presenter to delete *Error-inducing Conditions* which, in the unmodified model, are shown alongside *Deficient Barriers*. While an *error-inducing condition* can cause an *error*, an *error-inducing condition*, alone, cannot cause an *event*. An *event* occurs when *barriers* do not exist or are ineffective to *prevent error*, to *detect error* or the *hazard* activated by *error*, or to *mitigate and ameliorate the effects of the activated hazard*.

- If *barriers* do not exist to *prevent error which can activate a hazard with an intolerable effect*, to *detect the error or the activated hazard*, and to *mitigate and ameliorate its effect*, or if the these *barriers are ineffective*, their absence or ineffectiveness constitute *human error*. Very often, it's *cognition-based* or *value-based error*.

- For an intolerable *effect(s)*, there should be multiple *barriers*, unless the single *barrier* is automated and of sufficiently high *reliability*. A single, non-automated *barrier* would not have sufficient *reliability*.

- When *barrier* deficiencies (their absence or ineffectiveness) are aligned, an initiating error or an *initiating action* can activate the *hazard*. Kaboom! Remember, the *initiating action* may not be an *error*. Also, it may have been decided to accept the potential for an *initiating error* with the understanding that *barriers* would *mitigate / ameliorate*. But when the *mitigation / amelioration barriers* fail because of other *error*, kaboom!

- If the *mitigation / amelioration barriers* fail due to design inadequacy (their absence or ineffectiveness), that design *error* actually occurs **prior to** the *initiating error* or *initiating action*. Otherwise, if the *mitigation / amelioration barriers* fail due to *non-conformance* to design, that *non-conformance error* occurs **subsequent to** the *initiating error / initiating action*.

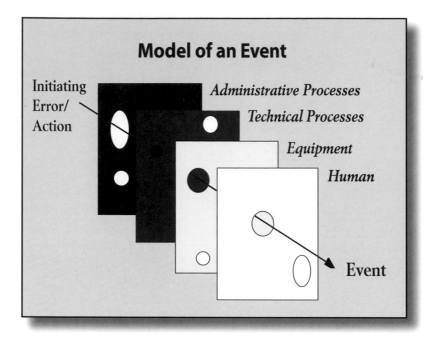

- This is another standard model of an *event*-the *Swiss cheese model*, modified by this presenter to recognize that the *direct cause* may be either an *initiating error* or an *initiating action* and to recognize the *four different types of barriers*.

- According to this model, when the deficiencies or holes (*errors*) in the *barriers* are aligned, an *initiating error* or an *initiating action* can result in the activation of the *hazard*, the red-arrowed line, leading to the *event*.

- It has been and will be shown in future case studies that equipment *barrier* failures due to poor equipment design are usually preceded by *administrative* and *technical procedure barrier* failures that allowed poor design, to begin with.

- For example, remember from the *Therac-25 Case Study*, Engineering Administrative Procedures did not assure that that the *fault tree* be constructed to account for the interface between the software and hardware. (See pages 56–61.)

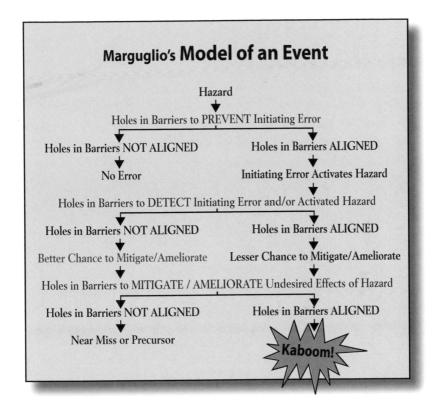

- This model shows *three levels of barriers* (in bright red font):
  - *First level—the barrier(s) to prevent an initiating error that can activate a hazard;*
  - *Second level—the barrier(s) to detect the error and / or the actuation of the hazard;*
  - *Third level—the barrier(s) to mitigate and ameliorate the undesired effects of the hazard.*
- An example of a *second-level barrier* is a building smoke detection system with an alarm. An example of *third-level barriers* are the building's fire suppression system and evacuation plan and evacuation drills in accordance with the plan.
- For some *events*, such as for a catastrophic bridge collapse, there are no *second-* and *third-level barriers* to give *warning* or to lessen the *significance* of the *event*. This statement is based on *in-service inspection* being categorized as a *first-level barrier* (*error / failure prevention*).
- For a manufacturing setting, the *first-level barrier(s)* is to prevent a defect. The *second-level barrier(s) is to detect the defect on a timely basis.* The *third-level barrier is to mitigate and ameliorate*—for example, to *prevent* shipment of *defective* product or, if shipped, to provide for the immediate notification to the customer, replacement of *defective* product, analysis as to the cause of the *first-* and *second-level barrier* breakdowns, and communication to the customer of the *corrective action* to *prevent recurrence* of the shipment of *defective* product.

- This model shows *four levels of error:*
  - *First level—the error in failing to have an effective first-level barrier(s) to the initiating error;*
  - *Second level—the initiating error;*
  - *Third level—the error in failing to have an effective second-level barrier for the detection of the initiating error or for the detection of the hazard activated by the initiating error;*
  - *Fourth level—the error in failing to have an effective third-level barrier for the mitigation and amelioration of the undesired effects of the hazard.*
- Failure to have an effective *barrier* may be due to *error* in the design of the *barrier* (quality of design) or *error* in the implementation of the *barrier* as designed (*quality of conformance to design*).
- Of course, failure to have an effective *barrier* does not constitute *error* when there is no technical or economic basis for the *barrier*. The establishment of a *barrier* in the absence of its need, itself, constitutes an *initiating error.*
- Sooner or later there will be an *initiating error.*
- Here are examples demonstrating the difference between an *initiating action* and an *initiating error.*
  - If an operator repositions a valve in accordance with an approved operating procedure, and if the result is an occurrence with a significantly adverse *undesired effect*, the operator took the *initiating action*, but did not make the *initiating error*. The *initiating error* occurred either in the design of the hardware system or in the preparation of the operating procedure. There should have been *first-*and *second-level barriers* to *prevent* and *detect*, respectively, any *error* in the hardware system design or in the procedure preparation. In addition, given the potential *significance* of the *undesired effect* and the potential for the failure of the first two levels of *barriers*, there should have been a *third-level barrier(s)* to lessen the *significance* of the *undesired effect.*
  - If an operator repositions a valve in violation of the approved operating procedure, the operator made the *initiating error.*
- The *direct cause* may be either an *initiating action* or an *initiating error.*

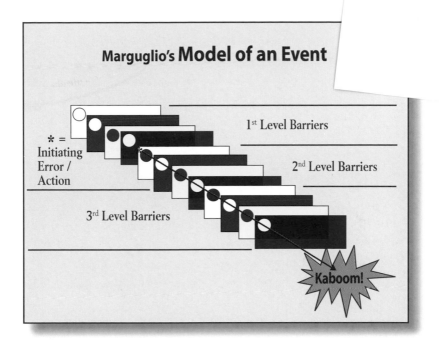

- In this slide, the model on page 64 is adjusted to recognize the *three levels of barriers*.
- (Forgive the *error* in that the red-lined arrow indicating the *hazard* is not drawn behind the upper left hand corners of the *barrier* boxes. This presenter couldn't do it such that the result would be a straight-lined arrow.)

When Holes in Barriers Align

CHALLENGER

- Challenger
- Chernobyl
- Valdez
- Bhopal
- SST / Concorde
- Secretary Brown's Aircraft

Source: NASA

- The crash of the aircraft carrying US Secretary of Commerce Ronald Brown and thirty-two others occurred in Croatia on April 3, 1996. All aboard were killed in the crash.

- The report released by the Air Force stated "...a combination of pilot mistakes, inadequate training, faulty landing procedures...and safety oversights...conspired to bring the flight to its grisly end. Had any one of those factors not been present...the crash never would have occurred."

- This portion of the report was quoted above for two reasons.

- First, the quotation reinforces the concept in the foregoing models that it takes a *combination* of failed *barriers* to yield an *event*. Had *any one* of these *barriers* not failed, *the crash never would have occurred*.

- Second, and more importantly, this quotation demonstrates the unfortunate tendency to apply *human error* only to the last person to touch the process, in this case the pilot. Notice *pilot mistakes*. Notice also, *inadequate training, faulty landing procedures, inadequate oversight*—the implication being that these are systemic and organizational issues, not attributable to *error* by a human or humans. Well, who's responsible for the adequacy of the training? Certainly not the entire Training Department. Rather, a specific individual or individuals failed to create and assure adequate training.

- There's a reluctance to recognize *human error* upstream in the process—to recognize it in the design of the administrative processes, in the design of the technical conversions processes, and in the design of the product—and to deal with the *root causes* of this *human error*. The correction is made to the design, itself, by fixing the procedure or the drawing. But, too often there is no correction to the human cause that resulted in the design *error* to begin with.

- The question *Why?* is no longer asked as soon as the *thing (other than the person) that has the problem* is fixed—e.g., the procedure or the drawing is fixed.
- Following are some other examples of this reluctance:
  - An article entitled *Most Airplane Crashes Caused by Human Error* was published in the November 2006 issue of *Quality Progress*, under the *Keeping Current* banner. Hopefully, some day, it will be recognized that all airplane crashes are caused by *human error*, possibly with the exception of lightening strikes and sabotage. It depends on how far upstream in the process one is willing to search.
  - In an otherwise excellent article entitled "Fixing Broken Election Processes" published in the November 28, 2006 issue of *Quality Digest Magazine*, under *IQ Principle 4*, it was written: "Defective products result from defective processes, not from defective people. Incorrect (wrong selection), unrecorded (under-votes), disqualified (over-votes) votes aren't the result of confused or uneducated—they're the result of confusing ballots, erroneous technology...." True enough. People are not *defective* but they do make *errors* in design. This author points out that people who vote, the last persons to touch the process, are not making knowledge-based or *cognition-based errors*. That's correct. But the author does not point out that people, upstream, who create confusing ballots or create erroneous technology are making knowledge-based or *cognition-based errors*. In this article, there's a subtle difference in perception between those who last touched the process and those who touch the process upstream.
  - Here's something from a consultant's website—incidentally, a consultant whom I much admire, who's articles I've read for years and from whom I learned.
    - "Do you ever waste time waiting...?
    - Do you ever redo your work...?
    - Do the procedures you use waste steps, duplicate efforts...?
    - Is information that you need ever lost?
    - Does communication ever fail?
    - Why?
    - **...Because it's processes, not people!**"

    Well, of course, people create the processes.
  - Last one. In an article entitled, *Handling the Human Side of Change*, published in the November 2003 issue of *Quality Progress*, the consultant, who's website is quoted immediately above, wrote: "Joseph Juran originally made the empirical observation that 85% of organizational problems are due to processes, while 15% stem from the people working in them. (At the end of his life, W. Edwards Deming thought that the ratio was closer to 96-to-4.)"

    Among the greatest quality theorists and practitioners, if not the greatest, were Drs. Joseph Juran (1904–2008) and W. Edwards Deming (1900–1993).

    Nevertheless, it would have been better stated that 85% or 96% of the *errors* are made by people working in the design and communication of the design of the processes, while 15% or 4% of the *errors* are made by people implementing the processes.

69

- Additional research is needed beyond this presenter's *Taxonomy of Human Error Causal Factors*—research to enable the identification of *errors* derived from various other categories of human *attributes* such as emotional, moral, ethical, perceptual, aesthetical, and spiritual.

A. V. Feigenbaum's Total Quality Function

	Prevention	Detection & Correction
Quality of Design	X	X
Quality of Conformance to Design	X	X

- The scope of the functions to which to apply *barriers* must be understood.

- The work of Drs. Armand V. (Val) Feigenbaum and Joseph Juran (among greatest quality theoreticians and practitioners) was revolutionary.

- Prior to their work, quality control was limited to the concern for conformance to the design, without sufficient concern for the quality of the design

- In his book *Total Quality Control*, Dr. Feigenbaum stressed the concept of *quality of design*. In his book *Quality Control Handbook*, Dr. Juran stressed the concept of *fitness for use*. Both authors pointed out that it is not sensible to limit one's concern to the quality of conformance to the design. One must expand one's concern to the quality of the design, itself, to begin with. A product that conforms to its design is not a quality product if it is unable to perform its intended functions, poses a threat to health and safety, fails frequently, has short life, is difficult to maintain, poses a threat to the environment, or costs a lot to operate.

- These books were first published in 1951. Since that time there has been an increasing concern for *quality of design*. However, in many enterprises, and still today, *quality of design* gets short shrift because it is limited to the product.

- Of course, the primary objective is *defect* or *problem prevention* but, in cases for which *problems* aren't *prevented*, the further objective is timely *problem detection and correction* of its *root* and *contributing causes*.

- The matrix in this slide indicates the need for *barriers* to:
  - *Prevent errors in design;*
  - *Prevent errors in conformance to design;* and
  - *Detect design and conformance errors on a timely basis and correct their causes.*

Marguglio's **Total EHS&Q Function**

	Prevention	Detection & Correction
Quality of Design	Administrative Barriers Technical Barriers Equipment Barriers Human Barriers	Administrative Barriers Technical Barriers Equipment Barriers Human Barriers
Quality of Conformance to Design	Administrative Barriers Technical Barriers Equipment Barriers Human Barriers	Administrative Barriers Technical Barriers Equipment Barriers Human Barriers

- In this slide, an *administrative (procedure) barrier, technical (procedure) barrier* or *equipment barrier* may used to create the product or it may be the product, itself. It makes no difference. A product is either a physical hardware item or a service or, with complex products, a combination of both.

- As stated in the notes for the previous slide, the concern for *quality of design*, even today, is limited in many enterprises to the product. More specifically, the concern for quality of design, even today, is limited to the design of a physical hardware product—as contrasted to concern for the design of a service product.

- Design quality analysis tools and techniques (e.g., *hazard-barrier-effects analysis*) are applied far less often to service products than to a physical hardware products.

- Design quality analysis tools and techniques are applied still less often to the administrative processes that govern the product design, and to the technical processes that convert the product design into the actual product.

- The matrix in this slide indicates the need for *barriers* to:

  - *Prevent errors in design of the administrative processes, technical processes, and equipment,* regardless of whether they are used to create the product or are the product;

  - *Prevent errors in conformance to design;*

  - *Detect design and conformance errors on a timely basis.*

- Remember, an error is *behavior* leading to the *undesired effect* or result. The desired result is (a) performance of the intended functions at the least cost within the constraints of *EHS&Q* criteria, and (b) *mitigation* and *amelioration* of any *undesired effects* should the intended functions not be performed or should *hazards* be activated.

Marguglio's **Total EHS&Q Function**

Quality of Design	Admin Barriers Tech Barriers Equip Barriers Human Barriers	Admin Barriers Tech Barriers Equip Barriers Human Barriers	Admin Barriers Tech Barriers Equip Barriers Human Barriers
Quality of Conformance to Design	Admin Barriers Tech Barriers Equip Barriers Human Barriers	Admin Barriers Tech Barriers Equip Barriers Human Barriers	Admin Barriers Tech Barriers Equip Barriers Human Barriers
	Prevention (Barrier Level 1)	Detection (Barrier Level 2)	Mitigation / Amelioration (Barrier Level 3)

Correction

- Taking the model one step further, the *three barrier levels* are added, recognizing the possible need for their correction—either with regard to *quality of design* or *quality of conformance to design*.

Administrative and Technical Process Barriers

- Law (e.g., legislation, agency rules and regulations, permit and license conditions, agency administrative law judge rulings)
- Commitments
- Values, mission, vision, goals and objectives
- Charters
- Policies
- Administrative procedures
- Technical procedures
- Training
- Management and supervision

- The slide gives a list of various types of *administrative* and *technical process barriers*.

- *Law* is the highest level of *administrative* and *technical process barrier*.

- *Enacted legislation* that establishes the general constraints and authorizes a regulatory agency to exist and to promulgate rules and regulations (constraints) is law. Among the rules and regulations are the requirements that an enterprise acquire a permit or a license as a prerequisite to a given action. For example, a utility must submit an application to and get approval from the Nuclear Regulatory Commission as a prerequisite to the construction and operation of a nuclear powered electricity generation plant. Or a pharmaceutical company must submit an application to and get approval from the Food and Drug Administration as the prerequisite to the public distribution and sale of a new drug. Any commitment given in the application or any condition stipulated in its approval constitutes law.

- Any *ruling made by a regulatory agency's administrative law judge* constitutes law. Of course, the issue could be taken to civil court and any resulting ruling would take precedence over the agency administrative law judge's ruling.

- Any *commitment* made voluntarily to a stakeholder group, such as environmental advocacy group, has the force of law.

- All of the *barriers* below the level of law are intended not only to comply with the law, but also to achieve the economic and technical benefits desired by the enterprise.

- *Values, mission, vision,* and *goals* or *objectives*, to the extent that they constrain, are *barriers*. This presenter's understanding is that in enterprise language, a *goal* differs from an *objective*, the former being that which is ultimately desired, and the latter being that which is desired as an intermediate position, like a milepost, along the way to the goal.

- A *charter* defines the roles, responsibilities and authorities of an organization and, as such, is a *barrier*.

- A *policy* is a general statement of intent, the purpose of which is to guide one toward a desired *behavior*, even in the absence of a procedure. Again, because it imposes constraints, it is a *barrier*.

- *Written procedures* communicate the design of the process by defining each step in the process, and for each step, further defining the specific requirement, specific method by which to achieve the requirement, and individual or organization responsible to implement the step.

- *Training* is a *barrier* that certainly provides constraints on *behavior*.

- The same is true of *management* and *supervision*.

- In all of the foregoing *barriers*, the constraints are intended to induce desired *behavior* such as to *prevent error, detect error or the hazard activated by error*, or to *mitigate and ameliorate the undesired effects of the hazard activated by error*.

- Understand that the desired *behavior* is not only that occurring at the point at which the process is last touched but equally, if not more importantly, is that occurring upstream at the point at which the process is designed.

Procedure Barrier Effectiveness
Process Design versus Process Communication

Process designed well Process communicated poorly	**Process designed well** **Process communicated well**
Process designed poorly Process communicated well	Process designed poorly Process communicated poorly

- The design of a process should be communicated by a written procedure(s). Although a *flow chart* may be used to describe the process in general or a *value chain diagram or table* may be used to describe the most important elements of the process, the written procedure is the only vehicle by which to communicate with sufficient specificity such that it can be implemented with its the technical and economic benefits.

- A process can be designed well and communicated in a well-written procedure. That's the ideal situation.

- A process can be designed well but communicated in a poorly written procedure. This is the easiest condition to detect.

- A process can be designed poorly and communicated in a well-written procedure, although given the former, the latter doesn't help very much. This situation provides a false sense of process quality and is the most difficult condition to identify.

- A process can be designed poorly and communicated in a poorly written procedure, the poor communication quality sometimes masking the poor design quality. This, too, is more easy to identify, but be sure to not limit the correction to merely the quality of communication, neglecting the *quality of the design of the process*.

Question: What types of *attributes* must be considered for a well-designed process?

Procedure Barrier Effectiveness (Cont'd)
Types of Design Quality Attributes for
Administrative and Technical Procedures

- Accuracy
- Adaptability to change
- Breadth of capability
- Capacity
- Flexibility
- Maintainability
- Memory
- Perceptibility
- Precision

- Predictability
- Processing speed
- Reasoning ability
- Repeatability
- Resolution
- Self-checking ability
- Sensory ability
- Simultaneous processing ability

- It seems that equipments are designed with far more knowledge and cognition regarding the types of *attributes* needed to meet *EHS&Q* criteria than are processes. It seems that some processes are designed with little or no design discipline or are not designed at all, but merely allowed to morph into whatever they will be.

- When designing an automobile, the types of *attributes* needed for *EHS&Q* criteria are well understood—even by laypersons. Crash survivability, acceleration ability, maneuverability, visibility, scratch and rust resistance, seating comfort, seating adjustability, gasoline mileage, minimization of carbon monoxide, etc. A layperson could go with this listing for half a page, a professional for much more.

- Administrative and technical process designers and procedure writers should be cognizant of the *attributes* listed on this slide and should be able to design processes and write procedures taking these *attributes* into consideration.

- Absent consideration of these *attributes*, there is the potential for holes in the *administrative* and *technical process / procedure barriers*.

- In addition, procedure writers should be cognizant of criteria or *good practices* for writing procedures

Question: What are some criteria or *good practices* for writing procedures?

Procedure Barrier Effectiveness (Cont'd)
Criteria for Procedure Preparation

- Requirements are consistent with higher level requirements, goals and objectives.
- Steps are effective.
  - Steps are clearly written.
  - Steps are properly sequenced.
  - Interfaces among the steps are matched.
  - Each step provides value—a technical or economic benefit.
  - Steps are sufficiently specific.

- This and the following few slides list only a few of the most important criteria. A thorough writer's guide should be available for use.
- A sub-tier drawing goes into a higher-tier drawing and, therefore, the requirements given in the sub-tier drawing have to be consistent with the requirements of the higher-tier drawing. Similarly, the requirements, methods and responsibilities in procedures should be consistent with the requirements, methods and responsibilities in higher-tier documents, such as in higher-level procedures or policies.
- In the second bulletin the slide, *effective* means two things:
  - *Adequacy*—i.e., no more and no less than that which is necessary to meet the requirements;
  - *Efficiency*—at the least cost with no loss of adequacy.
- Below the second bullet in the slide, all of the sub-bullets are necessary for effectiveness.
- For clarity, the procedure should be written using similar verbiage, language and format, an active voice and familiar language.
- Also, throughout the procedure, acronyms should be defined when they are used the first time, and acronyms should not be used if their use is occasional.
- Suggested reading: *Language in Action*; S. I. Hayakawa, PhD; Chicago: Institute of General Semantics; 1940; 106 pp. (Reprinted: New York: Harcourt Brace and Co.; 1941; 338 pp.)
- Step numbers are assigned to enable the performance of the steps in sequence. If any steps are permitted to be performed in an alternate sequence, permission should be indicated in a procedural *Note* placed immediately above the first of the affected steps.

- The output of a step should match the input of a subsequent step if the subsequent step depends on that output. For example, the output or result of Step 4.2.3 should match the required input for Step 5.1.7.

  A disproportionately large percentage of *errors* made in implementing procedures occurs from mismatched outputs and inputs, especially if there is a hand-off—i.e., when the organization providing the output is different from the organization using the input.

- Aside from steps that are merely connective, so to speak, each step should provide a value to the process. The value is in terms of either a technical or economic benefit.

- Technical and management expertise goes into the design of a step in order to achieve the value of the step—to achieve the technical or economic benefit. The step should be written with **specificity** so as to transfer this design expertise—to retain the technical or economic benefit. If the beneficial way of performing a step is not written with sufficient specificity, the step may be performed in a way that results in the loss of the benefit, or worse.

- There may be a conflict between specificity and simplicity. Certainly, the design of the process should be as simple as possible without loss of adequacy or efficiency. Given an adequate and efficient design, certainly it should be communicated faithfully—i.e., the written procedure should address each *attribute* of the design upon which the process adequacy and efficiency are based.

- Here's a parallel situation. Assume that the design of machined part has 50 dimensional *characteristics*, and that this design cannot be made any simpler. Certainly, the dimensional drawing for the part should show all 50 *characteristics*, each with its required dimension, either as a nominal measure plus and minus the tolerance or as a unilateral maximum or minimum measure.

  Now, assume that a process contains 50 steps, each a task for which actions must be taken in a specific way in order to get the desired adequacy and efficiency. Certainly, the written procedure for this process should show all 50 steps, each with its required specificity.

  None of part information would be omitted in the drawing for the sake of simplicity. Similarly, none of the process information should be omitted in the procedure. Alas, unfortunately, often the information needed for adequacy and efficiency is omitted in the procedure.

- Specificity need not include that which is considered to be "skill-of-the-trade". For example, for gas tungsten arc welding (TIG welding), the welder should have been trained and *qualified* and *certified* with regard to the manual dexterity techniques. Therefore, there is no need for the procedure to include details such as to **dip** the filler metal into the weld puddle and **not drip** the filler metal into the weld puddle, or to move the torch at a steady speed along the joint. These dexterity techniques are skill-of-the-trade.

- Incidentally, one is *qualified* if one has the ability to do the task, whereas one is *certified* if an *independent* third party has attested to one's ability to do the task, based on a formal demonstration of that ability.

- In a live setting, about 50 percent of seminar attendees indicate that they have been discouraged from incorporating specificity into the written procedure for fear of losing flexibility. Writing in generality for fear of losing flexibility is illogical.

Procedure Barrier Effectiveness (Cont'd)
Criteria for Procedure Preparation (Cont'd)

Specificity versus Flexibility

	Inflexibility	Flexibility
Specificity	Undesirable	**Desirable**
Generality	Undesirable	Undesirable

- The antonym of flexibility is inflexibility, not generality. The antonym of specificity is generality, not inflexibility. Therefore, specificity and flexibility are not mutually exclusive. It's entirely logical to expect both specificity and any necessary flexibility or options.

- For each option, the conditions that must apply to enter the option should be specified. The method for performing the option should be specified. The conditions for exiting from the option should be specified.

- Again, the argument that specificity precludes flexibility or options is illogical.

Procedure Barrier Effectiveness (Cont'd)
Criteria for Procedure Preparation (Cont'd)

- "IF" and "THEN"
- Designed to highlight the need for a specific action under a specific situation—e.g.:
  - IF such and such is the case,
  - THEN such and such is the action.

- Here's a technique to help clarify options.
- The use of bold and upper case font further facilitates the recognition that one is entering an option.
- In a procedure, there can be a series of IFs and THENs, each set addressing a different option.

Procedure Barrier Effectiveness (Cont'd)
Criteria for Procedure Preparation (Cont'd)

- Steps are effective. (Cont'd):
  - The method of performing each step is accurate.
  - In each step, inappropriate field decisions are avoided.
  - Each step is within the capability of the process.
  - In a single step, multiple or embedded actions are avoided.
  - Self-checks, peer checks, independent inspections, and contractually and regulatorily required third party inspections are appropriately placed in the process.

- Quantitative measurement *accuracy* is based on two factors—*lack of bias* and *precision*. Lack of bias means that the measures are distributed equally on both sides of the true measure, and that there is no predisposition to measures falling on one or the other side of the true measure. Precision means that the extent of the distribution around the true measure is minimal.

- For a written procedure, or for anything verbal, accuracy should be based on the same two factors, or their equivalents. The statement should be true—unbiased. But also, the statement should be precise or sufficiently specific such that it is reasonably understood in one and only one way, the way in which the writer intended. In other words, the precision or specificity of the language is such that there is no reasonable chance of any alternative interpretations beyond the intent of the author.

- When one reads a dimensional drawing, regardless of whether the dimensional requirement is given as a nominal with a bilateral or unilateral tolerance or as a maximum or minimum measure, the dimensional requirement is fully understood, without any reasonable possibility of any other understanding. There is no reasonable chance of alternative interpretations. It should be the same with a procedure.

- When a procedural step is written such that there can be alternative interpretations, by definition, the procedure, as a *barrier*, has failed.

- When a step is written with insufficient specificity or inaccuracy due to lack of precision or specificity, the procedure user has an option. The user may stop to get a procedural change to eliminate the need for interpretation, or the user may make an interpretation—basically a field decision. Stopping is the correct *behavior* because, too often, field decisions will be wrong—*reflexive-based error*.

- A step that inappropriately requires the making of a field decision, by definition, is a *procedure barrier* failure. The decision should be made in the design process, incorporating the contributions of all of the stakeholders, including those responsible for implementing the procedure.

- A capability study can be used to determine whether a design requirement or a procedural step is within the capability of the process.

- Any mental or physical requirements and methods imposed by the design or procedural step should be within human capabilities. Not only should *human factors engineering* be applied to the design of the hardware, it should be applied to the design of the process as well.

- Often, when this presenter refers to *human error prevention*, the response is "Oh, *human factors*". No, not *human factors, human error prevention*, the former being one of many very important contributors to the latter. The reader is encouraged to further study *human factors*.

- Each step should be limited to a single task for which there is a single individual or single crew, team or group responsible. Multiple tasks in a single step can lead to missing one of the tasks.

- A *warning* or *caution* should not be embedded in a step. It should be a separate and distinct notation preceding the step. If the *warning* or *caution* is embedded, it can go unrecognized until it's too late.

- There are many principles governing the placement of checks, *inspections* and reviews. The principles apply for 100 percent check and *inspection* and for *sampling inspection*. The principles are more complex for *sampling inspection*.

- For example, one simple principle is to place a check or *inspection* immediately preceding a step that necessitates a large expenditure for each item, the purpose being to avoid the large expenditure for any item that already may be *defective*.

- Another simple principle is to place a check or *inspection* immediately following a step for which there is not much *margin* between the process capability and the requirement, or for which there has been a higher than usual occurrence of *defects*.

- Another principle is to take fewer samples less frequently when the *inspection* cost is high relative to the *risk*—of course, within the constraints of a formal *sampling plan*.

- One should learn all of the principles regarding the placement of checks, *inspections* and reviews.

Procedure Barrier Effectiveness (Cont'd)
Criteria for Procedure Preparation (Cont'd)

- Steps are effective. (Cont'd):
  - If a step has the potential for a significant adverse undesired effect because of a human error or an equipment or material failure in the implementation of the process, a mitigation and recovery procedure is specified or referenced.
- Responsibility is assigned such as to provide single point accountability.
- The procedure is qualified.
- A process / procedure owner is assigned.

- Regarding the first sub-bullet, recall from the earlier exercise and case study, that upstream *human error* can be the cause of equipment or material failure in the process currently being implemented.

- In many, many processes, it should be technically and economically feasible for the process to be designed with *multiple barriers* against any *significant adverse undesired effect*—instead of designed with only the single *human* or *equipment barrier*.

- *Responsibility* is assigned either on a step-by-step basis or for the procedure as a whole. The latter usually occurs in maintenance procedures, for example, for which the entire procedure is to be implemented by a single person or a single crew.

- *Qualification of a procedure* means that there has been a formal demonstration that the procedure will yield success:

  - For the full range of operating levels (e.g., machine feeds and speeds);

  - For the full range of material types;

  - For the full range of material dimensions; (The fact that a spot-welding machine produces good welds for an assembly of extreme sheet thicknesses, does not mean the machine will produce good welds for other combinations of sheet thickness.)

  - With the given tools;

  - Under the full range of procedure use environments;

  - With the least *qualified* personnel. (A machine may yield a very high percentage of acceptable products with one operator and a lower percentage with another operator. The difference could be because the first operator knows how to manipulate the machine in a way that the second operator does not, even though both operators are *qualified*.)

- A *process owner* should be established for each procedure. The process owner should be responsible for assuring that the procedure:
  - Remains *qualified*;
  - Is changed to be consistent with hardware design engineering changes;
  - Is changed to take advantage of new technology for technical and economic benefits;
  - Is changed to correct *latent* design anomalies and deficiencies (*latent* because any such anomalies and deficiencies should have been identified in the procedure review and approval process and / or in the procedure *qualification* process.
- These criteria should be incorporated into the procedure on how to write a procedure or into the procedure writer's guide.
- How can it be that even with input from *qualified* users of the process, a *qualified* procedure writer, a *peer's review*, a supervisor's review, a manager's review and, sometimes even a safety engineer's or quality assurance engineer's review—how can it be with all of these that the procedure has design inadequacy?
- At this stage of the Bookinar™, an obvious answer should be that the process was not created using a disciplined design approach to begin with. *Hazard-barrier-effects analysis* and was not used in designing the process, as it should have been.
- Another answer is that the responsibilities of the reviewers are not specified, as they should have been. One logic for these responsibilities is as follows:
  - The proaycess designer, the single individual who makes the final decision on all of the inputs to the process design, is responsible for the:
    - Technical and economic quality of the design—i.e., the ability of the process to fulfill its objectives economically;
    - Accuracy of the process design's conversion into the written procedure.
  - The procedure writer (who should be the process designer) and the peer reviewer are each singularly responsible for:
    - The accuracy of the process design's conversion into the written procedure;
    - Compliance with the procedure on how to write a procedure or the procedure writer's guide.
  - The supervisor is responsible for:
    - Assuring that the procedure design, writing and review processes were implemented;
    - Checking the significant or *critical* procedural steps to assess their design reasonableness and conformance to the procedure on how to write a procedure / procedure writer's guide.
  - The manager is responsible for:
    - Ascertaining that the procedure design, writing and review processes were implemented;
    - Checking a sample of the *critical* steps to assess their design reasonableness.

Procedure Barrier Effectiveness (Cont'd)
Major Issues

- Procedures on how to design processes do not exist or are inadequate.
- Inputs to the design of processes are not obtained from process participants and other appropriate personnel.
- Personnel assigned to design processes, and write and review procedures are not qualified.
- Procedures on how to write procedures / writer's guides are inadequate.
- Procedures are not properly pre-production tested and qualified.
- Human error root causes for the inadequacy of process design and procedure preparation are not identified and corrected.
- Human error root causes for non-compliance with procedures are not identified and corrected.

Case Study—Lack of Consideration for Procedural Corrective Action

Assignment

From the following slide, identify the additional corrective actions that should have been taken or considered, particularly with regard to procedures.

Case Study—Lack of Consideration for Procedural Corrective Action (Cont'd)

Problem Statement:

"Measurements of Reactor Coolant System pressure are not as accurate as they should be because the pressure gauges are calibrated with pressure gauge standards that lack temperature compensation."

Action Taken:

"Procurement of temperature-compensated pressure gauge standards for the calibration of pressure gauges."

- The *problem statement* and *action taken* are from an actual *condition report*. The statement of the *problem* in this slide does not meet the criteria for such as described starting on page 237, but that's not the subject of this assignment.
- The pressure gauges are installed in the plant to measure pressure in a closed system. These installed gauges are *working instruments*. The pressure gauge standards that were procured are laboratory *working standards* or *company standards*.
- The action quoted on the slide is the only action that was recorded in the *condition report and corrective action tracking* tool.
- Some of the following additional actions were not taken; and some were, although not recorded.

Assignment Completion

- The technical procedure for calibrating the installed pressure gauge working instruments must be revised to require the use of the newly acquired pressure gauge working standards. The absence of this action was a lack of concern for procedural *corrective action*.
- It would have been conservative to verify that a requirement exists for the revision of any calibration procedure whenever there is a change to the working standard to be used for the calibration. If such a requirement is lacking, either the existing administrative procedure should be corrected or a new administrative procedure should be originated to establish this requirement. The absence of this verification indicated a lack of concern for procedural *corrective action*.
- The newly acquired pressure gauge working standards should be added to the calibration control system.

Assignment Completion (cont'd)

- It would have been conservative to verify the existence of an administrative process for incorporating any newly acquired measurement device (working instrument, working standard or higher level standard) into the calibration control system. If such a process is lacking, either the existing administrative procedure should be corrected or a new administrative procedure should be originated to establish this requirement, method and responsibility. The absence of this action indicated a lack of concern for procedural *corrective action*.

- The need to revise instrument loop setpoints based on the improved accuracy of the pressure measurements should be determined. (A set point is a measure at which at an action is to be taken—either an automated or manual action.)

- It would have been conservative to verify the existence of an administrative process for investigating the need for loop setpoint changes whenever there is instrumentation design change or accuracy change. If such a process is lacking, either the existing administrative procedure should be corrected or a new administrative procedure should be originated to establish this requirement, method and responsibility. The absence of this action indicated a lack of concern for procedural *corrective action*.

- The newly acquired temperature-compensated pressure gauge standards (the working standards), themselves, must be incorporated into the calibration control system.

- It would have been conservative to verify the existence of an administrative process for incorporating any newly acquired measurement devices into the calibration control system and for assuring that the means exist by which to perform their calibration or by which to acquire the performance of their calibration—rather than using the new devices to the point of their calibration expiration and then, belatedly, determining whether or not they, themselves, can be calibrated. If such a process is lacking, either the existing administrative procedure should be corrected or a new administrative procedure should be originated to establish this requirement, method and responsibility. The absence of this action indicated a lack of concern for procedural *corrective action*.

- There should be a search for any other measurements that are being made without necessary temperature compensation.

- Of course, the biggest questions are: What *attributes* were lacking in the humans who failed to take some of these actions and Why? Why? Why?

- -

- Often the poor quality of the **wording** of a *preventive corrective action* statement is such as to contribute to failure to correct a procedure or to correct the cause of the procedural inadequacy to begin with.

Case Study
Hose Cleaning Procedure

Assignment

In the following procedure:

- Identify each part or step in which one or more of the criteria for procedure preparation (addressed previously) was violated.

- Identify the violated criterion.

- Describe the nature of the violation.

Case Study—Hose Cleaning Procedure

The following procedure is given here verbatim except that the procedure basic number, the procedure revision number, approval titles and signatures, and change history have been deleted intentionally. A Fortune 100 company used this procedure. This is not an example from a small, newly developing company that might initially lack management and technical sophistication.

TITLE: Hose Cleaning Procedure.

APPLICABILITY: This procedure is to be implemented any time there are hoses to be cleaned of the various chemicals our equipment has transported.

PROCEDURE SUMMARY: The implementation of this procedure will affect the integrity and cleanliness of the hoses being cleaned as well as the safety of the personnel involved in the cleaning process.

SAFETY CONSIDERATIONS: The Tank Wash Technician(s) responsible for this procedure are to use all required protective equipment for all phases of this procedure. This includes but is not limited to Tyvek suit, rubber gloves, full-face respirator, hardhat and when not wearing the full-face respirator a face shield, safety glasses or splash goggles.

PROCEDURE ITEMS:

1.0 When drivers return from a trip with a trailer and hoses that need to be cleaned they are to park the dirty trailer in the designated area. Dirty hoses are to remain in the trailer's hose tubes. Dirty hoses will be removed by the Tank Wash Technicians, and moved to the hose cleaning area.

Case Study—Hose Cleaning Procedure (Cont'd)

2.0 Hoses are to be placed on the hose transport cart and moved to the hose cleaning area. Before loading hoses on the cart technicians are to check to insure caps and plugs are in place and secured.

3.0 Remove hoses from transport cart to hose cleaning staging area. With all protective gear on and in place carefully remove caps and plugs from the ends of the hoses.

4.0 Place one end of the hose in the appropriate residual materials drum and walk hose (rolled) towards the drum. This procedure is being completed in an attempt to remove excess or remaining materials left in the hose.

5.0 Using the fresh water hose (city supplied water) flush hose to remove remaining residual chemicals from hoses interior.

6.0 After flushing hose it is again to be walked (rolled) to remove excess water from hose prior to placing hose in the MEA Cleaning Vat.

7.0 The temperature of the material in the MEA Cleaning Vat is to be checked. The operating temperature of the MEA Cleaning Vat is to be maintained in the range of 200°F—215°F. If temperature is below the normal operating range adjust steam to heat cleaning medium to the desired temperature.

8.0 Open the protective covers on the Hose Cleaning Vat and attach the hoses to the circulating manifold. Arrange hoses so that they are laying flat and not touching each other. The exterior of the hoses is not to come in direct contact with the cleaning medium.

9.0 Open the inlet block valves to the attached hoses, insuring that the bleed valves are secured.

10.0 Close the protective covers on the Hose Cleaning Vat and turn on the Hose Cleaning Vats circulating pump. Check gauge to insure proper flow and circulation.

Note: Care must be used when opening or closing the covers on the Hose Cleaning Vat due to the weight of the covers and the possibility of extreme temperatures and fumes.

11.0 Circulation of the cleaning medium through the hoses should be maintained for a period of 30 minutes. This time will vary depending on the products that are being cleaned and the condition of the hoses after the initial flushing.

12.0 At the completion of the cleaning cycle, shut down the circulating pump. Disconnect the hoses from the circulating manifold and place hoses on pre-stage rack.

13.0 Using the Brightner wand, coat the interior of hoses that are removed from the Hose Cleaning Vat. This step is being completed to remove any residual MEA stains that might have adhered to the hose interior.

14.0 Flush hoses of all residual materials completely using fresh water (city-supplied water). Not under any circumstances is the pressure washer system or the high pressure Ken Jet System to be used for flushing of hoses. **Use of these systems can cause damage to the hoses interior linings.**

Case Study—Hose Cleaning Procedure (Cont'd)

15.0 After flushing, hoses are to be walked (rolled) to remove excess water. Hoses are then to be loaded on the transport cart and moved over to the hose testing area for the Hose Pressure Testing Procedure XXX (number intentionally omitted here).

Assignment Completion

- The following analysis may serve to complete the assignment:
- *Safety Considerations* Section:
  - There is a lack of clarity and specificity in the statement that personal protection equipment (PPE) "includes but is not limited to". The additional PPE that may be used and the conditions for its use are not described.
  - There is a lack of technical adequacy and specificity in the requirement to wear a "full face respirator, hard hat and when not wearing the full face respirator" the requirement to wear "a face shield, safety glasses or splash goggles". The conditions under which to use a full face respirator versus a face shield, safety glasses or splash goggles are not specified. The protection provided by a full face respirator is different than that provided by a face shield and glasses or goggles.
- *Step 2.0*:
  - There is an incorrect sequence in that the first task should be to check the caps and plugs.
  - Given that the two tasks are closely related, although not the best practice, it's permissible to have them both in the same step. Notice, however, that had they been in separate steps, the sequencing *problem* would have been obvious.
- *Step 3.0*:
  - There is an incorrect sequence in that the *warning* to use "protective gear" should come first, preferably as a *CAUTION* or *WARNING* (a separate section) preceding Step 2.0.
  - There is a lack of clarity and specificity in the requirement to "carefully remove" caps and plugs.. If the purpose of this is to prevent spillage of material from the hose, it should be so stated. Notice that the purpose of rolling the hose is appropriately stated in Step 4.0.
- *Step 4.0*:
  - There is a lack of specificity as to the method by which the technician is to determine what material is in the hose so that the end of the hose can be placed in the drum designated for that material, the objective being to prevent the mixture of pollutants and toxics.
  - There is a lack of specificity as to the method by which the technician can prevent or minimize the contamination of the hose exterior. This is desirable even though the hose will be cleaned later in a vat.
- Missing Step:
  - There is a missing task or step. In order to flush the hose, per Step 5.0, the hose must be unrolled.

Assignment Completion (cont'd)

- *Step 5.0*:
  - There is a question of the technical adequacy of this step from the perspective of environmental protection, since the flush is going to a drain.
- There's no need to continue with the analysis of this procedure. The points are made.

Points Demonstrated by Case Study:

- This is merely an example of the ways in which the criteria for the preparation of a procedure, the *good practices*, can be violated.
- Logic should indicate that these violations create the potential for *procedure barrier* failure. For example, because of lack of procedure specificity, if an technician is not informed of the conditions under which to use one PPE or another, the technician can be harmed.

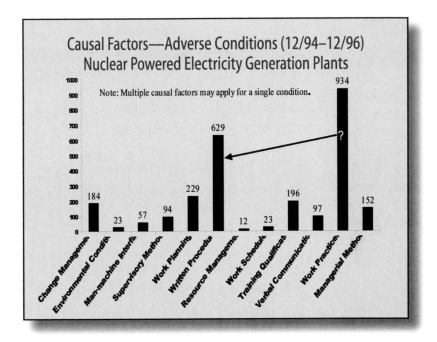

Causal Factors—Adverse Conditions (12/94–12/96)
Nuclear Powered Electricity Generation Plants

- This *bar chart* is taken from a study made by the Institute for Nuclear Power Operations (INPO).

- Reports of adverse conditions submitted to INPO by its member nuclear powered electricity generating facilities from December 1994 to December 1996 were analyzed. INPO found that *Work Practices* (practices employed by workers) contributed 35.5 percent (934 of 2630) of the total number of causes for the adverse conditions, and that *Written Procedures* contributed 23.9 percent (629 of 2630) of the total number of causes for the adverse conditions.

- Although INPO found *Work Practices* to be the most *problematic* and *Written Procedures* to be the second most *problematic,* in the experience of this presenter, based on reviewing literally hundreds, if not thousands, of similar types of reports (e.g., *condition reports, problem reports, incident reports, audit finding reports*) written procedure inadequacies contribute to a far greater extent than worker practice inadequacies. To reflect this experience. this presenter modified the *bar chart* by adding the question mark and arrow.

- Regardless of the difference, the data indicates that there is a large opportunity for reducing the frequency of adverse conditions (adverse effects) by reducing the frequency of procedure inadequacies.

Challenge

The best way
of reducing the frequency of events
is by identifying and eliminating
the causes of human error
in the management domain—
particularly with regard to
quality of the design
of the administrative and technical processes,
and
quality of the communication of the design
in the written procedures.

- Managers have the responsibility to *prevent* and to identify or *detect* and *correct* any poorly designed process and poorly written procedure prior to its use.

- Widespread failure to use and adhere to a written procedure may be caused by the failure to properly design the process and properly communicate the design in the written procedure.

- Just as management professionals long ago recognized the futility of *quality of conformance* in the absence of *quality of design*, so do first line workers.

Training Barrier

- *Training* is a type of *administrative process barrier*.
- Training must be well designed and well implemented. Otherwise, it will not be effective.

> ## Training Barrier Effectiveness
> ## Systematic Approach to Training
>
> - Analysis—Performance of job and task gap analyses
> - Design—Establishment of training requirements
> - Development—Preparation of training schedules, materials, etc in accordance with design
> - Implementation—Delivery of training
> - Evaluation—Assessment of the effectiveness of training

- The *Systematic Approach to Training* may be used to assist in the proper design and implementation of training.

- The *Systematic Approach to Training* may be known by other names or it may exist in an enterprise without a name.

- The broad steps in the *Systematic Approach to Training* very much follow the broad steps in the design of a hardware item.

- The initial step is the performance of *job and task gap analysis* to identify the jobs and tasks within a job for which training is required but for which training does not now exist. This might be akin to the enterprise Marketing Department identifying the need (or creating the need) for a product that does not now exist.

- One of the important causes of training ineffectiveness is the failure to perform a thorough *job and task analysis*.

Training Barrier Effectiveness (Cont'd)
Task Analysis

- Identifying needs for the performance of the task:
  - Information
  - Cognitive abilities
  - Physical abilities and skills
  - Certifications
  - Beliefs, values and attitudinal state

- For each task, as a minimum, the needs in the five areas shown on the slide must be identified

- These needs may apply to both employee selection and employee training.

- The information needed for the performance of the task must be identified, and the level of specificity of the needed information also must be identified. The latter is often overlooked.

- Recall the earlier discussion of Bloom's *levels of cognition* on pages 44–46. The cognitive abilities necessary for the performance of the task must be identified.

- The enterprise should not have to provide training for information and cognitive abilities that one should have acquired in high school or college. Rather, the enterprise must provide training for information and cognitive abilities that apply to processes that are unique to the enterprise. Of course, forward-looking enterprises help their employees to obtain additional schooling.

- Obviously, the necessary physical abilities and skills must be identified—e.g., the ability to differentiate among colors, or to lift and carry an item of a given weight and configuration for a given distance at a given frequency in a given period of time. Notice that the physical requirements are identified with specificity. Color blindness can't be overcome by training. Therefore, this need constitutes an employee selection requirement as contrasted to a training requirement. Likewise, an enterprise can't be expected to provide strength training at its own expense (other than the opportunity for it as an employee benefit). Strength is an individual responsibility. Therefore, any needed strength constitutes an employee selection requirement, not a training requirement.

- Recall from an earlier discussion, the difference between *qualification* and *certification*. (See page 80.) Any needed *certification* that is issued by an outside entity constitutes an employee selection requirement.

- Other often-overlooked *attributes* that may be required for a given task are one's *beliefs*, *values* and *attitude*. Certainly, the nature of each of these for a given task or set of tasks is much harder to determine but following are a couple of examples. For a senior reactor operator at a nuclear powered electricity generating plant, one would need *beliefs*, *values* and an *attitude* that are consistent with an *EHS&Q-conscious work environment* (particularly a nuclear safety-conscious work environment) as addressed on page 13—an *attitude* that encourage the identification of potential *problems* and strict adherence to procedure. For a high school counselor, one might want *beliefs*, *values* and an *attitude* that are consistent with helping a student to gain admission to a college or university based on the student's accomplishments, rather than on his or her social or economic status.

- All tasks, sets of tasks and jobs have needs that are universal and that go well beyond the five listed in the slide—e.g., ethics and morality. The criteria for these are reasonably well established. Although the very fine points of ethics and morality may be subjects for training provided by the enterprise, basically, these are employee selection criteria.

- Any task, set of tasks and job may have still additional needs that are not necessarily universal and that also go well beyond the five listed in the slide—e.g., perceptibility, aesthetic ability, spirituality. Of course, the criteria for these are quite subjective.

Training Barrier Effectiveness (Cont'd)
Systematic Approach to Training

- Analysis—Performance of job and task gap analyses
- Design—Establishment of training requirements
- Development—Preparation of training schedules, materials, etc in accordance with design
- Implementation—Delivery of training
- Evaluation—Assessment of the effectiveness of training

- For the given tasks in the given job, the requirements for the training must be established based on the results of the job and task gap analysis. The output from the this analysis is a training requirements document. This is akin to preparing the documents that describe the design of a hardware item.

- The training requirements document must specify: the job titles to which the training applies; whether the training is mandatory or optional; the prerequisites for the training; the training content in detail; the method and setting for the delivery of the training; the frequency of the delivery of the training; the method of assessing the effectiveness of the training; if by test, the test design criteria, including the methods for remediation; and, finally, the qualifications of those who will deliver the training.

- The development of the training materials is akin to the manufacture of the hardware item.

- Of course, the training must be implemented in accordance with its design, just as the hardware item must be used in accordance with its design.

- Training effectiveness may be evaluated by testing (the higher the test scores, the more effective the training), correlating test results with performance on the job (the higher the correlation, the greater the effectiveness), measuring training attendance, and making field observations of the delivery of the training.

- Failure to use the *systematic approach to training* will result in failure of training as an *administrative barrier*.

- Failure to use the *systematic approach to training* may be caused by *knowledge*-or *cognition-based human error*.

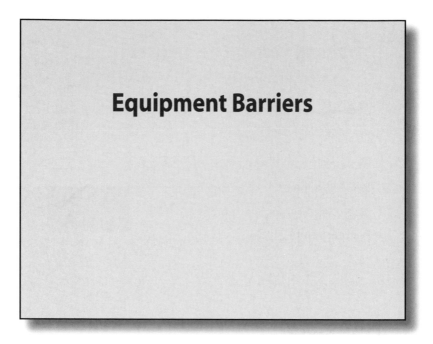

Equipment Barriers

- The *design attributes* for *administrative* and *technical process barriers* were addressed on pages 78–86.
- The *design attributes* for *equipment barriers* will be addressed in the next few pages but not in detail because the creation of these *attributes* is dependent upon the type of equipment and the design engineering discipline in question.

Equipment Barrier Effectiveness Design Attributes

- Abilities
  - Functionability
  - Ability to fabricate, assemble, install, construct (manufacturability and constructability)
  - Inspectability and testability
  - Reliability, maintainability and availability
  - Operability
  - Disposability
- Design margin—design ruggedness
- Single failure and common mode failure avoidance
- Fail-safe
- Human factored

- *Equipment* in this context means any item of hardware—e.g., a part, component, sub-assembly, assembly, module, sub-system, system, or structure.

- *Functionability* means that the requirements established for the equipment are such as to enable the equipment to work in accordance with requirements, expectations and needs.

- A functional *characteristic* is one that receives an input and provides an output.

- For example, an electrical component receives an electrical input and provides a voltage output. The component's specified voltage output of 120 volts + 5% is a functional *characteristic*.

- Or, a concrete pad receives a load from a truck and does not crack. The concrete's specified load bearing minimum of 3000 psi is a functional *characteristic*.

- *Manufacturability* and *constructability* (*workability*) mean that the requirements for the design *characteristics* of the equipment can be met in the manufacturing or construction process—i.e., attainment of the requirements is within the capability of the manufacturing or construction process.

- Similarly, *inspectability* and *testability* mean that conformance to the requirements for the *design characteristics* can be determined by *inspection* and *test*—i.e., determination of conformance is within the capability of the *inspection* and *testing* processes or techniques.

- *Manufacturability, constructability, inspectability and testability* can be enhanced by *poka-yoke* techniques. (See pages 108–109.)

- *Reliability* relates to the equipment's resistance to failure. *Reliability* is the probability that the equipment (or the human) will perform in accordance with functional requirements for a specified uninterrupted period of time under specified operating, maintenance and environmental conditions. *Reliability* is a specialized functional requirement. The duration of the *life* of an equipment and its *failure rate* are measures of its *reliability*.

- *Maintainability* relates to the equipment's ease of maintenance. *Maintainability* is the probability that a failed equipment can be restored to conform to its functional requirements within a specified period of time under specified maintenance and environmental conditions. The maintenance time in question is the time for: identification of the failure, location of the failure, isolation of the failure, correction of the failure, and verification that the correction has been effective. *Mean time to restore* is a measure of *maintainability*.

- *Availability* relates to the equipment's readiness for use. *Availability* is the probability that an equipment will be able to perform in accordance with its functional requirements when called upon. The ratio of *up-time* to *calendar-time* is a measure of *availability*.

- *Operability* relates to the equipment's ease of use. *Operability* means that the equipment can be operated in accordance with its functional requirements by a *qualified* operator under specified environmental conditions.

- *Disposability* is the ease with which the equipment, at the end of its life, or any part of the equipment, can be disposed of without violating environmental requirements or without excessive expenditure.

- *Design margin* is the amount of difference between the measure needed for an equipment *characteristic* versus the measure established for that *characteristic*. For example, if the maximum load on a concrete pad is 2,000 psi and the design document calls for the placement of 3,000 psi concrete, there is a 1,000 psi *margin* or 50% *margin*. The greater the *margin*, the more rugged the design.

- Almost always, it is standard practice to require that any design be such that a *single failure* cannot result in an *event*. If so, the design is almost always unacceptable unless the degree of design ruggedness is sufficiently great as to render the failure a probabilistic unreality, given compliance with the requirements, and given that compliance is determined by at least multiple *barriers*. *Fault tree* and *event tree analyses* should be used to identify any potential *single failure* that can result in an *event*. (See pages 323–332.)

- Similarly, it is standard practice to require that any design be such that any credible *common mode failure* cannot result in an *event*. A *common mode failure* is one for which some occurrence (often an act of God or an act of nature) results in the loss of all of the redundancy for a given function. For example, a pipe bursts, flooding a room in which there are redundant channels providing a critically important pressure measurement. The flood causes the loss of all of the redundant channels resulting in the necessity for plant shutdown.

- *Fail-safe* means that the design is such that any failure will not result in an *event*. Recall from the *Therac-25 Case Study* that the absence of an interlock rendered the design *non-fail-safe*. (See pages 56–61.)

- A design that is *human factored* is one for which equipment operating and maintenance requirements and/or process performance requirements are compatible with human capabilities and needs.

- The *International Ergonomics Association* and the *Human Factors and Ergonomics Society* provide the following definition: "Ergonomics (or human factors) is the scientific discipline concerned with the understanding of interactions among humans and other elements of a system, and the profession that applies theory, principles, data and methods to design in order to optimize human well-being and overall system performance. Ergonomists contribute to the design and evaluation of tasks, jobs, products, environments and systems in order to make them compatible with the needs, abilities and limitations of people."

- This definition recognizes that not only equipments should be designed, but that jobs and tasks (processes) should be designed, as well, and designed such as to be compatible with humans.

Administrative and Technical Barriers for Equipment Barrier Effectiveness

- Classification of design characteristics
- Design analyses and reviews
- Prototype inspection and testing
- Pre-production inspection and testing
- Environmental qualification
- Accelerated life testing
- Production inspection and testing
- Preventive and corrective maintenance
- Periodic in-service inspection and testing
- Configuration management

- In order to achieve effective physical *equipment barriers*, the processes listed on the slide must be effective. These processes must be well designed, and well communicated in written procedures, and the procedures must be consistently implemented.

- The proper design of these processes requires management and technical expertise based on a high level of knowledge and cognition so as to avoid *knowledge-based* and *cognition-based error*.

- Recall the *Therac-25 Case Study*, on pages 56–61, in which it was demonstrated that failures of physical *equipment barriers* are preceded by failures in the *administrative* and *technical process barriers* that govern the design, manufacture / construction, maintenance and use of the physical equipment.

- The design of the administrative and technical processes for each area listed in the slide is well beyond the scope of this Bookinar™. Each would require a Bookinar™ in itself.

- For example, for configuration management in a plant, to *prevent* an *event*, the process for returning a functionally modified equipment to service must require issuance of:

  - Documentation of *inspection* and *test* acceptance of the modified equipment;

  - Revised critical design documents and their placement in the Plant Central Control Room (CCR), with removal of any obsolete design documents;

  - Revised operating procedures (normal and off-normal operating procedures) and their placement in the CCR, with removal of any obsolete procedures;

  - Documentation of operator *walk-down* of and training for the modification.

This is merely one requirement, albeit an important one, among literally many, many dozens of requirements that must exist in the design of the configuration management process.

Human Barriers

- Abilities and skills
- Fitness for duty
- Behaviors to prevent human error
- Culture

- One's abilities and skills are human *barriers* to *error*. It's incumbent upon one to maintain these abilities and skills consistent with advancements in technology and the body of knowledge applicable to one's position.

- Also, it's incumbent upon one to maintain *fitness for duty* consistent with the criteria for that *fitness*.

- Unfortunately, the *barriers* (agency rules and regulations and corresponding enterprise policies and procedures) governing the number of hours that a worker may work in a given period are not wholly effective because there is no reliable method by which to *independently* ascertain whether or not the worker has had sufficient sleep and rest during his or her off duty hours. Therefore, it's imperative upon the worker to declare his or her unfitness in the absence of sufficient rest. Too often, this is not done because of economic considerations. (See pages 128–131.)

- *Behaviors* to *prevent human error* are acquired, not inherent. A progressive enterprise provides its employees with the opportunity to learn and practice these *behaviors* that, in large part, are the subject of the next section of this Bookinar™—starting on page 122.

- One's *culture* is critical to the effectiveness of one's *human barriers*. (See pages 11–15.)

Poka-Yoke

- Techniques intended to:
  - Minimize the potential for error
  - Prevent a process from being completed incorrectly, thereby minimizing the effects of error
  - Provide a signal indicating the erroneous state of a given characteristic or process, thereby minimizing the effects of error.

- *Poka-yoke* is a Japanese term which means *mistake proofing.* To some extent, the meaning is a misnomer. *Proofing* implies the absolute *prevention* of *error. Poka-yoke* does not absolutely *prevent error.* Nothing is capable of doing that.

- Rather, *poka-yoke* provides techniques that are intended to do the three things listed in the slide. Some of these techniques have been in existence long before the term *poka-yoke* came into popular usage.

- A technique for minimizing the potential for *error* is color-coding. For example, for cable connections, the plug and receptacle to be connected each may be the same color.

- A technique for *preventing* a process from being completed incorrectly is keying. For example, with one's lap top computer, one cannot incorrectly insert the CD Writer cable into the computer port because the cable and the port are keyed such that the cable can only be inserted correctly. However, the keying does not *prevent* the *initial error* which is made in trying to insert the cable 180° in reverse. Key provides assurance that the process can be completed only in the correct way.

- Here's a technique that both minimizes the potential for *error* and provides a signal indicating an *erroneous state.* An assembler is given a tray in which each of the 25 parts of the assembly is snugly fitted into its mold in the tray. Furthermore, the parts lay in the tray in the order in which they are to be assembled. The tray minimizes the potential for *error.* It provides all 25 parts, it indicates the likelihood that each part is the correct part given that it fits into its mold, and it provides the parts in their order of assembly. (Of course, a part may not be correct simply because it fits into its mold. A design change may have affected other than dimensional configuration.) Upon completion of the assembly, if there is a part remaining in the tray, it signals an *error* in assembly.

- Here's another example of a technique that provides a signal of an *erroneous state*. Using a stopwatch, the minimum time necessary to correctly perform a given operation on a moving line has been determined to be 20 seconds. It's humanly impossible to perform the task correctly with any greater speed. An installed device senses the duration of time between the completion of one movement of the line and the start of the next movement of the line. If that time is less than 20 seconds, the device also provides an audio signal indicating that an *error* has been made.

- An Internet search will yield *poka-yoke* techniques that have been designed for numerous products.

- The teaching of *poka-yoke* techniques is beyond the scope of this Bookinar™ because each technique is specific to the hardware or process design. The purpose of this limited coverage of the subject is to familiarize the reader with the three objectives of *poka-yoke* and to urge that these objectives be established for the design of hardware and processes.

	Higher ← Degree of Dependability → Lower					
	Equipment Barriers			Admin & Tech Proc Barriers		
Barrier Objectives	Automated Interlock	Manual Switch	PPE	Procedure	Training	Super-vision
Alert						
Warn						
Prevent						
Detect						
Protect						
Contain						
Recover						
Escape						
Mitigate						

- This slide has a few purposes.

- First, the slide indicates that *administrative* and *technical procedure barriers* are less dependable than equipment *barriers*.

- Second, the slide indicates that the greater the extent to which the *equipment barrier* interacts with an *administrative* and *technical procedure barrier*, the lesser the dependability of the *equipment barrier*.

- Personal protective equipment (PPE) is an *equipment barrier* of lesser value when the corresponding procedure (an *administrative barrier*) lacks specificity as to the conditions for which each item of PPE is to be used. Recall the exercise for the hose cleaning procedure for which there was just such a lack of specificity. (See pages 91–94.)

- A switch may be a part of an *equipment barrier*. If a fire suppression system is designed with a manual on/off switch, it's possible that the switch could be in the *off* position at the time that the system is needed, as happened on the *Piper Alpha* oil and gas rig. (See pages 168–174.)

- Recall that for the *Therac-25 Case Study* an automated interlock certainly would have saved the day. (See pages 56–61.)

- Third, this slide indicates that *barriers* may have any of nine objectives, as follows:

- To *alert* means to create awareness. For example, a poster or flag may create an awareness of a given subject.

- To *warn* mean to go a step further than to *alert* or create awareness. A *warning* may be for something that has either greater potential for occurrence or greater adverse effect. For example, a *statistical process control (SPC) chart* showing a string of measures above the prior *arithmetic average measure*, may be a *warning* that the *average measure* may be shifting or has shifted. Or a statement in a procedure immediately preceding an environmentally hazardous operation may provide a *warning*.

- To *prevent* means to avoid the occurrence of something. The example in the preceding bullet can be expanded. The *SPC chart* may be used in conjunction with a procedure. The procedure may require that if *x* number of measures occur in sequence above the *average*, the process is to be stopped and adjusted to re-center the measures, thereby avoiding a future measure that is beyond the control limit and avoiding the creation of a *defective* unit. The combination of the chart and procedure constitutes a *prevention barrier*.

- The lines of demarcation among these terms (*alert, warn* and *prevent*) may not always be clear. However, that's not very important. In the model on page 65, the *first level of barriers is for the prevention of human error*. At this level, the *barrier* objectives may exist in combination—to *alert, warn* and / or *prevent*.

- To *detect* means to identify the occurrence of something. A sensing device may *detect* an off-normal condition. A recording device in a Control Room may communicate the *detection*. It may be communicated further by an alarm.

- Continuing with the *SPC chart* example, a measure outside of a *control limit* may indicate an *out-of-control process*. The chart communicates the *out-of-control condition*.

- In the model on page 65, the *second level of barriers is for the detection of human error*, either upon the occurrence of the *error* or upon the occurrence of its *undesired effect*-hopefully, the former.

- To *protect* is to *prevent* injury or damage.

- To *contain* is to limit an uncontrolled discharge or release or to minimize the discharge or release or to minimize the number of *defects* produced, once a state of *defectiveness* is detected.

- To *escape* is to place out of harm's way or to be removed from the *undesired effects* of a hazard.

- *Protection, containment, recovery, escape* and other *mitigation* and *amelioration* techniques are all objectives within the scope of the *third level of barriers* in the model on page 65.

Exercise
Type of Barrier and Barrier Objective

Assignment

For the barriers on the following slide:

- Identify the type of barrier (administrative process, technical process, or equipment).

- Describe the objective of the barrier.

- Using the *Marguglio's Model of an Event* (page 65), identify the level of the barrier—first, second or third.

Exercise
Type of Barrier and Barrier Objective (Cont'd)

- Valve tag-out / isolation
- Low tank level alarm
- Pressure sensor
- Boundary sign
- Reactor containment building
- Confined space sign posting
- Confined space monitor
- Emergency plan

- Pre-job briefing
- Switchyard fence
- Written process description
- Emergency operating procedure
- Safety injection pump
- Anti-contamination clothing
- Designated challenger
- Reactor safe shutdown system

Assignment Completion—Following are samples of the completion of the assignment:

- *Valve tag-out / isolation*
  - Type of *barrier: Equipment,* in conjunction with an *administrative procedure*
  - Purpose: *Prevention*
  - Level in the model on page 65: *1st level, preventing error.*
- *Low tank level alarm*
  - Type of *barrier: Equipment,* in conjunction with an *administrative procedure*
  - Purpose: *Detection*
  - Level in the model on page 65: *2nd level, detecting error or detecting the adverse effects of error*
- *Reactor containment building*
  - Type of *barrier: Equipment*
  - Purpose: *Containment,* obviously
  - Level in the model on page 65: *3rd level, mitigation and amelioration of the effects of the hazard activated by the error*
- *Pre-job briefing* (See pages 138–140.)
  - Type of *barrier: Administrative procedure*
  - Purpose: *Prevention*
  - Level in the model on page 65: *1st level, preventing error*

Automation

- Operation with greater precision
- Operation with greater consistency, less variation
- Operation with greater speed
- Operation for a longer continuous time
- Operation with less failure

- -

- Operation with higher safety and quality at less expense

- The slide provides a list of the reasons for automating a step or steps in a process.
- The reasons all boil down to enabling the operation to be performed with higher *EHS&Q attributes* at less expense.
- Given the availability of the technology and an appropriate return on investment, automation is the way to go, except when the task requires sensitivities (such as perceptibility) beyond the ability of an automat. The next slide gives an example of that.

On the Other Hand—Over Automation

Can a computer read the following?

The hmuan mnid has phaonmneal pweor. Aoccdrnig to rscheearch at Cmabrigde Uinervtisy, the oredr of the ltteers in a word deosn't mttaer. The olny iprmoatnt tihng is that the frist and lsat ltteer be in the rghit pclae. The rset can be a taotl mses and one can still raed it wouthit a porbelm. This is bcuseae the huamn mnid deos not raed ervey lteter by istlef, but the wrod as a wlohe.

Case Study—Stator Bar Removal

Assignment—For the following scenario:

- Identify each failed barrier.
- Categorize each failed barrier as to its type—i.e., administrative process, technical process, equipment or human.
- Describe why the barrier is considered to be a failure.
- Determine whether the failed barrier was due to inadequate design or non-conformance to design.
- Determine whether the barrier failure could have been detected and corrected earlier.
- Using postulated scenarios and the *Human Error Causal Factor Taxonomy*, determine the possible human error causal factors for each failed barrier.

Case Study—Stator Bar Removal

A member of a generator stator bar removal crew was injured during the process of removing a stator bar from the stator of a generator.

Written Procedure:

Presenter's Note: The following steps constitute the body of the written procedure in toto. Anything not stated in the following steps did not exist in the written procedure.

Procedure Title: Stator Bar Removal

1. Lift the turbine end of a stator bar out of its slot using an overhead chain hoist.
2. Insert a glass fiber wedge (4' long and 1 ½' wide) half way or 2' under the stator bar. The weight and return flexing force of the bar holds the wedge in place.
3. Using another hoist, an air driven mechanical winch or "tugger", with a wire rope, attach a sling to the end of the rope.
4. Wrap the sling around the notch in the back of the wedge.
5. Increase tension with the tugger, such that the wedge is pulled toward the tugger, underneath the bar, raising the bar out of its slot.
6. When the bar is sufficiently out of its slot, remove the bar by hand.
7. Remove the wedge by hand.
8. Repeat Steps 1–7 for each stator bar.

Case Study—Stator Bar Removal (Cont'd)

Photograph #1—Crew-Member Holding Wedge

Photograph #2—Tugger

Case Study—Stator Bar Removal (Cont'd)

Problem:

The stator is designed with slide ripple springs that are used to retain the stator bar in its slot. The ripple springs are positioned between the edge of the bar and the wall of the slot. As the wedge is slid under the stator bar, the leading edge of the wedge has a tendency to "capture" the side ripple springs. If enough springs are captured, the wedge becomes jammed in the slot. This occurs a minimum of 10 times and a maximum of 15 times per stator. When this occurs, the stuck wedge is removed by hammering it up and out with a mallet, sufficiently to create "grip points" enabling the manual removal of the wedge.

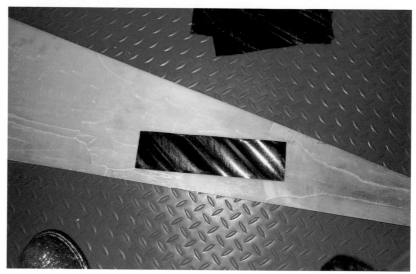

Photograph #3—Side Ripple Spring

Accident Scenario:

For this stator bar, Step 1 of the procedure was accomplished by (a) attaching a sling to the overhead hoist chain, (b) using a prying tool to raise one end of the stator bar, (c) putting the loop end of the sling around the raised end of the stator bar, and (d) pulling down on one end of the hoist chain such as to raise the other end of the chain, with its attached sling, thus raising the end of the stator bar—readying it for insertion of the wedge.

Per Step 2, the wedge was inserted.

Per Step 3, one end of a sling was attached to the end of the tugger wire rope

Per Step 4, the other loop end of the sling was looped around the notch at the back of the wedge.

Per Step 5, (a) tension was applied to the tugger rope and to the sling causing the wedge to traverse in the slot, raising the stator bar sufficiently out of the slot, (b) tension was released from the tugger rope / sling, and (c) the sling was removed from the slot in the wedge.

Case Study—Stator Bar Removal (Cont'd)

Accident Scenario (Cont'd)

Per Step 6, the stator bar was manually removed.

However, per Step 7, the wedge could not be removed, not even by hammering. It had captured enough ripple springs to cause it to jam in the slot. It was decided to use the tugger to remove the wedge. The loop end of the sling was re-inserted into the wedge's slot. The slack was taken up and the rope / sling was tensioned thinking that the wedge would pivot up and out of the slot sufficiently to create "grip points" for its manual removal.

The wedge did not budge. More tension was applied until the tugger's air motor was heard to strain. A *stop* hand signal was given to the tugger operator. At that instant, the wedge became free of the slot, rotated up and out of the slot, pivoting along the jammed leading edge. There was enough force to snap the tip of the wedge. The broken wedge became airborne, tumbling end-over-end toward a crew-member.

The crew-member was standing about 15' from the original position of the wedge, not in a direct line between the wedge and the winch. The airborne, tumbling, broken wedge struck the crew-member in his chest and in the lower part of his face. The crew-member collapsed upon impact. His injuries were bruising of the chest and sternum and lacerations of his lower face. (He was lucky.)

This Stator Bar Removal Procedure had been used for about 70 stator jobs. For this stator, bar 143 of 144 was in the process of removal when the accident occurred.

Assignment Completion

- The results given on the next two pages demonstrate how the assignment may be completed. In a live seminar, not all of these results will be obtained using merely a brainstorming technique.

- Later in this Bookinar™ this same case study is addressed using a formal, more robust *root cause analysis* technique—namely *hazard-barrier-effects analysis*. (See pages 278–289.) Using this formal analytical technique, chances are far better for arriving at all of the results given on the next two pages.

Case Study—Stator Bar Removal (Cont'd)

Accident Scenario (Cont'd)

- *Failed Barrier:* Stator Bar Removal Procedure
  - *What is the type of this barrier?* Technical process procedure
  - *Why is this barrier considered a failure?* It did not provide the method for the removal of a stuck wedge.
  - *What is the type of failure?* Design
  - *Could the failure have been detected and corrected earlier?* Yes, especially because the requirement should be to follow procedures. When a wedge got stuck, this procedure couldn't possibly be followed because this procedure did not address a stuck wedge condition. In order to adhere to the requirement to follow procedures, the need for change to the Stator Bar Removal Procedure should have been obvious.
  - *Using the taxonomy, what is the causal factor?*
    - Possibly it was a knowledge-based or a *cognition-based error*. Given that the procedure was prepared prior to its first use, there was no prior knowledge and no recognition of the potential for stuck wedges.
    - Possibly it was a *value-based error*. It might have been thought that there was no benefit in changing the procedure because there hadn't been an earlier *problem*. Complacency.
- *Failed Barrier:* Trade Skills
  - *What is the type of this barrier?* Human
  - *Why is this barrier considered a failure?* The crew-member should have recognized the *risk* in standing in the proximity of the wire rope, were it to become unattached from the sling or break when under tension. Even not being in a direct line can be dangerous because the wire rope can whip. The crew-member might not have been expected to anticipate the *risk* from a broken wedge.
  - *What is the type of failure?* Not applicable
  - *Could the failure have been detected and corrected earlier?* Yes, either by the injured crew-member, himself, or by other crew-members operating under the principle of *mutual accountability for safety*. While each employee is responsible primarily for his or her own safety, members of a crew certainly should look out for one another.
  - *Using the taxonomy, what is the causal factor?*
    - Possibly it was *value-based*. The injured crew-member could have been thinking that there was never a *problem* in the past and, therefore, that there was no need for concern in the current situation.
    - Possibly it was a combination of *cognition-based* and *error-inducing condition-based*, in that the crew-member failed to recognize the *hazard* in the *error-inducing condition* created by the jury rig approach to the removal of the wedge, and failed to behave accordingly.

Case Study—Stator Bar Removal (Cont'd)

Assignment Completion (Cont'd)

- Also, consider the following:
  - *Administrative procedure barrier failure*—Lack of a procedure(s) requiring engineering analysis of a process in which there are significant forces, stored energy and loads, such as in the stator bar removal process. (It's understood that "significant forces…" is ill-defined. However, at least it will raise the question in the process owner's mind and a decision can be made on a process-by-process basis.)
  - *Equipment barrier failure*—Lack of designed constraint on the tugger's torque.
  - *Combined equipment barrier and technical procedure barrier failures*—Lack of a maximum allowable limit on the distance between the tugger and the load, so as to limit the range and speed of the whiplash if the tugger's wire rope should it break or become disconnected from the sling or should the sling become disconnected from the slot in the wedge.
  - *Combined equipment barrier and technical procedure barrier failures*—Lack of an adequate mechanism by which to communicate with the tugger operator given that recognition of and response to a hand signal is too slow.
  - *Technical procedure barrier failure*—Lack of a designated safety zone in the Stator Bar Removal Procedure.
  - *Administrative procedure barrier failure*—Lack of effectiveness of training with regard to procedure compliance.
  - *Human barrier failure*—Consistent lack of compliance with procedure.

Points Demonstrated by the Case Study:

- *Administrative process, technical process, equipment* and *human barriers* fail.
- For an *event*, multiple *barriers* fail.
- For an *event*, *administrative* and *technical process barriers* failures almost always contribute very significantly.
- Whenever there are multiple *equipment barrier* failures, almost always there are *administrative* and *technical process barrier* failures allowing the *equipment barriers* to be non-existent or ineffective. In this case, a maintenance *administrative procedure barrier* failed to require engineering analysis of the stator bar removal process—yielding *equipment barrier failure*.
- The *Human Error Causal Factor Taxonomy* applies to the causes of *barrier* failure.
- *Human errors* are made upstream of the last person or persons to touch the process.

Error-inducing Conditions and Counteracting Behaviors

- This is the *Error-inducing Conditions and Counteracting Behaviors* Section of the Bookinar™.

- An *error-inducing condition* or *error-likely situation* is anything at the job-site that can reduce the probability of the successful performance of the task.

- *Error-inducing conditions* and *error-likely situations* and *counteracting behaviors* are the *second field of focus* or major areas of interest in the *prevention* of *human error.*

- The following will be addressed in this section:

  - Sources of *error-inducing conditions* and *error-likely situations;*

  - Types of *error-inducing conditions* and *error-likely situations;*

  - *Behaviors* to *counteract error-inducing conditions* and *error-likely situations.*

- Additional terms will be defined in this section.

Sources of Error-Inducing Conditions and Error-Likely Situations

- Task demands
- Work environment
- Human attributes—inherent and acquired

- The probability of the successful completion of the task may be reduced by:
  - Task demands:
    - The difficulty of the mental or physical requirements for the accomplishment of the task.
  - Work environment:
    - Inappropriate cultural, organizational and systemic conditions under which the task is accomplished;
    - Man-made physical conditions in the area in which the task is accomplished;
    - Natural conditions in the area in which the task is accomplished.
  - Human *attributes*:
    - Acquired and inherent mental and physical limitations of humans relative to the mental and physical requirements for the accomplishment of the task.

Question: What are some *error-inducing conditions* that may exist in the demands of a task?

Task Demands—Error-inducing Conditions and Error-likely Situations

- Time constraint
- Monotonous repetition
- Prolonged task
- Physical load
- Recollection
- Multi-tasking
- Unexpected equipment condition or system response
- Out-of-service status indication equipment and lack of an alternative
- Confusing display
- Procedure interpretation
- Creation of method

- The slide shows a list of some *error-inducing conditions* that frequently exist in a task.

- The *error-inducing conditions* on the list are not in order of frequency of occurrence, although it may be concluded that *time constraint*, if not the most frequent, is among the most frequent. In the experience of this presenter, having reviewed hundreds, if not thousands of high technology enterprise *condition reports*, *procedure interpretation* and *creation of method* are among the most frequently occurring *error-inducing conditions*.

- Very often, an *error-inducing condition* is created by a *barrier* failure.

- The first six listed *error-inducing conditions* may or may not be the result of failed *barriers*. It depends on whether or not it is reasonable for the *process* or *equipment barrier* to be designed better. For example, if a procedure imposes a *time constraint* that could have been designed out, the procedure is a failed *administrative barrier*. It unnecessarily introduces the *error-inducing* time constraint. In this example, substitute any of the other five of the first six conditions. For example, if a procedure requires *multi-tasking*, the simultaneous accomplishment of multiple tasks, when, in fact, the process could have been designed to avoid multi-tasking, then the procedure is a failed *administrative barrier*. It unnecessarily introduces this *error-inducing condition*.

- The seventh and eight listed items are *equipment barrier* failures—equipment malfunction—if the equipment was not intended to be *run to failure*.

- The ninth listed, *confusing display*, is also an *equipment barrier* failure.

- The last two listed, *procedure interpretation* and *creation of method* are *administrative* or *technical procedure barrier* failures.

Question: What are some *error-inducing conditions* that may exist in the work environment?

Work Environment—Error-inducing Conditions and Error-likely Situations

- Temperature
- Humidity
- Altitude
- Air pollution
- Wind velocity
- Noise
- Vibration
- Distraction

- The slide shows a list of some *error-inducing conditions* that may exist in the work environment.

- If the task is to be performed out-of-doors, the *error-inducing conditions* of *temperature, humidity, altitude, air pollution,* and *wind velocity* cannot be eliminated and *administrative process barriers, technical process barriers, equipment barriers* and *human barriers (human behaviors)* are needed to *counteract* these *conditions. Barrier* failure exists to the extent that any needed *barriers* are not provided, or are ineffective. Beyond the limited available *barriers* to *counteract* these *error-inducing conditions,* there are only *human behaviors.*

- Similarly, the last three listed *error-inducing conditions* may or may not be the result of failed *barriers.* Again, it depends on whether or not it is reasonable for the *administrative* and *technical process barriers* or *equipment barriers* to be designed better. For example, if *noise, vibration* or *distraction* exist but could have been designed out of the work place, there is a failed *barrier(s).*

Question: What are some *error-inducing attributes* of humans?

Human Attributes—Error-inducing Conditions and Error-likely Situations

Inherent
- Level of intelligence
- Level of mental ability depending on age
- Level of physical ability depending on age
- Level of physical ability depending on gender

Acquired
- Mental and physical fitness
- Attitudes
- Habit patterns
- Complacency / overconfidence
- Communication ability
- Physiological clock
- Assumptions / mindsets
- Mental shortcuts
- Biases

- The slide shows a list of inherent and acquired *error-inducing* human *attributes*.
- *Stress* may adversely impact one's *mental fitness*.
- One's level of *motivation* may fall under the category of *mental fitness* or *attitude*.
- A lot more study is needed to fully understand the implications of one's physiological clock and circadian rhythm.
- *Assumptions / mindsets, mental shortcuts and bias* will be addressed in the *Non-Conservative Decisions…Section,* the next major section of this Bookinar™ starting on page 176.

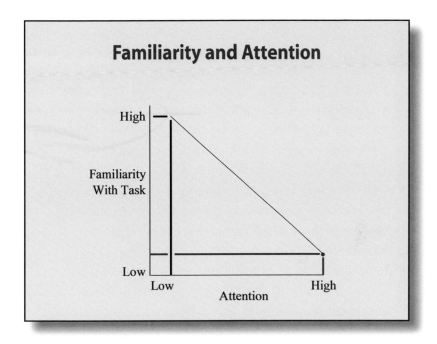

- This slide shows the inverse relationship between one's degree of *familiarity* with a task and one's *level of attention* in performing the task. The higher the familiarity, the lower the level of attention paid in the performance of the task and vice-versa.

Example—Fatigue

- Railroad accident
- Des Plains, IL
- October 21, 2002
- Collision between Union Pacific trains MPRSS-21 and AJAPRB-21

- -

The National Transportation Safety Board determined that the probable cause of the collision was that the "train MPRSS-21 engineer fell asleep at the controls of his locomotive.... Contributing to the engineer's falling asleep was likely his use of prescription medications that may cause drowsiness, as well as his lack of sleep in the 22 hours preceding the accident".

- In this case, *fatigue* contributed to the *event* but, in the opinion of this presenter, it was not the *root cause* of the *event*, as will be explained below.
- Certainly there are federal controls governing the hours to be worked by an engineer, but that *barrier* may be ineffective if an engineer does not rest during his or her time off. Also, for financial reasons, an engineer may refrain from exercising his or her right to claim unfitness for duty because of lack of rest.
- In this case, the engineer awoke at about 12:15 AM on the day of the accident. He laid down at 1:30 PM (13¼ hours later). He was called to work at 3:00 PM (1½ hours later). The accident occurred at 10:38 PM (almost 7¾ hours later). The elapsed time between 12:15 AM and 10:38 PM was 22 hours and 23 minutes. He was awake for all of this time with the possible exception of the 1½ hours during which he laid down.
- Following is the Union Pacific's transcript of the conversation between the dispatcher and the engineer, prior to the engineer's reporting to work:
  - Dispatcher: Calls engineer.
  - Engineer: Yeah.
  - Dispatcher: Hey, how you doing man?
  - Engineer: I'm sleeping (Of course, he means that he was sleeping.)
  - Dispatcher: Did you get some rest?
  - Engineer: No.
  - Dispatcher: They wanna run that MPRSS at 5 o'clock.
  - Engineer: Um hum. Who's the conductor?

- Transcript (Cont'd)
  - Dispatcher: You and (Dispatcher names another employee.)
  - Engineer: Again.
  - (Non-significant dialog omitted.)
  - Engineer: Where is (Engineer names another employee.)? He was supposed to be ahead of me.
  - Dispatcher: He is laid off sick.
  - Engineer: Oh, really!
  - Dispatcher: Yeah.
  - Engineer: Oh, that's pretty interesting. The last four weekends in a row he has laid off sick. Do you think he is sick now?
  - Dispatcher: Um hum.
  - Engineer: Do you realize this is twice in one day I've been to work? (Of course, he means that this will be twice in one day that he will be going to work.)
  - Dispatcher: That's not good.
  - Engineer: No it ain't.
  - Dispatcher: No it ain't.
  - Engineer: No it ain't, alright!
- Following is a photograph of the aftermath of the accident.

Source of photograph: National Transportation Safety Board

129

- From the transcript, it's apparent that both the dispatcher and engineer were or should have been aware of the potential for fatigue.

- The following was excerpted from an article published by the Office of Research and Development, Office of Safety, in November 2006:

"The Federal Railroad Administration (FRA) has, historically, managed the *risk* of fatigue in the railroad industry through enforcement of the Hours of Service Act of 1907 as amended through 1989. The current Hours of Service Act (49 U.S.C. §21101 *et seq.*) stipulates that train service employees may work no longer than 12 continuous hours followed by a minimum of 10 hours off duty, and that they be given at least 8 consecutive hours off duty in every 24-hour period. Consequently, an individual can work 11 hours and 59 minutes, be off duty for 8 hours, and return to work at the end of that 8-hour period. Moreover, such a pattern could continue for many consecutive days, so that the individual's work schedule would never develop a consistent circadian pattern. Crew-members are generally called approximately 2 hours before reporting time, so that the maximum duration of uninterrupted sleep could be between 6 and 7 hours. However, since the required 8 hours off-duty time includes commuting, leisure and personal time, the duration of any sleep would be even less than that. Further, actual periods of work, which may include traveling in "deadhead" status to a work site, waiting on a train for transportation and traveling back to the point of final release, can greatly exceed 12 hours. Furthermore, as noted by the National Transportation Safety Board and other concerned parties, the statutory maximums and minimums are not based on science.

The FRA is the only modal administration within the Department of Transportation whose hours of service are mandated by Congressional statute and, therefore, may not be adjusted or modified by administrative procedures. Thus, FRA is restricted in its efforts to aggressively initiate an appropriate range of fatigue mitigation measures. This limitation on FRA's administration authority has resulted in an environment wherein:

A commercial airline pilot can fly up to 100 hours per month. A truck driver can be on duty up to about 260 hours per month. Shipboard personnel, at sea, cannot operate more than 360 hours per month and only 270 hours per month when in port. Locomotive engineers can operate a train up to 432 hours per month, which equates to more than 14 hours a day for each day of the month."

- For this accident, if one were to ask why an engineer, in a state of fatigue, was allowed to operate the train, based on the foregoing excerpt, the answer would be because of the ineffectiveness of the *barrier* for hours of service—basically, the failure of the *administrative law barrier*, addressed on page 75—coupled with the absence of any other *barrier* to address the situation. *Barrier* failure is closer to the *root cause* than fatigue, itself.

- In addition, in most contracts between railroad companies operating under federal jurisdiction and unions, there exists a clause(s) allowing an engineer to refuse an assignment because of his or her lack of *fitness for duty* or for any other personal reason, such as for illness—there being no sick leave. The maximum number of such refusals is specified for a given calendar period (3 times in 30 days, 5 times in 90 days, 11 times in 12 months, as an example). In this case, the engineer either did not avail himself of this opportunity to refuse the assignment or had expended all such opportunities—in either case, *human barrier* failure.

130

- The fundamental point of this example is that whenever there is a *event* (an intolerable adverse effect), there always must be a failure of at least one *barrier*. An *error* attributable to an *error-inducing condition*, alone, cannot result in an *event*. Such an *error* is at the first level in the model on page 65. Such an *error* activates the *hazard*, but in order for the *hazard* to rise to the level of an *event*, there must be a failure of *second*-and *third-level barriers*—failures to *detect the hazard* and to *mitigate and ameliorate the undesired effects of the hazard*.

- Some locomotives provide an *equipment barrier*, requiring the engineer to periodically give *alert* signals, such as by sending an electronic signal of his or her state of alertness. Each signal must be given within a limited time following the immediately preceding signal. The absence of a signal within the required time limit results in an automated *corrective action*. This *equipment barrier* mostly overcomes *errors* due to fatigue, inattention (e.g., talking on a cell phone while operating the train) and other similar conditions.

- Stated differently, as a corollary, the fundamental point is as follows. IF there is the potential for an *error* attributable to an *error-inducing condition*, and IF the effect of the *hazard* activated by this *error* would be an *event*, THEN there should be a *barrier(s)* to *mitigate* the *hazard's undesired effect*. The absence of a *mitigating barrier(s)*, itself, constitutes a *human error*.

- (In older locomotives, there was a *dead man's* pedal which had to be continuously depressed, otherwise the *alert signal* would be sent. However, this was an uncomfortable foot position and, therefore, it was customary to use a heavy toolbox to continuously depress the pedal—*human barrier* failure defeating the *equipment barrier*. New locomotives automatically recognize the engineer's manipulation of the controls and within a given time period following the last manipulation, the locomotives automatically signal the engineer to depress an *alert button*. If the engineer fails to depress the button, the locomotive is automatically put into a safe operational status.)

Examples—Error-Inducing Conditions

- Turning the charging pump switch instead of the dilution valve switch
  - Identical looking switches—both pistol grip style
  - Side-by-side switches—one inch apart
  - Repetitive task—done several times during plant start-up
- Isolating the wrong flow transmitter
  - Poor lighting—incandescent light, casting shadows
  - Repetitive task—several transmitters being calibrated
  - Procedural call-out by nomenclature, not by number
  - Small lettering—black on gray

- To reemphasize the penultimate point on the preceding page, if isolating the wrong flow transmitter could result in an *event* (serious injury to or death of a technician), there should be a *barrier(s)*—possibly an *independent inspection* of the isolation and a *test* of the isolation prior to doing the physical work.

- The *error-inducing conditions* noted in the slide may cause the wrong transmitter to be isolated but, given the potential consequences of the *error*, failure to *detect* it and *correct* it prior to doing the physical work constitutes, itself, a *barrier(s)* failure.

Top 10 Error-Inducing Conditions

- Time pressure
- Distracting environment
- High workload
- First time evolution
- First working day after days off
- One-half hour after wake-up or meal
- Vague or incorrect written procedural guidance
- Overconfidence
- Imprecise oral communications
- Work stress

- The list in this slide was published by the Institute of Nuclear Power Operations.
- From the perspective of this presenter, *vague or incorrect written procedural guidance* is the most frequent *error-inducing condition*. The condition constitutes a failed *administrative barrier*—the procedure.

Exercise
Thunderbolt—Redesigned Instrument Panel

Assignment

Describe the error-inducing conditions and barrier failure in the following scenario:

The instrument panel of the P-47 Thunderbolt was redesigned during WW II—an improvement from an engineering perspective. Instruments and controls such as the altimeter, manifold pressure gauge, fuel gauge, and ignition switch were redesigned.

One story cited in a 1947 study, "Psychological Aspects of Instrument Display: Analysis of 270 Pilot-Error Experiences" recounts the following:

During a Japanese air raid on an U.S. held island, a pilot who had selected the newly redesigned P-47 failed in his take-off attempt and ended up taxiing his plane zigzag around the runway to avoid the strafing machine gun fire. He and his plane survived.

- Given the survival of the pilot, the passage of time, and the successful outcome of the war for both the United States and the Japanese, this may be somewhat humorous.

Assignment Completion—*Error Inducing Conditions / Barrier Failure*

- Stress of enemy fire
- New design of instrument panel
- Poor condition of the runway due to enemy bombing and strafing
- Again, however, there was a corresponding *administrative barrier* failure—training.

Behaviors to Eliminate Error-Inducing Conditions and Error-Likely Situations

- Simplify tasks.
- Increase allowable time.
- Improve task written descriptions in procedures.
- Establish realistic expectations.
- Eliminate distractions.
- Improve lighting.
- Provide physical shields against environmental conditions.
- Properly match workers to their tasks.
- Provide awareness aides—e.g.:
  - Color coding;
  - Highlighting.

- The slide lists a few actions that can be taken to eliminate *error-inducing conditions* and *error-likely situations*.

- *Simplif(ing) tasks* is often abused. The concept of "KISS", "keep it simple, stupid", is often the culprit—for example, by over simplifying a communication (a written procedure) to the point at which important process design information is lost. Removing specificity needed to attain technical excellence or economic benefit for the purpose of simplicity is over simplification. (See pages 79–82.)

- *Properly match(ing) workers to their tasks* is dependent on good *task analysis*. (See pages 98–100.)

- *Provid(ing) awareness aides* now falls under the umbrella of *poka yoke* techniques. (See pages 108–109.)

- Very often it is decided that it is not economically worthwhile to eliminate the *error-inducing condition* or *error-likely situation*. In some cases, the cost of eliminating the condition may exceed the cost of living with its effect. In other cases, with limited capital, the return on the investment needed to eliminate the condition or situation may not be competitive with the return on other investments.

- In the foregoing cases, the only remaining recourse is to practice *behaviors* by which to counteract the *error-inducing conditions* or *situation*.

Question: What are some *behaviors* by which to *counteract error-inducing conditions* and *error-likely situations*?

135

Behaviors to Counteract Error-Inducing Conditions and Error-Likely Situations

- Walk-down
- Pre-job briefing / Kick-off meeting
- Post-job assessment
- Turn-over meeting
- STAR
- QVV
- Time-out
- Three-part communication
- Universally accepted acronyms
- Phonetic alphabet
- Procedure use and compliance
- Checklists
- Place-keeping
- Verbalization
- Designated challenger
- Peer checking
- Independent verification
- Situational awareness
- Field observations / Coaching
- Defense in depth

- In contrast to actions that can be taken to eliminate *error-inducing conditions* and *error-likely situations*, this slide lists actions that can be taken to *counteract* the *conditions* and *situations*, when eliminating them is impossible or does not make economic sense.

- Essentially, this slide is a table of contents. In the following pages, each of these *behaviors* will be addressed.

Question: In the context of a modification to the design of a facility, what is meant by the *behavior* referred to as *walk-down*?

Walk-down

- Pre-requisite to modifying the design of a facility
- Coaching opportunity

- *Walk-down* is an individual *behavior* used to *prevent error* in the modification of the design of a facility, particularly an older facility, in which there may exist the *error-inducing condition* of loss of configuration control.

- At some locations in the facility, the actual physical hardware configuration (i.e., the *as-is* or *as-built* configuration) may not be correctly reflected in the official design documentation.

- Therefore, the administrative procedure governing modification of the design of such a facility should require, as a prerequisite, that the design engineer perform a *walk-down* of each location to be modified. The purpose of the *walk-down* is to verify the consistency between the as-built configuration and the drawing or, absent this verification, to *red-line* the drawing to reflect the as-built. The design document with which the modification is initiated must be consistent with the actual as-built configuration. Were it not, for example, the engineer might design an added component to be installed in a physical space that is already occupied by another, existing component.

- Of course, the administrative procedure would not require the prerequisite *walk-down* for every type of design document change. For example, a *walk-down* would not be required to change a note on a drawing. Or, for example, a *walk-down* would not be required to replace a component with a like-for-like component—i.e., a component that has identical envelope and installation and functional *characteristics*. The administrative procedure should itemize these kinds of exceptions.

- *Walk-down* also is used to create a *coaching* opportunity. (See pages 207–219.)

Questions: What is a *pre-job briefing?* What kind of information does it cover?

137

Pre-job Briefing

- Objectives and expectations
- Prerequisites, cautions and warnings
- Special requirements—e.g., asbestos
- Recent process changes
- Operating experience
- Error-inducing conditions / error-likely situations
- Error prevention behavioral tools
- Critical tasks
- Data to be taken
- Potential for significant adverse outcomes (What can go wrong?)
- Response to significant adverse outcomes (Abort criteria?)
- Recovery techniques

- *Pre-job briefing* is a group *behavior.*
- This slide lists the types of things that should be covered for a construction, manufacturing, operations or maintenance *pre-job briefing.* The listed subjects would not apply to an engineering or administrative type of job. That will be covered in the next slide.
- Giving workers information about the *objectives* of a job enhances worker motivation.
- Any process change of *significance* should have been covered by training. Addressing the *recent process change* in the *pre-job briefing* is a worthwhile redundant reminder.
- *Operating experience* (See page 242.)
- *Critical tasks* are those which bear most significantly upon the success of the job.
- There should be an administrative procedure for *pre-job briefing.* It should specify the:
  - List of topics to be covered in the briefing, as given on this slide, for example.
  - Conditions for which a *pre-job briefing* is mandatory, such as for the following, for example:
    - A process being implemented for the first time;
    - A process to be implemented by new personnel for the first time;
    - A process that was substantially changed;
    - A process for which there are significant hazards of the kind listed on page 28;
    - A process for which there is no *recovery* for the attainment of the objective.
  - Personnel who are to arrange for and conduct the briefing.
  - Personnel who are to attend the briefing.

- Rules of conduct for the *briefing* or a reference to such rules—e.g., timely start, use of a checklist to cover all the points, interaction, attentiveness, absence of side-bar conversations, criteria for resolution of concerns, criteria for *parking lot* items.

- In some nuclear powered electricity generating stations, the *pre-job briefing* precedes almost every field maintenance and field modification job.

Question: How does a *pre-job briefing* for an engineering job differ from the preceding?

Pre-Job Briefing—Engineering / Administrative Job Considerations

- What requirements are difficult to achieve?
- What information needs to be obtained?
- What decisions need to be made?
- What are the concerns?
- What concerns should be worked on first?
- What are the next tasks?
- When are these tasks to be performed?
- Who is in responsible for each task?
- Who needs to be kept informed?
- Who may be unavailable?

- With regard to the types of subjects covered, notice the significant difference between an *engineering / administrative pre-job briefing* and, as described in the preceding two pages, a *manufacturing / construction / maintenance / operations pre-job briefing*.

- For an engineering or administrative job, the term *pre-job* is somewhat of a misnomer because the kinds of questions listed in the slide should be asked not only as a prerequisite to the start of the job but also, periodically, throughout the duration of the job.

- The word *briefing* is also somewhat of a misnomer because it's far less a briefing than it is a questioning, the questions designed so as to induce the identification of potential *problems*.

- Rather than an administrative procedure addressing engineering *pre-job briefings* (or administrative *pre-job briefings*), the administrative procedure that addresses engineering project planning should cover the things relating to those listed in the slide. For example, the procedure should require the engineering project plan to contain, among other things:

  - Issuance of a requirements-type document, the name of the individual responsible for its issuance, and the date scheduled for its issuance;

  - Design input information that is to be received from external sources, and for each item of information, the name of its source, and the date scheduled for its receipt;

  - Design input information that is to be exchanged among cross-disciplines, and for each item of information, the name of the responsible individual, and the date scheduled for the exchange;

  - Milestone design decisions, and for each decision, the individual responsible for the decision, and the date scheduled for the decision.

Question: What information should be covered in a *post-job assessment?*

Post-Job Assessment

- Identification of problems and good practices
- Determination of recommended corrective actions
- Identification of responsibilities for preparation of Condition Reports for problems and good practices that should be institutionalized

- *Post-job assessment* is a group *behavior*.
- The administrative procedure for post-job assessment should require the following:
  - The performance of the assessment either:
    - Immediately following the completion of the job, so that the job experience is fresh in the minds of the workers; or
    - Immediately following a significant interruption of the job because of an *EHS/Q problem*.
  - The job supervisor's and the job planner's participation in the assessment.
  - The identification of any *problems* for which the causes should be corrected, and the identification of any *good practices* that may be exported to other jobs involving the same and similar processes.
  - The identification of any worker-recommended *corrective actions*. (See pages 335–336 for descriptions of the various types of *corrective actions*.)
  - For any job involving a *problem* or *good practice*, the assignment of a *condition report* originator. The *condition report* format requires the entry of any recommended *corrective actions*. (See page 240.)

Question: What information should be covered in a *turn-over meeting?*

Turn-over Meeting

- Facility status
- Job or activity status
- Changes anticipated for the on-coming crew / worker
- New evolutions anticipated for the on-coming crew / worker
- Problems that may be experienced by the on-coming crew / worker
- Unusual actions that are coming due for the on-coming crew / worker
- Problems experienced by the off-going crew / worker
- Review of the Control Room log (for facility operations)

- A *turn-over meeting* is a group (two or more persons) *behavior*.
- A *turn-over meeting* can occur at the end of one shift and the beginning of another between the off-going and on-coming operating crews, construction or maintenance crews, manufacturing machine operators, or any two people performing at a given position in a manufacturing process.
- The purpose of a *turn-over meeting* is to provide the opportunity to communicate important, specific information.
- The administrative procedure for *turn-over meetings* should require that:
  - A *turn-over meeting* be held for:
    - Any shift change;
    - Any crew or individual worker change, regardless of whether or not it occurs during a shift change.
  - Each of the items listed in the slide be addressed during the *turn-over meeting*.
- *Facility status* may include, for example, the identification of: out-of-service equipment; devices providing alternative measurements and indications; temporary installations; work-arounds; and alarms that have been recognized.

Question: What is the practice of *STAR*?

STAR

- **S**top
- **T**hink
- **A**sk / Act
- **R**eview / Resolve / Remediate

- *STAR* is a *behavior* of an individual, either working alone or working as a member of a crew. It's something that's done introspectively.

- **S**: *Stop* is a deliberate and conscious pause prior to performing the task, so as to enable the remainder of the process to be accomplished. Without stopping, the following can't happen.

- **T**: *Think* is a thought process to assure one's self that the requirements and methods for performing the task are understood and are within one's capability, and that one is ready to correctly perform the task. If not, the thought process leads to asking instead of acting.

- **A**: *Ask or Act*. Ask is the acquisition of any additional information or clarification necessary to enable the task to be performed correctly. Act is the performance of the task.

- **R**: *Review* is a deliberate and conscious self-check or self-verification to confirm that the required or expected results have been obtained. If one is authorized, one may also resolve and remediate any *problem* identified in the review.

- If one has to ask for additional information or for a clarification of the existing information, then, by definition, the document(s) providing the information is inadequate and constitutes a failed *barrier*. A *condition report* should be originated for the inadequacy.

- In an enterprise with a *EHS&Q culture*, addressed on pages 11–15, a large majority of the *problems* should be found by one's self-check in the think and review steps. (See pages 363–367.)

- *STAR* is used frequently in the performance of both personal and business tasks. However, it is not used consistently. Midway into a task, how often does one recognize that one doesn't fully understand the written instruction or doesn't have a necessary tool?

Questions: What is a *time-out*? How does it help to *prevent human error*?

Time-out

Brief stoppage of the task-allowing workers to:

- Acquire more accurate information regarding the work situation;

- Discuss the task, specifically with the intent of creating a shared understanding of the task requirements and methods, task conditions and task environment.

- *Time-out* is very similar to *STAR*, except that *time-out* is often used following the start of a task, whereas *STAR* is used immediately preceding the start of a task. Also, *time-out*, although requested by an individual, is taken by a group, whereas the "ask" step in *STAR* is taken by an individual. Obviously, as a result of the "ask" step in *STAR*, an individual may call for a group *time-out*.

- In an *EHS&Q-conscious work environment*, basically, any member of a work group is encouraged to call *time-out* when he or she needs additional information or clarification, feels the need to assure a common understanding of the work requirements or methods, or recognizes something in the task conditions or task environment that warrants discussion by the group. A *time-out* may lead to a change to a document.

Question: What's the difference between a *time-out* and a *stop work order?*

Answer:

- *Time-out* is self-imposed by the work group; a *stop work order* is imposed by a second party—e.g., an inspector from the internal Quality Control Department.

- In some enterprises, the administrative procedure authorizes any employee to issue a *stop work order* if proceeding would create an *EHS/Q problem*. The procedure would require adherence to such an order.

- An order given by a regulatory agency to stop operations or stop the shipment of product is the ultimate *stop work order*. It's referred to as an *enforcement action*.

- An internal *stop work order* is almost always given orally because of the immediacy of the need to stop and followed-up in writing. An enforcement action is always communicated in writing because of it legal implication.

QVV

- Question / Qualify
- Verify
- Validate

- *QVV* is a *behavior* taken by an individual. It's used frequently in design engineering work, although it should be used in all types of work.

- **Q**, *Question / Qualify*: Question any information that doesn't seem reasonable or lacks clarity. Use information only from a *qualified* source. Be assured that the source is valid and authoritative. For example, an individual in the Engineering Department of an enterprise supplying a specialty designed hardware item, would assure that the design requirements for that item are received from an official source within the customer's enterprise (and received in the official form). Or, for example, an electrical engineer receiving mechanical design interface information, would assure that the information is received from the correct source (and in the correct form).

- **V**, *Verify*: Verify the accuracy of the information. This can be done by getting the same information from a second *qualified* source, or by assessing or testing the accuracy of the information in some way. For example, in a plant, often, a field-walk or *walk-down* is performed to verify the accuracy of the plant's design information prior to modifying the plant's design. An engineer would not want to make a modification design requiring the installation of a electrical junction box where a pump is now installed.

- **V**, *Validate*: Validate the logic with which data is being used. A good example of this is in design calculations. Often, a second, alternative calculational method is used to validate the logic of the primary calculational method. Software that yields the sum of "six" from inputs of "three" and "three" is arithmetically correct. However, the solution may be "nine" instead of "six". Summation may be an incorrect solution. Multiplication may be the correct solution.

Question: What is *three-part communication?*

Three-Part Communication

- Technique creates improved understanding.
  1. Sender initiates the message.
  2. Receiver repeats the message.
  3. Sender confirms the accuracy of the repeat-back.
- Technique characterized by:
  - Use of specific nomenclature and alpha-numerics;
  - Paraphrased repeat-back of general information;
  - Verbatim repeat-back of nomenclature and alpha-numerics;
  - Use of phonetic alphabet.

- *Three-part communication* is a *behavior* practiced with two or more persons in a conversation.

- The purpose of *three-part communication* is to help to reduce communication *error*.

- Following is an example of the use of *three-part communication*. Assume that the sender of the message, Mary, is a Central Control Room (CCR) operator, and that the recipient of the message, John, is a field operator, physically located in the plant outside of the CCR. Assume that the two are communicating by radio. Assume that the purpose of the communication is to reposition a component as a step in a plant operating evolution.

  1. Mary: "John, on my count of three, switch *Air Operated Valve 43 Bravo* to the *on* position." (In the *phonetic alphabet*, *bravo* stands for the letter *b*.)

  2. John: "I understand, Mary, that on the count of three, I'm to switch on *Air Operated Valve 43 Bravo* to the *on* position."

  3. Mary: "That's correct."

- Also, if a co-worker were in the field with John, concurrent with his Step 2 (repetition of Mary's instruction), he might well point to the switch. In so doing, he would be indicating his intended action and giving his co-worker, who is listening in, the opportunity to verify the correctness of the action. This is a form of *verbalization*. (See page 154.)

- Notice that the component nomenclature, *Air Operated Valve* was repeated verbatim, as was the numeric-alpha, *43 Bravo*. It would be acceptable to use the commonly understood acronym, *AOV* in lieu of *Air Operated Valve*.

- Another frequent use of the *phonetic alphabet* is in conversations between an airline ticket agent and a ticket purchaser. For example:

  1. Agent: "Your reservation locator identifier is *Lima, Hotel, Alpha, Charlie, Whiskey, Bravo.*" (The agent may use a different *phonetic alphabet.*)

  2. Purchaser: "My locator ID is *Lima, Hotel, Alpha, Charlie, Whiskey, Bravo.*"

  3. Agent: "Correct."

- Sometimes, four part or *five-part communication* may be better. For example:

  1. Locomotive engineer: "We just passed an *Approach* signal."

  2. Conductor: "Confirm, *Approach* signal."

  3. Locomotive engineer: "Reducing speed to 30 mph."

  4. Conductor: "Confirm, Reducing speed to 30 mph is required."

  5. Locomotive engineer: "Speed reduced to 30 mph."

- The benefit of the fifth part of the communication is that it provides greater assurance that the action has been taken—especially if there has been an interruption or other impedance to the required performance.

Use of Three-Part Communication

- Use three-part communication when:
  - Immediate action is to be taken.
  - A record is to be made.

- Notice from the preceding slide that *three-part communication* was used in the example for which the field operator had to take immediate action and for which the ticket purchaser had to make of record of his or her locator ID.

- The use of *three-part communication* could be considered overkill in any case for which action is not intended to be taken immediately or a record is not intended to be made. On the other hand, its consistent use, regardless of the need for immediate action or a recording, might be considered a *good practice* as a means of ingraining its use.

- Notice that *five-part communication* was used when the locomotive engineer had to take immediate action. It might help in the following circumstance. Assume that following the recognition, action and confirmation of action in response to the *Approach* signal, the engineer has to stop the train at a depot to discharge and take on passengers. Further assume that upon leaving the depot the engineer might forget that he or she is still under the *Approach* signal, except for the potential of *five-part communication* providing a better memory jogger for both the engineer and conductor.

- In the foregoing scenario, considering the need for the *error-inducing* interruption—i.e., the need to stop at the depot—possibly the equipment situation would be considered a poor design because of the absence of another *Approach* signal immediately upon departing from the depot. This signal would constitute a *barrier* to overcome the *error-inducing* interruption and reinforce the required 30 mph limit.

Phonetic Alphabet

A - Alpha	J - Juliet	S - Sierra
B - Bravo	K - Kilo	T - Tango
C - Charlie	L - Lima	U - Uniform
D - Delta	M - Mike	V - Victor
E - Echo	N - November	W - Whiskey
F - Foxtrot	O - Oscar	X - X-ray
G - Golf	P - Papa	Y - Yankee
H - Hotel	Q - Quebec	Z - Zulu
I - India	R - Romeo	

- This slide provides the most frequently used *phonetic alphabet*, officially known as the *International Radiotelephony Spelling Alphabet*. This is the alphabet used by many international and national organizations.

- The purpose of the *phonetic alphabet* is help to reduce the potential for *error* in oral telephone and radio communications for which the transmission may be subject to static or break-up, or in any oral communications in a noisy environment. It's also used to compensate for different accents that may be heard in pronouncing English words.

- In some organizations, such as in some nuclear powered electricity generating plants, the *phonetic alphabet* is used consistently, regardless of the type of oral communication, the noise level or any other environmental conditions.

- The *phonetic alphabet* should be used when the alphabetical character is a distinguishing feature between two items.

- For example, in referring to radiation monitors in a nuclear plant, one would say *R 42 Alpha* (not *R 42 A*), *R 43 Alpha* (not *R 43 A*), *R 43 Bravo* (not *R 43 B*), etc.

- Notice that among rad monitors *R 43*, the letters (*Alpha, Bravo,* etc.) are the only distinguishing feature.

- Notice, also, that *Romeo* was not used for the *R* because, in this case, all rad monitors are designated as *R* something or other. The *R* is not a distinguishing feature. However, in some organizations, to further emphasize the use of the *phonetic alphabet*, one might hear *Romeo 43 Bravo,* for example. It's a toss-up between unnecessary usage of the alphabet and ingraining its consistent usage.

- While recognizing the unquestionable benefit of this *phonetic alphabet,* especially as contrasted to its absence, this presenter has concerns with its design. In raising these concerns, this presenter recognizes that there may be substantive disagreement with the concerns.

  - *Golf* sounds too much like *Off.* This is a concern for obvious reasons.

  - There is a lack of a consistent theme in the words used to represent the letters. A consistent theme would considerably help understanding, especially among those whose primary language is not English.

  - There is a lack of consistency in the number of syllables in each word. Some are one, some are two, and some are three syllable words. Consistency in the number of syllables coupled with the concern stated in the next bullet would help understanding.

  - The emphasis is not necessarily on the syllable that most represents the letter. For example, in the word *November,* the emphasis is on the second syllable, *vem.* In speaking the word out loud, one almost slurs over *Nov.* Using words all of two syllables with the emphasis consistently on the first syllable would help understanding.

  - *Sierra* sounds like a C word. Someone whose primary language is not English might not know that *Sierra* is spelled with the letter S. Speak the letter and the word out loud—C / *Sierra.* The C and the first syllable of *Sierra* are identical.

- For the reader's consideration, here's an alternative *phonetic alphabet* with:

  - A theme of people's first names;

  - Two syllables in each name, with emphasis consistently on the first syllable (with two exceptions); and

  - For each vowel, an initial syllable of the name that sounds like the vowel. For example, *A / Adolph.* Speak the letter and the name out loud. The letter and the first syllable of the name are identical. Furthermore, each name in the alphabet cannot be mistaken for any letter other than that intended. For example, *Adolph* cannot be mistaken for other than *A.* There are no such names as *Bedolph, Cedolph, Dedolph, Edolph, Idolph, Odolph,* or *Udolph.* This principle is applied consistently below.

A - Adolph	J - Jacob	S - Susan
B - Bradley	K - Kathy	T - Thomas / Tatum
C - Cedil	L - Lila	U - Ulysses*
D - David	M - Mimi	V - Victor
E - Egon	N - Nancy	W - Walter
F - Freeda	O - Ophra	X - Xavier*
G - Gigi	P - Peter	Y - Yogi
H - Henry	Q - Queenie	Z - Zena
I - Ida	R - Rhoda	*Exception, three syllables

Procedure Use

- Procedures control behavior, to enable consistent performance.
- Some types of procedures are "qualified" prior to use for production.
- Procedures are corrected and approved prior to use.
- Work is performed in accordance with the approved procedures.
- Work is not altered by oral directives differing from the procedures.
- Procedures are categorized for use:
  - At the job-site-referred to on a step-by-step basis;
  - At the job site-referred to as necessary;
  - Not at the job site-referred to as necessary.

- Adherence to procedure is an individual *behavior*.

- *Consistent performance* means the minimization of *variation*—variation being the antithesis of quality.

- This presenter remembers reading a children's story in which, as is often the case in children's stories, an inanimate object takes on human *attributes*. In this story, the inanimate object was a train. No matter what, the train ran on the track. No matter what, procedures are followed.

- There are only two exceptions:

  1. Avoid *malicious compliance*. (See page 20.)

  2. Give the chief operator an option along the following lines:

     IF an unavoidable, undesired condition exists, a condition which cannot be corrected by operation in accordance with the existing procedure(s) and

     IF the condition can lead to an *event* or can exacerbate an *event*,

     THEN the chief operator has the responsibility and authority to take whatever action is necessary to avert the *event* or to *mitigate* and *ameliorate* its level of severity.

- The need for the second exception may arise if a *hazard* was not recognized or a condition was not pre-postulated in the design of the operating process.

- In an enterprise with an *EHS&Q-conscious work environment*, addressed on pages 11–15, the process is designed and the procedure is written with the input of those who have overall responsibility for the process, who will implement the process, who have subject matter expertise, and who have procedure writing expertise. That's a lot of expertise.

- Anyone who knowingly violates a procedure indicates, essentially, that he or she believes himself / herself to have more expertise that the group's expertise. That's *risky* and egotistical. Although, sometimes, the violator may be correct, often he or she is not. In addition, although the procedure may be erroneous, the action taken by the violator in lieu of the procedure, also may be erroneous.

- Given that a procedure needs to be changed, and given the dilemma of either waiting an inordinate length of time for the necessary change or going forward in the absence of the change, many will make a *value-based* or *reflexive-based error* by going forward.

- For there to be consistent adherence to procedures, there must be a process enabling a procedure to be officially changed in quick-time. The administrative procedure governing the performance of a quick-time procedure change should assure that each step in the change process is performed (none omitted), BUT performed in quick-time—each step performed IMMEDIATELY following its preceding step. One of the keys to the success of quick-time procedural change is designating a sufficient number of back-up personnel for each different required functional and management review and approval.

- Procedures that are required to be used at the job-site and referred to on a step-by-step basis are often used in conjunction with *place-keeping.*

Question: In the context of procedure implementation, what is meant by *place-keeping?*

Place Keeping

Keeping track of the completion status of a process, step-by-step—e.g., a signature applied to the each step in the written procedure immediately following the completion of the step

- *Place-keeping* is an individual *behavior*.
- The purposes of place keeping are to (a) help to avoid *errors* due to interruptions, (b) signify the importance of the job, and (c) provide the means of identifying the person who performed each task of the job to facilitate *investigation*, should it become necessary in the aftermath of an *event*.
- *Place-keeping* should be used for jobs:
  - That are prone to interruption—e.g., that extend beyond a single shift;
  - For which different crew-members may perform different tasks of the job;
  - For which there are *inspection hold points*, such as for a mandatory inspection by a Quality Control Inspector, ASME Boiler and Pressure Vessel Code Authorized Nuclear Inspector, or any other regulatory inspector;
  - That are of sufficient importance to warrant the identification of the individual responsible for the implementation quality and safety of each step.
- Sign-offs or signatures are better than initials which are better than mere check marks (check-offs).
- If signatures or initials are to be used, in the procedure or in a central location, there should be an official cross-reference between the printed name of each individual and his or her signed name or initials. This cross-reference enables the identity of each individual, which would not be possible given an illegible signature or initials only.

Questions: What is meant by *verbalization*? What is the purpose of *verbalization*?

Verbalization

Stating out loud one's thoughts and intentions, or otherwise indicating one's intentions, before acting.

- *Verbalization* is an individual *behavior* performed when working with another person or with a group.
- *Verbalization* is performed in order to:
  - Accentuate *focus*. (See page 188.)
  - Give other members in a group the opportunity to challenge the intended action;
  - Allow the group to arrive at a common understanding of the requirement for a procedural step and the method for the attainment of the requirement.
- An example of *verbalization* was given on page 146 in which both words and finger-pointing were used to indicate the intention to reposition a specific air operated valve.
- The three non-concentric, partially overlapping circles may represent three workers each having a different understanding of a task requirement or method. With *verbalization*, the three circles may become concentric and wholly overlapping, representing a common understanding.
- As noted earlier, if a written procedure reasonably can be interpreted in different ways, it should be changed to eliminate the potential for the different interpretations.

Challenge / Designated Challenger

- An EHS&Q-conscious work environment fosters a questioning attitude.
- Anyone may question or challenge any action or decision, without invitation or fear of reprisal, regardless of his or her organizational rank.
- Recognizing the importance of a questioning attitude, a decision-maker may assign a "designated challenger".

- Assigning a *designated challenger* is a *behavior* that is taken by a decision-maker.
- In lieu of *designated challenger*, the term *devil's advocate* is used too often, unfortunately, to convey the same responsibility. The former is a term which implies value added; the latter is a term which has a negative connotation. The latter may mean a person who upholds the wrong side, perversely, or for argument's sake.
- As noted in the slide, anyone should be able to challenge, designated or not.
- A *designated challenger* should be a subject matter expert, assigned specifically to challenge the accuracy of the data as well as the logic being applied to the data in decision-making.
- It's the responsibility of the decision-maker to resolve each challenge or difference of opinion.
- In an enterprise environment, there should be only two acceptable reasons for disagreement. Those who disagree are either using different data or applying different logic to the data. By comparing the data being used and the logic being applied, the decision-maker should be able to achieve a resolution—either by facilitating the convergence of the data and logic or by recognizing the fallacy in the data or logic of one of the differing parties.
- One objective of the *designated challenger* is to *prevent* convergence from being achieved by *groupthink*.

Question: What is meant by *groupthink*?

Avoiding "Groupthink"

- "A pattern of thought characterized by self-deception, forced manufacture of consent, and conformity to group values and ethics."
Source: Merriam-Webster's dictionary

- A classic case of "groupthink" is thought to have resulted in the 1986 space shuttle "Challenger" explosion.

- *Groupthink* is a word coined in 1972 by psychologist Irving Janis.
- *Groupthink* occurs when the decision-maker is insulated from different points of view—either by allowing one, two or a few members of the group to dominate the group's input to decision-making, or by constructing the group such that it is homogeneous to the point of, basically, having a single perspective. This may be coupled with the group's zeal for a given decision
- Janis documented eight conditions existing in a group that lead to *groupthink*:
  1. Illusion of invulnerability—Excessive optimism encourages greater *risk-taking*.
  2. Collective rationalization—Warnings are discounted; assumptions are not reconsidered.
  3. *Belief* in inherent morality—*Belief* in the rightness of the cause encourages disregard of the ethical or moral consequences of the decisions.
  4. Stereotyped views of dissenters—Dissenters are viewed as enemies, making responses to conflict seem unnecessary.
  5. Direct pressure on dissenters—Dissenters are under pressure not to express arguments against any of the group's views.
  6. Self-censorship—Doubts and deviations from the perceived consensus are not expressed.
  7. Illusion of unanimity—Majority views and judgments are assumed to be unanimous.
  8. Self-appointed "mindguards"—Information that is *problematic* or contradictory to the group's cohesiveness and views is kept from the group.

- This presenter has difficulty with some of the literature on *groupthink* that implies that groups make decisions. They do not. Enterprises give individual leaders the responsibility and authority to make decisions, except at the level of the Board of Directors or Board of Trustees. A decision-maker, in a group setting, may make a less conservative decision than he or she would make in a non-group setting but it is, nevertheless, the individual who makes the decision. Also, if a decision were truly a group decision, in contrast to an individual decision, the potential would be even greater for an even less conservative decision.

- The Space Shuttle Challenger disaster in 1986 is often referred to as a classic example of *groupthink*.

- As will be seen from the following the discussion, the engineers at Morton Thiokol Inc (Thiokol) who recommended postponement of the shuttle's flight, did not themselves, have any of the eight conditions documented by Janis and were not subject to any of these conditions, except, possibly, for pressure. The Thiokol engineers never changed their positions to conform to any group. *Groupthink* did not occur at the engineering level. However, the Thiokol manager who made the decision to recommend that the flight not be postponed may, himself, as a member of a higher level group, been the victim of *groupthink*.

Source: Report of the Presidential Commission on the Space Shuttle Challenger Accident, June 1986

- The cause of the shuttle's disastrous ninth mission was the failure of an "O-ring" seal in the solid rocket booster on the right hand side of the external tank. The seal failure allowed flames to leak from the booster. As the seal failure got worse, the flame leak got larger. The flames from the booster then burned through the shuttle's external fuel tank and through one of the supports that attached the booster to the side of the tank. That booster broke loose and collided with the tank, piercing the tank. The booster also collided with the right wing of the orbiter. The assembly (orbiter, external fuel tank and boosters) swerved off course. Aerodynamic forces destroyed the assembly.

- Certain O-rings that sealed various sections of the solid rocket boosters were found to be eroded following the shuttle's second mission. The failure cause could not be found. O-ring damage had not been found during extensive pre-flight tests or following the shuttle's first mission.

- Prior to the disaster, Thiokol engineers argued that the likely temperature at the time of scheduled lift-off would be between 20° and 30° Fahrenheit and that the O-rings were not *qualified* at any temperature below 50° Fahrenheit. Higher authorities and customers required them to prove that the O-rings would fail at the lower temperature. They could not provide this proof.

- Requiring proof of inadequacy as a prerequisite to postponement, as contrasted to requiring proof of adequacy, is a violation of the *precautionary principle*. Under this principle, which applies to items and processes governed by the US Food and Drug Administration, the US Nuclear Regulatory Commission, and until this point in time, the NASA Space Shuttle Program—under this principle, the burden of proof with regard to safety rests with those who would take the action—in this case with those who wanted to go forward with the flight without postponement. The burden of proof should not have rested with the Thiokol engineers.

- The following is from the Report of the Presidential Commission on the Space Shuttle Challenger Accident (commonly called the Rogers Commission Report), June 1986: "At approximately 11 P.M. Eastern Standard Time, the Thiokol / NASA teleconference resumed, the Thiokol management stating that they had reassessed the *problem*, that the temperature effects were a concern, but that the data were admittedly inconclusive. (A Thiokol manager) [name intentionally omitted] read the rationale recommending launch and stated that it was Morton Thiokol's recommendation. (A Thiokol manager) [name intentionally omitted] requested that it (rationale recommending launch) be sent in writing by telefax both to Kennedy and to Marshall, and it was."

- The Commission concluded that Thiokol management "reversed its position and recommended the launch of 51-L (ninth mission), at the urging of Marshall and contrary to the views of its engineers in order to accommodate a major customer". (From the testimony reproduced in the Report, some Marshall Space Flight engineers had the same concerns as the Thiokol engineers.)

- This is an extreme example with tragic results. It provides valuable lessons. When participating in a group discussion leading to decision-making, beware of the *groupthink* trap. Sometimes the collective desire to *get it done* or *stay on schedule* can lead to *groupthink* even without its realization.

Peer Check

- Timeliness
- Independence
  - Hands off the job
  - Equivalence of knowledge and cognitive abilities
- Acceptance of peer check responsibilities

- *Peer check*, either *peer review* of a document or *peer inspection* of a hardware *characteristic*, is a *behavior* performed by an individual and in accordance with a procedure.

- By definition, a *peer* is one who is equivalent in knowledge and cognitive abilities. *Peer check* is of little benefit if the creator of the document or hardware *characteristic* is *unqualified* and the peer is equivalent—equally *unqualified*.

- A peer checker is assigned as such on a part time basis. The majority of his or her time is spent originating documents (rather than *peer reviewing* documents) or producing hardware quality or safety *characteristics* (rather than *peer inspecting* hardware *characteristics*). Today the person is an originator / producer, tomorrow a peer reviewer / peer inspector.

- Here are examples of *peer review*: one engineer checking a calculation made by another engineer; one maintenance planner checking the *corrective maintenance* procedure prepared by another maintenance planner.

- Here are examples of *peer inspection*: one machine operator *inspecting* the set-up of another operator's machine; one member of an electrical maintenance crew inspecting the cable terminations made by other members of the crew.

- Obviously, a *peer check* is not going to *prevent* a *problem*, its purpose being to *detect* any *problem*. However, feedback from the peer checker may *prevent recurrence* of a *problem*.

- *Timeliness* is required for the effectiveness of the check.

- *Hands off the job* means that the peer checker took no part in the origination of the document to be *peer reviewed* or in the creation of the quality or safety *characteristic* to be peer inspected. For *peer review, hands-off* also means that the peer did not contribute to any assumptions made for the origination of the document—for example, assumptions as might be made for an engineering calculation.

- A bargaining unit may demand a wage rate increase as a condition for adding *peer inspection* to the responsibilities of construction, maintenance or manufacturing workers. Although the workers already may be responsible for performing related functions such as self-checking their work, recording data, and originating *condition reports*, in the final analysis, the bargaining unit's argument is that *peer inspection* adds the responsibility of officially determining acceptable versus non-acceptable items. Judging the validity of this argument is difficult. (See the list of responsibilities of an inspector on the next two pages.)

- This presenter became involved with a situation in which some maintenance supervisors, at a certain age nearing retirement, because of the strenuousness of the field job, were reassigned as maintenance procedure writers. This practice had existed for a long time. Whereas the maintenance supervisors were excellent in their field supervisory jobs, they were poor in their reassigned procedure writing and *peer reviewing* jobs. The procedures that they originated were substantially flawed. The *peer reviews* that they performed were equally flawed. Subsequent to *peer review*, quality engineers reviewed the procedures. At that point the procedures were essentially rewritten. This was not a very effective process because neither the procedure originators nor the peer reviewers were *qualified*. The quality engineering review was enabling the continuation of this ineffective process. It had to be corrected.

- The near-retiring personnel were re-reassigned to mentor new field maintenance supervisors and maintenance crews (which they did successfully). Competent procedure writers who also served as peer reviewers were assigned. Quality engineering reviews were reduced to a *sampling* level, and following *process qualification*, eliminated in favor of *quality audits* only.

- The greatest difficulty in achieving the success of peer check is getting the peer checker to fully accept the responsibilities of the role, especially if one of those responsibilities is to record the types of *problems* found in the document being *peer reviewed* or to record the *defects* found in the hardware *characteristic* being peer inspected. This may be a recording of a co-worker's *error* (a buddy's *error*). Tomorrow, the peer checker may be in the same position as his or her co-worker. A tacit non-disclosure agreement tends to arise between or among the co-workers.

- One way by which to improve the success of document *peer review* may be to have it performed *blind*, so to speak, such that the peer reviewer does not know the name of the originator of the document being reviewed or the name of the worker who created the hardware *characteristic*. Usually, this is impractical. A peer is a part of the group and, as such, he or she knows who originated the document to be *peer reviewed* or who created the *characteristic* to be peer inspected—or can easily get that information. There is no way to keep people from talking to one another.

Independent Verification

- Timeliness
- Independence
  - Hands off the job
  - Equivalence of knowledge and cognitive abilities
  - Not responsible for earlier decisions
  - Not in the same organizational hierarchy

- *Independent verification* is a review or an *inspection* performed in accordance with an administrative or technical procedure by someone who has greater *independence* than a peer checker.
- An *independent* verifier is one who:
  - Did not create the document or hardware *characteristic* to be verified;
  - Was not responsible for any decisions made earlier with regard to the creation of the document or hardware *characteristic* to be verified;
  - Does not organizationally report to anyone who either:
    - Was responsible for the creation of the document or *characteristic* to be verified; or
    - Previously made decisions regarding the creation of the document or *characteristic* to be verified.
- Inspectors, either peer inspectors or *independent verification* inspectors, have the following responsibilities:
  - Maintain physical and mental *fitness for duty*
  - Maintain technical excellence in the use of the tools and documents necessary to perform the job.
  - Help to assure calibration control.
  - Identify *problems* with documents, especially hardware design and procedure documents.
  - Implement *sampling plans*.

- Make measurements without *flinching*. *Inspection* policy must require that only those *characteristics* that demonstrably meet requirements may be accepted—rather than requiring proof of unacceptability. In the absence of such a policy, an inspector may *flinch*—accepting a *characteristic* that exceeds its requirement by a very small amount—for fear that he or she can't prove it *defectiveness*. This is similar to the *precautionary principle*. (See page 158.)

- Distinguish acceptable from unacceptable *characteristics*.

- Record data.

- Recommend *corrective actions*.

- Set the standard for ethical *behavior*. This is a difficult responsibility to describe. First, there needs to be a clear distinction between *ethical* and *moralistic behavior*. Only *ethical behavior* is being addressed here. Probably the responsibility for this *behavior* can best be described by exemplification from the aircraft manufacturing industry. A flight line inspector is responsible, above all, for assuring the integrity of the quality and safety *characteristics* created on the flight line, before allowing the test flight of the airplane. Traditionally, this inspector is a hard-nosed, uncompromising, rigidly honest, experienced, thorough, well disciplined, systematic, and highly regarded individual, who is ethically incorruptible. Of course, these traits should apply to all peer checkers and *independent* verifiers.

- *Independent verification inspection* is best accomplished when the *inspection* steps are integrated with the construction, fabrication, assembly, installation and maintenance steps in the written procedure.

- Here are some techniques by which to improve *inspection* effectiveness, in no particular sequence of importance:

  - Increase inspector *qualifications*.

  - Rotate inspectors.

  - Increase *inspection* procedure specificity and clarity.

  - Eliminate *error-inducing conditions* in the *inspection* process and environment—e.g., time constraint, distraction.

  - Inspect for a single *characteristic* at a time. For example, if, at a given *inspection* station, 25 parts are to be *inspected* for *characteristics* x, y and z, it's more effective to inspect all 25 for x, then all 25 for y, then the 25 for z, rather than to inspect the first part for x, y and z, then inspect the second for x, y and z, and so on.

  - Inspect the *characteristics* in the sequence of their potential for rejection—from greatest to least. Going forward with the example from the preceding bullet, if y had the highest rejection rate, and x the next highest rejection rate, all 25 parts should be inspected first for y, then all 25 for x, and last, all 25 for z. Otherwise, there's the potential for wasting *inspection* effort on parts that will later be rejected.

  - Use *inspection* visual aids—e.g., pictures, templates.

  - Increase visibility—e.g., magnification, lighting.

  - Increase accuracy and resolution of measuring devices relative to tolerance limits.

- Use *go—no-go* gages.
- Use *statistical acceptance sampling inspection.*
- Perform greater than 100% *inspection.*
- Automate *inspection.*
- Use the highest *qualified* inspectors for *characteristics* that are of the highest *criticality.*
- Place *inspections* at the appropriate points in the process—e.g.:
  - Inspect machine set-up.
  - Inspect the first part completed in a step.
  - Inspect the parts immediately preceding a very expensive step. There's no sense in incurring the expense of the forthcoming step for parts that already may be *defective.*
  - Inspect the parts immediately following a step for which the process capability is limited relative to the design requirement for the *characteristic* in question or for which, historically, there is a high percent *defective*—again, to avoid downstream expenditure on already *defective* parts.

Questions: What is the *blame spiral?* What are its effects?

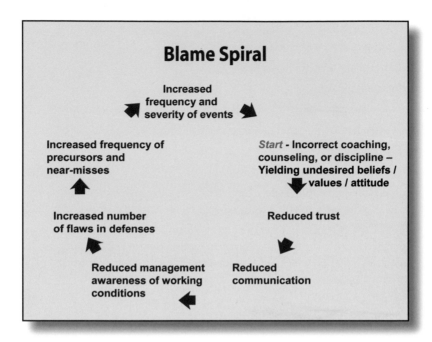

- Although it's not drawn as such, the intent of the slide is to convey a spiral that's ever widening for the worse.

- Recall the model of *human performance* on page 17 in which it was noted that the kind of information given to the employee, the way in which it is given, and the way in which it is processed by the employee's cognition—that these factors will contribute substantially to the employee's *beliefs*, from which his or her *values* are derived, from which an *attitude* is formed, which, in turn, is reflected in the employee's *behavior* leading to *results.•* *Coaching*, *counseling* and *discipline* are important kinds of information given to an employee. These and other kinds of information should be such as to build a high level of *trust* in the employee, employee-by-employee, throughout the enterprise, to encourage collaboration, and the identification and reporting of *problems*.

- There is less chance for the existence of this spiral when there is a *no fault* policy with the intent to learn from mistakes, not blame. Having learned, an employee is of greater value to himself or herself and to the enterprise.

- Those who can't learn or refuse to learn must be reassigned to roles in which they can and do learn or, failing that, discharged.

- This Bookinar™ does not cover supervisory skills, but appropriate supervisory *behavior* in giving *coaching*, counseling and discipline are needed for the *prevention* of *error* and the *prevention of error recurrence*.

Reinforce / Discourage

- Reinforce behavior that:
  - Gets desired results;
  - Avoids undesired results.
- Discourage behavior that:
  - Does not get desired results;
  - Does not avoid undesired results.

- This is *behavior* expected of a supervisor, peer and subordinate. All should participate in *reinforcement* and *discouragement*, as appropriate.
- Reinforcement may be done in large part by public recognition and, possibly, by reward.
- Discouragement should be done privately but with appropriate documentation and, possibly, consequences.
- Regardless of whether its reinforcement or discouragement, management and technical excellence, honesty and fairness must prevail—consistently.

Additional Tools

- Human error clock
- Excellence Room
- Special day
- Visual awareness aids

- *Human error clock*:
  - A clock may be established for the enterprise as a whole, or for any organization within the enterprise, at any level in the enterprise.
  - The clock measures the time that has transpired between *human errors* resulting in *events*, *near misses* or *precursors* that offer a particularly learning opportunity. When there is such an occurrence, the clock is reset. For *precursors*, the organization establishes its own threshold for the kinds of occurrences that are to result in clock reset.
  - When a clock is reset, the organization may call an *all-hands* meeting or a *stand-down* to review the circumstances of and the lessons to be learned from the occurrence. Unfortunately, sometimes the focus is on the last *error* that occurred in the process without sufficient attention to the *errors* that occurred upstream. Or, referring to the model on page 65, the focus may be on a *Level 1 error*, as contrasted to higher level *errors*. Of course, the organization conducting the all-hands meeting or stand-down should focus on the types of *error* for which it has or could have responsibility.
  - Resetting the clock too frequently may indicate a serious *problem* within the organization. Resetting the clock too infrequently may result in lost learning opportunities.
- *Excellence Room*-A dedicated room in which are posted enterprise *values, certifications,* awards, major accomplishments, achievements toward goals, *human error prevention* information, and similar information. The room provides the *values* and performance underpinning that excellence. The room is usually used for team building, and to house *self-assessment* teams, *root cause analysis* teams, *independent* third party assessment teams, and regulatory agency inspection teams. For outsiders, the room provides a positive setting.

- Some nuclear powered electricity generating stations periodically have a *Human Error Prevention Day*, it's purpose being to stimulate awareness of the principles and practices of *human error prevention*, particularly the *counteracting behaviors* covered in this section of the Bookinar™.

- A variety of *human error prevention* visual aids may used—e.g., *human error prevention* flags; banners and posters. A banner or poster may list *counteracting behaviors* adjacent to each of the ten top human *error-inducing conditions*. Newsletters may be used to predominantly cover *human error prevention* items of interest.

Case Study—Piper Alpha

Assignment—For the following scenario, for each function listed, identify:

- Failed barriers;
- Error-inducing conditions / error-likely situations;
- Non-conservative decisions.

	Failed Barriers	Error-Inducing Conditions	Non-Conservative Decisions
Design Engrg	1	2	3
Operations	4	5	6
Maintenance	7	8	9
Training	10	11	12
Emergency Preparedness	13	14	15

Case Study—*Piper Alpha*

Background:

- *Piper Alpha* was an oil and gas production platform located in the North Sea, approximately 120 miles Northeast of Aberdeen Scotland. The *Claymore* and *Tartan* platforms were nearby. Occidental Petroleum Company owned the platforms.

- Originally, *Piper Alpha* was an oil production facility. In 1980, it was modified for gas production, as well.

- On July 6, 1988, gas explosions and oil fires on *Piper Alpha* caused its total destruction and the loss of 167 of the 229 roughnecks who were aboard.

- The Gas Compression Module was located near the Control Room. The design provided Firewalls between the Module and the Control Room to protect against an oil fire. The Firewalls were not designed to protect against a gas explosion.

- Gas Compressors A and B were used for compressing gas for its transport to the on-shore collection and storage facility. Gas Compressor A was in Gas Compression Line A and Gas Compressor B was in Gas Compression Line B. Within the Module, Line A ran about 15 feet above floor level in an area that was not well lit.

- Gas pipelines ran between *Piper Alpha* and *Tartan*, and between *Piper Alpha* and the gas-compressing platform, about 30 miles away.

- Two years prior to the accident, a study warned of the dangers of these gas lines. Due to their length and diameter it would take several hours to reduce their pressure, so that it would not be possible to fight a fire fueled by them. The report recommended the installation of a safety system to protect against such an occurrence.

Case Study—*Piper Alpha* (Cont'd)

Background (Cont'd):

- Prior to the accident, it had been three years since an evacuation drill had been performed on *Piper Alpha*. Many of the men were new to the platform. However, the men were trained to assemble at the Life Boat Stations.

- *Piper Alpha* had a Helicopter Pad.

- The Fire Suppression System could be switched to either automatic or manual operation. The System's Diesel Pumps could suck in sufficient sea water to put out a fire. When divers were in the water, it was customary for the System to be switched from automatic to manual operation, regardless of whether or not the divers were near the intakes. On the day of the accident, the System was switched to manual operation. (This presenter does not know whether or not divers were in the water at the time.)

- *Piper Alpha*, *Claymore* and *Tartan* fed oil into the same pipeline used to export the oil to an on-shore collection and storage facility. The oil pipelines were such as to allow backflow to *Piper Alpha*.

- *Piper Alpha* was closer to shore than some other platforms in the area. It had two Gas Risers from those platforms. The Risers were 24 to 36 inch diameter steel pipes. The gas in the Risers was pressurized to two thousand pounds per square inch. *Piper Alpha* processed the gas from the Risers and the oil drilled from it own platform, and then piped the final products to shore.

Accident Scenario:

- The Line A Pressure Relief Valve was due for its routine bi-weekly preventive maintenance. This maintenance had not yet begun. For this work, in the Control Room there existed a **Bi-Weekly PM Form**.

- On the shift immediately preceding the shift on which the accident occurred, the Pressure Relief Valve was removed from Line A to undergo an overhaul. For this work, there existed an **Overhaul Form**. (This presenter does not know the intended difference between the PM and the overhaul.)

- *Note: The titles of these forms, above, are not actual titles, but have been ascribed by this presenter to provide a clear distinction between the forms.*

- The overhaul of the Line A Pressure Relief Valve could not be completed on this shift. Therefore, at the end of this shift, a temporary Cover Plate was installed to cover the Line A opening that was created by the removal of its Pressure Relief Valve. The Plate was black.

- Also, at the end of this shift, the Maintenance Foreman completed the **Overhaul Form** (as contrasted to the already existing **Bi-weekly PM Form**). The **Overhaul Form** indicated that the Pressure Relief Valve was removed from Line A. The Maintenance foreman hand carried the **Overhaul Form** to the Control Room. The Control Room operator was busy with others. Therefore, the Maintenance foreman placed the **Overhaul Form** on a desk and left the Control Room. There was no acknowledgement or recognition of the **Overhaul Form** by the Control Room operator.

Case Study—*Piper Alpha* (Cont'd)

Accident Scenario (Cont'd):

- On the next shift, the shift on which the accident occurred, Compressor B failed and it could not be restarted. The *Piper Alpha*'s Power Supply depended on the operation of either Compressor A or B or on the operation of the Diesel Generator. However, the Diesel was considered to be unreliable. Therefore, the switchover to the Diesel was not made. If compression continued to be unavailable, within a few minutes the *Piper Alpha* would lose power completely. Without power, the Drill could stick. *(The cost to recover from a stuck Drill is very high.)*

- A search was made for documents to determine whether Compressor A could be started in place of the failed Compressor B. The **Bi-weekly PM Form** was found. It indicated that the bi-weekly preventive maintenance for the Line A Pressure Relief Valve had not started.

- Unfortunately, the **Overhaul Form** was not found. Therefore, the Control Room operator had no indication that the Pressure Relief Valve was removed from Line A. In the absence of this knowledge, he ordered the start-up of Compressor A.

- Compressor A was started. When the gas flowed into Compressor A, over-pressurization occurred due to the missing Pressure Relief Valve. The temporary Cover Plate could not *contain* the gas. It leaked past the Plate. Then the gas ignited and exploded. The explosion ignited oil fires. Oil and gas production was stopped.

- The gas explosion breached the Firewalls between the Module and the Control Room and destroyed some Oil Lines. The Control Room, including Central Communications, was destroyed and abandoned.

- The fire prevented the men from reaching the Lifeboat Stations. Therefore, many of the men assembled in the fireproof Living Accommodation Block which was located beneath the Helicopter Pad—hopefully awaiting evacuation by Helicopter. A Helicopter landing was prohibited because of the black smoke being blown over the Pad. Smoke began to fill the Accommodation Block. Many of the men jumped 100 feet from the Accommodation Block into the water. Some survived.

- There was a failed attempt to activate the Fire Suppression System.

- Oil from *Claymore* and *Tartan* was forced by backpressure into *Piper Alpha*. This continued to fuel the fire. Although the smoke from *Piper Alpha* was seen, *Claymore* and *Tartan* continued to pump following the initial emergency call. The *Claymore* operations manager was not authorized to shut down. The *Tartan* operations manager received direction from his superior to continue pumping. A blast on *Piper Alpha* destroyed communication with the coast.

- The *Tharos* firefighting and rescue ship was nearby. It drew close to *Piper Alpha*. The Fire Fighting System was switched on prematurely and the System tripped. A delay of a few minutes was necessary to restart the System. The Evacuation Gangway was activated. It rose at the speed of two feet in five minutes.

- Within a short time of its positioning near *Piper Alpha*, about twenty minutes into the accident, the fires melted the Gas Risers. The gas in these Pipelines was released and exploded engulfing *Piper Alpha* entirely. The heat caused *Tharos* to back away.

Case Study—*Piper Alpha* (Cont'd)

Accident Scenario (Cont'd):

- *Claymore* and *Tartan* shut down, but it was too late. *(Had Claymore and Tartan stopped pumping when the initial emergency call was heard, very possibly the fire could have burned itself out. When production is stopped for whatever reason, at least a few days are needed to regain full production.)*
- The Generation and Utilities Module, which included the Accommodation Block, fell into the sea, followed by the largest part of the platform.

Before

After

Source of photographs: The Report of the Public Inquiry

171

Case Study—*Piper Alpha* (Cont'd)

Summary of Losses:

- 167 men.
- The reputation of Occidental's management team which was accused of negligence and callousness toward safety. The Public Inquiry was led by the Hon. Lord William Douglas Cullen, a renowned Scottish judge. The Report of the Public Inquiry indicated that the *event* occurred because of what was tantamount to management's blatant disregard for safety.
- $1.0 billion platform.
- $700,000 to the family of each victim—almost $117 million.
- Loss of production for five years. (Alpha was replaced with Bravo, five years later.)
- Total dollar losses of $2.8 billion.

Assignment Completion

Cell # 1. Design Engineering—Failed *Barriers*:

- *Equipment barrier* failure—Absence of Blast Walls to protect against gas explosion.
- *Equipment barrier* failure—Absence of Check Valves to prevent backflow of oil into *Piper Alpha*.
- *Equipment barrier* failure—Inadequate separation of Gas Compressor Module and Control Room.
- *Equipment barrier* failure—Inadequate speed of *Tharos* Gangway escalation.
- *Equipment barrier* failure—Absence of a safety system to protect against fire due to gas in Risers.
- *Equipment barrier* failure—Absence of a back-up system for communication.
- *(Although the location of the Pressure Relief Valve, 15 feet above the floor, presents the challenge to its bi-weekly maintenance, it is not considered an equipment barrier failure because a Relief Valve must be located where its relief would be safe.)*
- *Administrative procedure barrier* failure—Given the numerous *equipment barrier* failures, it's obvious that there did not exist adequate administrative procedures for *hazard* or *risk analysis* of equipment design.

Cell # 3. Design Engineering—*Non-Conservative Decisions*:

- Given the recommendation made two years in advance, absence of a safety system to protect against fire due to gas in Risers. This could have been a *value-based error*. The testimony indicated that the recommendation was never communicated to the highest decision-making level. Therefore, this could have been a case in which fear played a role—middle management's fear of even communicating such a recommendation to higher management—a form of *value-based error*. It's not worth exposing oneself to rejection.
- If there existed knowledge and cognition of the need for Blast Walls and greater separation between the Gas Compression Module and the Control Room, failure to act probably constituted a *value-based error*—e.g., the needed modifications weren't worth the cost.

Case Study—*Piper Alpha* (Cont'd)

Assignment Completion (Cont'd)

- The same applies for check valves and back-up communication.

Cell # 4. Operations—Failed *Administrative Procedure Barriers*:

- The administrative procedure for equipment status was backwards and not failsafe. It required Maintenance to inform Operations of the out-of-service condition of an equipment and, in the absence of any such information, allowed Operations to operate the equipment. In other words, the *tag-out* process was non-existent or very flawed.

- Although the accident had the potential for happening at some time, given the absence of a well designed tag-out process, the accident could have been averted at this time had the Maintenance foreman positively informed the Control Room operator by handing him the **Overhaul Form**. It's not known whether or not this was procedurally required. If it was, it constitutes a *barrier* failure due to non-compliance.

- The inappropriate start-up of the *Tharos's* Fire Fighting System leading to the loss of valuable time was a *non-conformance* to procedure.

Cell # 5. Operations—*Error-Inducing Condition*:

- Location of the Line A Pressure Relief Valve coupled with the blackness of the Cover Plate and relative dimness of the lighting, making it difficult to recognize the condition of the line.

Cell # 6. Operations—*Non-Conservative Decisions*:

- Switching the Fire Suppression System to the position requiring its manual operation. Probably, this was a *value-based error*.

- Following the initial emergency call, continuing to pump oil and gas from other Platforms. This was a *value-based error* and a non-conservative, *reflexive-based error*.

- Continuing to accept the *unreliability* of the Diesel Generator, without causing its modification to improve its *reliability*.

Cell # 9. Maintenance—*Non-Conservative Decision*

- Placing the **Overhaul Form** on a table rather than giving it to the Control Room operator. *(Although a Maintenance person made the decision, the Operations function was impacted.)* This was a non-conservative, *reflexive-based error*.

Cell # 10. Training—Failed *Administrative Procedure Barriers*:

- Failure to perform evacuation drills with sufficient periodicity—either an inadequacy in the design of the procedure, failing to specify sufficient periodicity, or *non-compliance* with the procedure. An inadequacy in the procedure would be caused by a *cognition-based error*. Consistent *non-compliance* with the procedure would indicate a *value-based error*—e.g., the drills aren't worth the time lost for their performance..

- The same applies to drills for other than full evacuation.

Case Study—*Piper Alpha* (Cont'd)
Assignment Completion (Cont'd)

Cell # 13. Emergency Preparedness—Failed *Administrative Procedure Barrier.*
- There was no procedure requiring:
  - Identification of each plausible type of occurrence that could threaten worker safety.
  - For each such type of occurrence, the identification of the various levels of severity.
  - For each such level of severity, the establishment of the appropriate response or action.
  - For each such response or action, the assignment of responsibility and authority.

  Consequently, the Operations managers on *Claymore* and *Tartan* could not act in a timely manner. Probably, this *administrative procedure barrier* failure was due to *cognition-based error*. Possibly, there was not even a recognition of the need for such a procedure.

  Of course, as stated above, even in the absence of such a procedure, the decision to keep pumping was a non-conservative, *reflexive-based error*. The response to the immediate stimulus of the fire and mayday communication was non-conservative.

Overall:
- Certainly, there was a lack of an *EHS&Q culture* and *EHS&Q-conscious work environment*. The Report of the Public Inquiry stated that the *event* was not an "accident" but, rather, was caused by the *behavior*, or lack of proper *behavior*, of the management.

Single Cell Input—Cell #1

		Failed Barriers		
		Admin/Tech Proc Barrier?	Equipment Barrier?	Human Barrier?
Design Engrg	Design Problem?	Preventable?	Preventable?	Preventable?
		Detectable Earlier?	Detectable Earlier?	Detectable Earlier?
	Conform Problem?	Preventable?	Preventable?	Preventable?
		Detectable Earlier?	Detectable Earlier?	Detectable Earlier?

- This slide shows how a single cell from the preceding slide may be further broken down to more definitively complete the assignment. For example, for the Design Engineering function, one would want to know whether the:

  - Failed *barrier* is either an *administrative process, technical process, equipment* or *human barrier;*

  - Failed was due to the inadequate design of the *barrier* or to *non-conformance* to the design;

  - Inadequacy or *non-conformance* could have been *prevented* or, if not *preventable*, whether it could have been *detected* and *corrected* earlier.

- There will be a lot more on this in the section on *Error Recurrence Prevention*, the *fourth field of focus*, a large part of which deals with *root cause analysis*.

Non-Conservative and Conservative Decision-making

- This is the *Non-Conservative and Conservative Decision-Making* Section of the Bookinar™.

- *Non-Conservative and Conservative Decision-Making* is the *third field of focus* or major area of interest in *human error prevention—Hazards and Barriers* having been first, and *Error-Inducing Conditions and Counteracting Behaviors* having been second.

- The objectives in order to achieve conservative decisions are as follows:

  - Reduce the need for field decisions.

  - Reduce the pressures that contribute to non-conservation field decisions.

  - Learn to recognize thought processes and *behaviors* that lead to non-conservative decisions—field decisions or otherwise.

  - Learn thought processes and *behaviors* that lead to conservative decisions.

  - Consistently avoid *non-conservative* thought processes and *behaviors* and consistently use *conservative decision* thought processes and *behaviors*.

- Is the *risk* of the action worth the benefit of the action?

- People take *risks* and people make mistakes.

Non-conservative Decision-making Pressures

- Financial incentives
- Opportunity for profit
- Cost constraints
- Schedule constraint
- End of shift
- Approaching weekend or holiday
- Pride
- Job survival

- Some of these pressures are the same as *error-inducing conditions* or *error-likely situations*.
- *Financial incentive* or *opportunity for profit*—Shipment is made even though the lot, based on final *sampling inspection*, has an outgoing percent *defective* that is higher than the customer allowable. Shipment is made because otherwise the goal for the month is not achieved, adversely impacting the bonus.
- *Cost constraint*—The causes of the *problem* are not corrected. There is no budget for their correction.
- *Schedule constraint*—The document is submitted on schedule, without *independent* review. There is no time for its *independent* review.
- *End of shift* or *approaching weekend or holiday*—If the job is not completed on the current shift, it may have to be completed using overtime or time that cuts into the weekend or holiday. Can't have that. Take a short-cut; complete the job on the current shift.
- *Pride*—There's no need for input to the decision. The boss, the decision-maker, knows best.
- *Job survival*—It's done either when or how the boss wants it or else.
- Many of these pressures act in combination with one another.
- In an *EHS&Q-conscious work environment*, these pressures are largely eliminated. Don't misunderstand; there are still schedules and cost constraints, but they don't take precedence over *EHS&Q* issues of *significance*.

Non-conservative Decision-making Sources

- Bias
- "Satisficing"
- Operational loafing

- These, too, are thought processes and *behaviors* that lead to *non-conservative decision-making.*
- Each will be covered in following slides.
- It's not necessarily important for one to learn the name or title of each type of *bias* and operational loafing, but it is important for one to learn their underlying concepts and avoid the *behaviors* they represent.

Frequency and Similarity Bias

- Tendency to define the problem in terms of past experience
- Tendency to use solutions from past experience
- Tendency to use solutions that are used frequently
- Tendency to give greater weight to frequently occurring information
- Tendency to give greater weight to recently acquired information

Over-simplification Bias

- Tendency to oversimplify the problem definition
- Tendency to settle on a simple solution or course of action that appears satisfactory, giving undue weight to available data

- This is very similar to *satisficing*. (See page 185.)
- This occurs frequently in the preparation of administrative and technical process procedures and, sometimes, in the selection of *preventive corrective actions*.

Close-in-time Bias

Tendency to establish a correlation between or perceive a cause and effect relationship between two occurrences that are close together in time, even if the occurrences are unrelated

- A *spurious correlation* is one for which there is no cause and effect relationship—a correlation in which the relationship is mere coincidence. Assigning cause and effect on the strength of the correlation, when cause and effect do not exist, is erroneous.
- An often used, jocular example of a spurious correlation is as follows: For years, each year, there has been an increase in the number of storks flying over the city and, for the same years, each year, there has been a corresponding increase in the number of child births in the city. The correlation is strong. Can it, therefore, be concluded that storks bring babies? Well, of course.

Confirmation Bias

Reluctance to change one's mind even in light of conflicting information, tending to see only evidence that supports the original solution and to ignore or rationalize conflicting data

• Often, this is referred to as *pigheadedness* or *bullheadedness*.

Overload Bias

Tendency to attend to only parts of a problem due to insufficient resources or insufficient attention span

- This is very much akin to yielding to one or more of the pressures listed in an earlier slide in this section—e.g., time pressure or budget pressure.

Order Bias

- Tendency to fill in data gaps with perceptions
- Tendency to put data in a preconceived order

- As will be seen in the next section, acquiring data for *root cause analysis* on a process step-by-step basis or on a time-line basis, helps to avoid this bias.

"Satisficing"

- Selection of the first alternative that meets a need, without consideration of other alternatives, such that the best or a better alternative may not even be considered

- Selection of an alternative that meets most, if not all of the needs, such that an alternative that meets all of the needs may not even be considered

- The word *satisficing* was coined by Herbert Simon, who was a political scientist, professor at Carnegie Mellon University, and the 1978 Nobel Prize winner for economics (mainly for his study of decision-making in organizations and his theory of "bounded rationality"). He was referred to as the father of artificial intelligence.

- *Satisficing* is drawn from the words *satisfy* and *suffice*.

- *Satisficing* is an economic concept, in its simplest form addressing the question of whether or not it's worthwhile to spend the resources necessary for the best or a better solution. In this context, it has no negative connotation. If a solution suffices, by definition it's adequate—i.e., no more and no less than is necessary to do the job. There's nothing wrong with that. Spending more than is necessary for adequacy makes no sense, and this senselessness is conveyed by the statement that *best is the enemy of good enough*.

- However, *satisficing* has transitioned to take on the connotation of the acceptance of a less than best or less than better solution because of the decision-maker's lack of care, rather than lack of cognitive ability or cost-benefit considerations.

- *Satisficing* is a seriously flawed thought process when the potential consequence of a less than best or better solution is intolerable.

- When *satisficing* is wrong, because of lack of care, it's an *attribute* of *groupthink*. (See page 156.)

Operational Loafing

- Mostly, failing to take steps to get or to provide more information
- Different types of operational loafing:
  - Co-piloting
  - Dropping guard
  - Free-riding
  - Outward neutralizing
  - Unsharing
  - Group thinking
  - Risky-shifting

- *Co-piloting*—Worker feels that it is not his / her place to challenge the actions of the leader. If this is the *attitude* of a large number of workers, the kind of *culture* that exists is obvious.

- *Dropping guard*—Worker trusts his / her experienced partner to do the job correctly, and lowers his / her own guard.

- *Free-riding*—Worker benefits from the efforts of the other group members while contributing no effort to the task, and taking a lackadaisical approach to the job.

- *Outward neutralizing*—Worker does not contribute a position for fear of being wrong. Some will not contribute even in a highly *EHS&Q-consciousness work environment*.

- *Unsharing*—Worker takes information from others but does not share his or her information, an especially unacceptable *behavior*, derived from the idea that he or she who has the most information has the *leg up*. It doesn't take long to identify this kind of worker. Such a worker should be *coached* to a sharing *attitude* or, if that's unsuccessful, dismissed.

- *Group thinking*—Workers' desire for unanimity or consensus overrides the need to consider alternative courses of action. (See page 156.)

- *Risky-shifting*—As a group, workers accept a decision that invokes a *risk* greater than that which they would take as individuals on their own. Input to decisions should be provided by groups; decisions should be made by individuals. The only exception is decisions made by Boards of Directors or Boards of Trustees.

- While avoiding *risky-shifting*, managers also should *empower* employees with the authority to make decisions commensurate with their abilities.

- Managers and co-workers have a responsibility to create an environment in which these *behaviors* are eliminated or minimized.

Team Involvement

- Keep all members of the team involved.
- Get different perspectives.
- Prevent the shut-down of valuable input.
- Resolve disagreement.
  - Identify differences in the information / data being used.
  - Identify differences in the logic being used.

- For *conservative decision-making*, the decision-maker should adopt a *participative style*.
- The value of the input is based on the quality of the data being inputted and on the sensibility of the logic applied to the data.
- The value of input is independent of the (a) organizational level of the contributor, or (b) type of department to which the contributor is assigned. Input contributed by persons of lower organizational rank or from supporting departments should not be prejudged and devalued based on the person's rank or department.
- Inputs contributed by persons from different organizational levels and different departments may provide the variety of perspectives needed for *conservative decision-making*.
- The decision-maker should assure that the *behavior* of those with strong, dominant personalities does not preclude the contributions of those who are timid or reticent. The decision-maker should solicit input from those who are timid or reticent.
- The decision-maker should resolve disagreement. There are only two acceptable bases for disagreement—either a difference in the data used by the differing parties or a difference in the logic applied to the data by the parties. By comparing the data or by comparing the logic being used by the disagreeing parties, a decision-maker may be able to identify the source of the disagreement and resolve it. Disagreement should be resolved on the basis of either of these two factors—data or logic.
- Otherwise, the disagreement may be rooted in a personality conflict that is unacceptable in a decision-making environment.

Questions: What is *situational awareness*? What are its *attributes*?

Situational Awareness

- Ongoing vigilance
  - Focus without fixation
    - Awareness of environment and surroundings
    - Anticipation of change

- *Situational awareness* is an individual *behavior* that can be practiced when one is performing alone or as a part of a team.

- *Situational awareness* is widely practiced—for example, while driving a car or playing a sport. Unfortunately, it's practiced inconsistently or incorrectly.

- Take tennis. The good player keeps his eye on the ball and is focused on the point being played, not on the previous point in which he or she might have made an *error* and not on the next point which may be needed to win the game. Depending on the pace of his or her shot, its depth, its angle, is type (flat, slice or topspin) and the skill of the opponent, the good player recognizes the "percentages" (as they are referred to) and positions himself / herself to receive the return accordingly—anticipating the pace, depth, angle and type of return.

- Take handball. The good player recognized the opponent's position on the court, his or her stance (upright or bending over), the direction in which his / her feet are pointing, and whether the ball is to be struck with his / her stronger or weaker hand. Based on these factors, the good player positions himself / herself to receive the return accordingly. Were he or she to be fixated on the flight of the ball without recognizing these other factors, the player probably would not be positioned in the best place according to the "percentages".

- While driving a car, if one becomes fixated on the road ahead, oblivious of the cars to the side or rear, one has lost *situational awareness* and is more likely to be involved in an accident.

Question: What are some practices that will help to maintain *situational awareness* for a group or team?

Tips for Good Situational Awareness

- Predetermine the roles of each team member.
- Develop a plan and assign responsibilities for handling potential problems and distractions.
- Monitor and evaluate the current status relative to the plan.
- Solicit input from all team members.
- Focus on the task, but be aware of the state of the facility, environment, and people; don't fixate.
- Look ahead and consider contingencies.
- Create visual and/or aural reminders of interrupted tasks. Place keep.
- Speak up when you see situational awareness breaking down.

Question: What are some conditions that indicate the loss of *situational awareness* for a group or team?

Clues to Loss of Situational Awareness

- Lack of focus on operational activities
- Fixation-focusing on any one thing to the exclusion of everything else
- Confusion-uncertainty or bafflement about a situation (often accompanied by anxiety or psychological discomfort)
- Data inconsistency or conflict
- Personal conflict
- Unresolved conflict
- Vague or incomplete oral or written communication
- Non-compliance with standard operating procedures, system limitations or settings

Conservative Decision-making Behaviors

- Remain conservative when facing non-conservative decision-making pressures (e.g., financial incentives).
- Avoid the biases, "satisficing", and operational loafing.
- Demonstrate respect for the barriers that assure human and equipment safety, and process and product quality.
- Expect procedure compliance. It is not optional.
- Maintain plant safety margins and operate within design criteria.
- Do not accept or live with known problems—e.g., high backlogs, procedure and equipment deficiencies, operator work-arounds.
- Maintain an environment in which questions are appreciated.
- Be self-critical and objective.

- ADVOCATE for ENVIRONMENTAL PROTECTION, HEALTH, SAFETY and QUALITY!

  Repeatedly, history has shown that leading to an *event*, there are multiple opportunities for the advocacy of *EHS&Q*, and that a single action in response to any such an opportunity to advocate would have *prevented* the *event*.

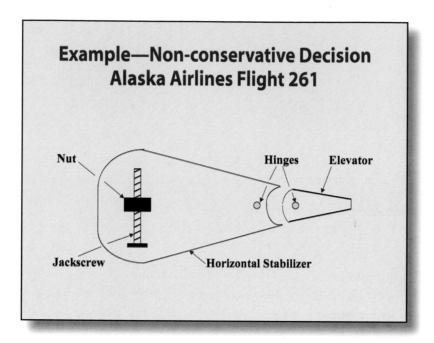

Example—Non-conservative Decision
Alaska Airlines Flight 261

Nut　　　　　　　　　　Hinges　　Elevator

Jackscrew　　　　　　Horizontal Stabilizer

- The sketch in the slide is a gross simplification of the configuration.

Executive Summary—National Transportation Safety Board Report:

"On January 31, 2000, about 1621 Pacific Standard Time, Alaska Airlines, Inc., Flight 261, a McDonnell Douglas MD-83, N963AS, crashed into the Pacific Ocean about 2.7 miles north of Anacapa Island, California. The 2 pilots, 3 cabin crew-members, and 83 passengers on board were killed, and the airplane was destroyed by impact forces.

The National Transportation Safety Board determines that the probable cause of this accident was a loss of airplane pitch control resulting from the in-flight failure of the horizontal stabilizer trim system jackscrew assembly's acme nut threads. The thread failure was caused by excessive wear resulting from Alaska Airlines' insufficient lubrication of the jackscrew assembly."

- Starting on page 193, selected conclusions from the National Transportation Safety Board Report are provided.

- Notice from the last bullet on page 194 that the lubrication interval had been almost doubled from the original interval. The interval extensions were non-conservative decisions resulting from *cognition-based error* in conjunction with *value-based error*.

- Notice from the first bullet on page 194 that a single missed or inadequate lubrication would possibly put a flight in danger. Therefore, the new interval was an insufficient *barrier*. Notice from the penultimate bullet on page 194 that the interval extensions were not "supported by adequate technical data to demonstrate that the extension would not present a potential hazard." This indicates a *barrier* failure. Since there were multiple interval extensions without analysis, there appears to have been an absence of an administrative procedure to require such analysis. This, too, appears to be a *cognition-based error*.

Description of the Acme Screw and Nut—National Transportation Safety Board Report:

- "Movement of the horizontal stabilizer is commanded either automatically by the autopilot when it is engaged, or manually by the flight crew by depressing either set of dual trim switches (located on each control wheel), moving the dual longitudinal trim handles on the center control pedestal, or moving the dual alternate trim control switches on the center pedestal…. Any of these commands activates one of the two electric motors that rotate the acme screw by applying torque to the titanium torque tube that is held fixed inside the acme screw. The motors are deenergized whenever either the autopilot senses that the horizontal stabilizer has reached the desired pitch trim condition, when pilot commands are terminated, or when the horizontal stabilizer reaches its maximum travel limits. Electrical travel limit shutoff switches (also known as the electrical stops) stop the motors at the maximum limits of travel. The MD-80 horizontal stabilizer's design limits are 12.2° leading edge down, which results in airplane-nose-up trim, and 2.1° leading edge up, which results in airplane-nose-down trim, as set by the electrical stops."

Selected Conclusions—National Transportation Safety Board Report:

- "The worn threads inside the horizontal stabilizer acme nut were incrementally sheared off by the acme screw and were completely sheared off during the accident flight. As the airplane passed through 23,400 feet, the acme screw and nut jammed, preventing further movement of the horizontal stabilizer until the initial dive."

- "The airplane's initial dive from 31,050 feet began when the jam between the acme screw and nut was overcome as a result of operation of the primary trim motor. Release of the jam allowed the acme screw to pull up through the acme nut, causing the horizontal stabilizer leading edge to move upward, thus causing the airplane to pitch rapidly downward."

- "The acme screw did not completely separate from the acme nut during the initial dive because the screw's lower mechanical stop was restrained by the lower surface of the acme nut until just before the second and final dive about 10 minutes later."

- "The cause of the final dive was the low-cycle fatigue fracture of the torque tube, followed by the failure of the vertical stabilizer tip fairing brackets, which allowed the horizontal stabilizer leading edge to move upward significantly beyond what is permitted by a normally operating jackscrew assembly. The resulting upward movement of the horizontal stabilizer leading edge created an excessive upward aerodynamic tail load, which caused an uncontrollable downward pitching of the airplane from which recovery was not possible."

- "The acme nut threads on the accident airplane's horizontal stabilizer jackscrew assembly wore at an excessive rate."

- "There was no effective lubrication on the acme screw and nut interface at the time of the Alaska Airlines Flight 261 accident."

- "The excessive and accelerated wear of the accident jackscrew assembly acme nut threads was the result of insufficient lubrication, which was directly causal to the Alaska Airlines Flight 261 accident."

Selected Conclusions—National Transportation Safety Board Report (Cont'd):

- "Alaska Airline's extensions of its lubrication interval for its McDonnell Douglas MD-80 horizontal stabilizer components and the Federal Aviation Administration's approval of these extensions, the last of which was based on Boeing's extension of the recommended lubrication interval, increased the likelihood that a missed or inadequate lubrication would result in excessive wear of jackscrew assembly acme nut threads and, therefore, was a direct cause of the excessive wear and contributed to the Alaska Airlines Flight 261 accident."

- **Note**: The Boeing / McDonnell Douglas merger was approved by the Federal Trade Commission on July 1, 1997. "Boeing" was the name of the merged company.

- "When lubricating the jackscrew assembly, removal of used grease from the acme screw before application of fresh grease will increase the effectiveness of the lubrication."

- "A larger access panel would facilitate the proper accomplishment of the jackscrew assembly lubrication task."

- "If the jackscrew assembly lubrication procedure were a required inspection item for which an inspector's signoff is needed, the potential for unperformed or improperly performed lubrications would be reduced.

- "Alaska Airline's extension of the end play check interval and the Federal Aviation Administration's approval of that extension allowed the accident acme nut threads to wear to failure without the opportunity for detection and, therefore, was a direct cause of the excessive wear and contributed to the Alaska Airlines Flight 261 accident."

- "Alaska Airline's end play check interval extension should have been, but was not, supported by adequate technical data to demonstrate that the extension would not present a potential hazard."

Continuous Airworthiness Maintenance Program—National Transportation Safety Board Report

- Alaska Airlines' initial check interval was 2,500 flight hours. In 1988, it was extended to every 13 months (which, based on the average airplane utilization rate at Alaska Airlines at the time, was about 3,200 flight hours). In 1996, the check interval was extended to 15 months (which, based on the average airplane utilization rate at Alaska Airlines at the time, was about 4,775 flight hours).

Source of photograph: National Transportation Safety Board

Example—Non-conservative Decision
Alaska Airlines Flight 261 (Cont'd)

Maintenance Procedure

A. Open access doors 6307, 6308, 6306 and 6309

B. Lube per the following...
   3. JACKSCREW
     Apply light coat of grease to threads, then operate mechanism through full range of travel to distribute lubricant over length of jackscrew.

C. Close doors 6307, 6308, 6306 and 6309

- Notice the failure of this procedure as a *barrier*:
  - There is no requirement to remove any remaining lubricant as a prerequisite to applying the new lubricant. Such a requirement would make the new lubricant more effective.
  - A *light coat* is not defined. However, possibly it need not be defined if it is *skill of the trade*.
  - The type of lubricant is not specified. Although it was the practice to use *Aeroshell 3* and *Mobilgrease 2*, the lubricant should be specified because, ostensibly, it's a design requirement. Absent its specification in the procedure, who knows when a cost reduction initiative could result in the procurement of a less effective lubricant.
  - Although the NTSB Report indicated that the differences in wear rates using two different lubricants, *Aeroshell 3* and *Mobilgrease 2*, could not have caused the failure, given the difference, one would assume that the longer lasting lubricant would be economically preferred and, therefore, specified.

Case Study—Greeneville and Ehime Maru

Assignment

Identify the:

- Failed barriers;

- Error-inducing conditions / error-likely situations;

- Non-conservative decisions.

Emphasize the latter.

Case Study—*Greeneville* and *Ehime Maru*

- Case study information obtained from the:
  - Report of the "Court Inquiry Into The Circumstances Surrounding The Collision Between The USS Greeneville (SSN 772) And Japanese M/V Ehime Maru That Occurred Off The Coast Of Oahu, Hawaii on 9 February 2001" dated 13 April 2001.
  - US Navy Greeneville Incident Image Gallery

***USS Greeneville*—Los Angeles Class:**

- Builders: General Dynamics Electric Boat Division.
- Christened by: Tipper Gore on September 17, 1994.
- Power plant: Nuclear reactor, single shaft, 33-year lifetime.
- Gross tonnage: Approximately 6,900.
- Length: 110 meters.
- Speed: 20+ knots.
- Crew: 17 Officers, 125 Enlisted.

***Ehime Maru*:**

- Builder: Hashihama Works.
- Delivery Date: June 1996.
- Main engine: Akasaka E28BFD
- Gross tonnage: 741.

Case Study—*Greeneville* and *Ehime Maru* (Cont'd)

- Length: 55 meters.
- Max Speed: 15.05 knots.
- Color: White.
- User: Uwajima Fisheries High School.
- Purpose: Cadet training for fisheries and oceanographic research.

Greeneville—Source of Photograph: Navy Buddies

Ehime Maru—Source of Photograph: Navy Buddies

Case Study—*Greeneville* and *Ehime Maru* (Cont'd)

Size Comparison:

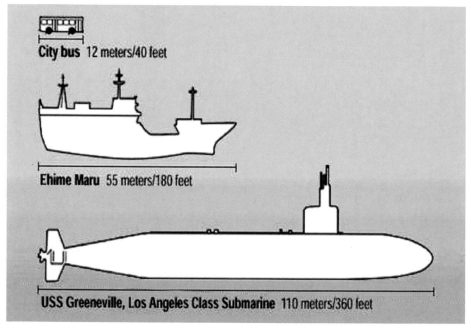

City bus 12 meters/40 feet

Ehime Maru 55 meters/180 feet

USS Greeneville, Los Angeles Class Submarine 110 meters/360 feet

Source of sketch: Navy Buddies

Recent History:

- *Greeneville* was in dry-dock for maintenance from September to December 2000, and then underwent sea trials on December 21, 2000.
- After sea trials, *Greeneville* entered a holiday, stand-down period.
- From January 5 to February 2, 2001, *Greeneville* went to Ketchikan, Alaska, did normal underway training, and made a port call in San Francisco. While in San Francisco, *Greeneville* was asked to support a SUBPAC Public Affairs embarkation from Honolulu to take place on February 9, 2001, with civilian VIP guests aboard.

Staff:

- Commanding Officer (CO): Commander (CDR) (name intentionally omitted)
- Executive Officer (XO): Lieutenant Commander (LCDR) (name intentionally omitted)
- Navigator (NAV): Lieutenant (LT) (name intentionally omitted)
- Officer of the Day (OOD): Lieutenant Junior Grade (LTJG) (name intentionally omitted)
- Submarine Pacific (SUBPAC) Chief of Staff: Captain (CAPT) (name intentionally omitted)

Case Study—*Greeneville* and *Ehime Maru* (Cont'd)

Staff (Cont'd):

- The crew of *Greeneville* respected CO's technical proficiency, admired him as a CO, and had grown accustomed to receiving praise under his leadership. Having the CO in the Control Room gave watch standers a sense of security.
- The CO's theme of *Safety, Efficiency, Back-up* was well known on board the *Greeneville*.

Mission of the Day:

- To demonstrate the performance capabilities of the *Greeneville* to the group of civilian, distinguished visitors.

Plan of the Day:

- 0230 hours: Brief and start-up reactor.
- 0715 hours: Station maneuvering watch.
- 0800 hours: Underway.
- 1000 hours: Deep dive.
- 1100 hours: Lunch.
- 1130 hours: Relieve the watch.
- 1230 hours: *Angles* and *high-speed maneuvers*.
  - Angles are vertical movements in the water column, an evolution whereby the submarine cycles through a series of increasing ups and downs ranging to a maximum of 30°, while changing depths between 150 and 650 feet. Angles are conducted to demonstrate the submarine's ability to rapidly change depth.
  - High-speed maneuvers involve horizontal movements in the water column, hard turns left or right, up to flank speed and full rudder. These are conducted to demonstrate a submarine's maneuverability in a tactical setting.
- 1300 hours: Emergency blow. Emergency blow will be done at about 12 knots, rather than at full speed, because *porpoising* is rather violent and may induce motion sickness in the visitors.
- 1330 hours: Station maneuvering watch.
- 1500 hours: Back to port. If not back into port at the scheduled time, port authorities must be notified to reassign tugs, line handlers, etc.

Case Study—*Greeneville* and *Ehime Maru* (Cont'd)

Orders of the Day:

- It is critical to verify that the surface is clear prior to surfacing.
- Fire Control (FC) will verify the location of surface contacts prior to coming to Periscope depth (PD).
- Tracking Surface Contacts:
  - Sonar is passive, listening for ships on the surface.
  - Acquiring sonar is difficult when changing directions rapidly.
  - In order to obtain reliable contact data from the passive sonar system, the submarine must maintain a stable course and depth, with a speed of about 10 knots (slow enough to minimize interference from the submarine's own noise, yet fast enough to drive across the line of sight to a contact).

- **Standing Orders for Coming to PD:**

1. Periscope brief with FC, Sonar and others. Periscope Brief:
   - As the submarine ascends to PD, an underwater search is made, whereby the Periscope operator aligns the view of the Periscope directly in front of the submarine, looking for shadows, which may indicate a collision threat.
   - As the Periscope breaks the surface, the operator conducts three 360° sweeps of approximately eight seconds per sweep in low power, to quickly determine if there are close contacts. This is to defend the submarine against imminent collision. If safe operation is indicated, the announcement *no close contacts* is made.
   - Following the initial search, an aerial search involving several sweeps in low power, at different elevations, is conducted.
   - Following the aerial search, a continuous visual search is conducted. This involves a series of 360° horizon sweeps in low power, followed by successive 90° quadrant searches in high power. Each sweep takes approximately 45 seconds.
   - All totaled, more than three minutes is required for proper Periscope use when first reaching PD.

2. Two good *Target Motion Analysis (TMA) legs*:
   - TMA is the study of relative motion, by which to determine the bearing, range, course, and speed of surface contacts relative to the submarine. The process takes sonar data and develops parameters of movement through a coordinated, logical series of assumptions, solutions, and refinements of the solutions. The computer solutions provide assistance and confirmation to human mental analysis, training and experience.

Case Study—*Greeneville* and *Ehime Maru* (Cont'd)

Standing Orders for Coming to PD (Cont'd):

2. Two good *Target Motion Analysis (TMA) legs* (Cont'd):

- Generally, development of contact solutions requires data from two different courses or legs of about three minutes each. The second leg also allows the submarine to *clear the baffles*, and identify contacts in an area where the submarine is acoustically deaf. If a contact is identified during the baffle clear, an additional leg as to that contact is generally necessary. In addition to an appropriate length of time, a *good leg* requires a steady course, at a steady depth, at a speed of about 10 knots.

3. Report to CO and obtain permission for ascent.

4. Make ascent.

Operational Area:

- East of *Submarine Test and Trial Area*, South of Honolulu.

- Current *National Oceanic and Atmospheric Administration* charts (specifically chart 19340), used by civilian mariners, show a "Submarine Test and Trial Area" South of Oahu. This area was designated at Navy request in the 1960's.

- This area no longer has any special meaning or relevance under the Hawaiian Operations Area System, and this designation has been removed from National Imagery and Mapping Agency charts used by the military.

The Cruise:

- *Greeneville* embarked with 11 of 17 officers and 95 of 125 enlisted men—106 of the 142 full staff.

- Among those left ashore to attend training, were six sonarmen and the Leading Chief Petty Officer (LCPO) for the Sonar Division. Relatively new onboard, the LCPO had specifically identified the need to work on the Sonar Room's ability to conduct TMA and ranging techniques.

- A map of the *Greeneville* and *Ehime Maru* cruise paths from 1230 to 1343 hours is given on the next page.

- Through Periscope #2, the NAV observed a hazy, off-white sky—"probably the worst I've ever seen it, where you could actually see a long, long distance, but not see clearly very far at all."

- The NAV saw two trawlers at 10,000 yards. Both surface contacts had similar range and bearings. One was dark hulled, the other white hulled. As the contacts came to 8,000 yards, the NAV had no difficulty in quickly reacquiring the dark hulled vessel during Periscope sweeps, but concerted effort was required to relocate the white-hulled vessel. This information was not passed on to the OOD, XO or CO.

Case Study—*Greeneville* and *Ehime Maru* (Cont'd)

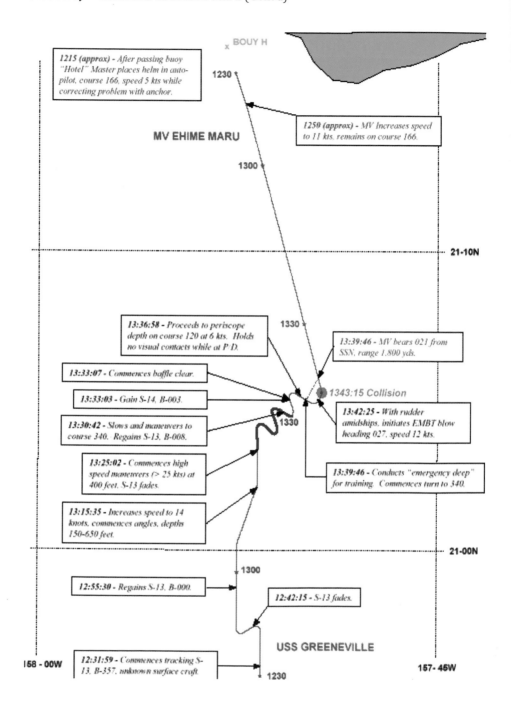

x BOUY H

1215 (approx) - *After passing buoy "Hotel" Master places helm in autopilot, course 166, speed 5 kts while correcting problem with anchor.*

1230

1250 (approx) - *MV Increases speed to 11 kts, remains on course 166.*

MV EHIME MARU

1300

- **21-10N**

13:36:58 - *Proceeds to periscope depth on course 120 at 6 kts. Holds no visual contacts while at P/D.*

1330

13:39:46 - *MV bears 021 from SSN, range 1,800 yds.*

13:33:07 - *Commences baffle clear.*

1343:15 Collision

13:33:03 - *Gain S-14, B-003.*

13:42:25 - *With rudder amidships, initiates EMBT blow heading 027, speed 12 kts.*

13:30:42 - *Slows and maneuvers to course 340. Regains S-13, B-008.*

1330

13:25:02 - *Commences high speed maneuvers (> 25 kts) at 400 feet. S-13 fades.*

13:39:46 - *Conducts "emergency deep" for training. Commences turn to 340.*

13:15:35 - *Increases speed to 14 knots, commences angles, depths 150-650 feet.*

- **21-00N**

1300

12:55:30 - *Regains S-13, B-000.*

12:42:15 - *S-13 fades.*

USS GREENEVILLE

158 - 00W

12:31:59 - *Commences tracking S-13, B-357, unknown surface craft.*

1230

157- 45W

Case Study—*Greeneville* and *Ehime Maru* (Cont'd)

The Cruise (Cont'd):

- The Fire Control Tech (FCT) was relieved for a 10 minute smoke break. In the absence of the FCT, the relieving FCT was told to *alert* the OOD if bearing rates of the contacts got higher. This was not passed on or repeated to the FCT when he returned for duty.
- An *unqualified* individual was manning one of the three positions in the Sonar Room.
- At 1314, sonar data indicated the *Ehime Maru* (S-13) bearing to be 007 and maintaining—i.e., not drawing left or right.
- The Fire Control System solution entered for S-13 was bearing 007, range 15,000 yards, course 024, speed 11 knots. In actuality, S-13 was at a range of approximately 15,000 yards, course 166, speed 11 knots, and closing.
- The OOD was "excited, tight" during angles and high-speed maneuvers. Further, he had no previous experience with emergency surfacing evolutions.
- Without formally assuming the watch, the CO directed the angles evolution. He told the OOD the angle of attack and the depth that were to be achieved.
- During the high-speed maneuvers, the CO stated that he would challenge any other boat to perform these maneuvers so well.
- Dynamic maneuvers, such as high-speed large rudder turns, negatively impact Sonar displays. The Sonar supervisor described the effect as making the Sonar Screens look like *spaghetti*. Putting the contacts into the baffles during the submarine's large turns, and the noise of the submarine, itself, during high speeds, also caused the contacts to lose track or fade.
- The CO ordered a dive to 400 feet, which initially surprised the forward Watch Standers, as well as the XO and the CAPT. The CO then stated the emergency dive was for training, and directed the OOD to make a depth of 400 feet.
- The CO told the OOD to make preparations to proceed to PD and be there in five minutes. It was CO's intent to make this a training evolution for a slow and methodical OOD. Others in the Control Room thought this was aggressive, if not impossible, but said nothing.
- The CO then went the Sonar Room.
- Starting with *Greeneville's* preparations to come to PD, the CAPT harbored concerns over the pace of events. His thoughts were that these evolutions were happening quicker than he would have done them. However, the CAPT did not voice his concerns at the time; he felt the CO was performing within his capabilities and was actively involved in showcasing his submarine and the prowess of his team. The CAPT decided to instead discuss his concerns with the CO after returning to port.
- The OOD did not do a Periscope brief. The XO saw the CO left the Sonar Room and assumed that the CO was aware of the contact picture.
- Sonar began to see S-13 as a close contact, but when the *Greeneville* turned, S-13 looked distant again. A new contact appeared, for a total of three.

Case Study—*Greeneville* and *Ehime Maru* (Cont'd)

The Cruise (Cont'd):

- When the OOD asked for a contact report, Sonar reported three contacts. The CO and OOD heard only two. Fire Control was never consulted.

- As they ascended to PD, Fire Control was still assembling contact information, which already should have been done. Fire Control updated S-13 from 15,000 yards to 4,000 yards, but didn't notice it as significant. Fire Control was busy determining the new contact and setting up a video display of the Periscope view for the distinguished visitors.

- PD was attained in seven minutes. Once there, quick sweeps were made as required by the OOD. Waves were hitting the Optics. The CO took the Periscope and focused on the area to the rear of the boat. Total scan time at PD was 66 seconds, far less than three minutes. Radio did not have time to pick up a radar signal from the S-13.

Collision:

- The *Greeneville* impacted *Ehime Maru* aft of the submarine's sail (tower), just outside and adjacent to the Control Room, on the port side at about 2 o'clock. The submarine's rudder then sliced through *Ehime Maru* from starboard to port.

- The *Ehime Maru* sank within 10 minutes.

***Greeneville* Repairs at Pearl Harbor:**

- In the following photograph, the circle identifies the damaged area of the *Greeneville*.

Source of Photograph: Navy Buddies

Case Study—*Greeneville* and *Ehime Maru* (Cont'd)

Ehime Maru Recovery:

- The cost to recover the victims and selected artifacts was $40 to $60 million.

- The overall cost was estimated to be slightly less than $1 billion, excluding good will.

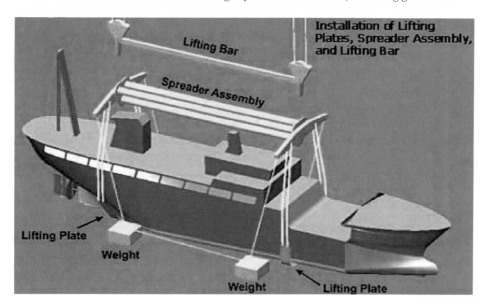

Assignment Completion

- *Non Conservative Decision* / Ineffective *Administrative Procedure Barrier*—Process implementation *non-compliance* in that Periscope scan was performed in 66 seconds rather than three minutes.

- *Non Conservative Decision* / Ineffective *Administrative Procedure Barrier*—Procedure implementation *non-compliance* in making Periscope depth in too short a time.

- Ineffective *Administrative Procedure Barrier*—Procedure inadequacy or procedure implementation *non-compliance* for not alerting OOD of bearing rates and contacts.

- Ineffective *Human Barrier:* The question of three versus two contacts was not resolved.

- Ineffective *Administrative Procedure Barrier:* Use of an *unqualified* sailor to man a position in the Sonar Room.

- Unresolved Question: What caused Fire Control to be in *error* with regard to course?

- *Error-Inducing Conditions* / *Error-Likely Situations:*

  - Presence of VIPs and a desire to impress them may have cause over exuberance.

  - Presence of VIPs may have caused Fire Control's distraction with display.

  - Hazy day, white hulled *Ehime Maru* and high waves in combination.

- In the absence of the failed *barriers* (first four bullets) the accident might not have occurred.

Error Recurrence Prevention

- This is the *Error Recurrence Prevention Section* of the Bookinar™.
- *Preventing the recurrence of error* is the *fourth field of focus* for *human error prevention*.
- The following will be covered in this section:
  - *Coaching*, to reinforce existing requirements;
  - Criteria for the design and use of a *condition report and corrective action tracking tool*;
  - Processes that constitute a *condition reporting, root cause analysis, corrective action, and performance and status measurement system*;
  - *Root cause analysis* techniques;
  - *Quantitative performance and status indicators*.
- Additional terms will be defined in this section.

Field Observations-Coaching

- A *field observation and coaching system* may be established requiring leaders to:
  - Spend a specified portion of their time in the field (e.g., on the floor, in the shop, in the plant, at the construction site);
  - Make *observations* of the work being performed in the field;
  - Perform *coaching* based on their observations;
  - Complete a document describing the results of the *observation* and *coaching*; and
  - Submit the document to an organization that categorizes the results, tallies the categorized results, and prepares and distributes periodic reports of the results, with analyses.

- The main purpose of this system is to help to assure that *coaching* is performed, given its importance to the *prevention of the recurrence* of *error*. Otherwise, the concern is that supervisors and managers will remain desk bound and that this important technique will not be utilized to the extent desired.

- A distortion of the system sometimes occurs in that supervisors and managers tend to perform a disproportionate number of the required field observations at the end of the period, to fill their quota, and at that time, also choose to observe jobs of the kind that allow them to do other work simultaneously.

- For example, as the end of a month approaches, a disproportionate number of classroom training sessions may be subject to field observation. As the field observation is being made, the observer / *coach* may be seen doing paperwork totally unrelated to the training session. Not good.

- The system's analyst easily should recognize the mal distributions of the (a) timing of observations and (b) types of jobs observed, and get these corrected.

- Another *problem* with the implementation of the system is that an observation may be performed inadequately, merely to fill the quota (sometimes referred to as a *drive-by observation*). An astute analyst may be able to identify the consistent absence of meaningful results from a given observer.

- There is an important difference between the type of *coaching* that occurs in an enterprise to reinforce known standards and requirements and the type of coaching that constitutes a teaching process.

- In an enterprise, a worker assigned to a job already should have the knowledge, cognitive abilities, skills and other *attributes* with which to perform the job and should know the performance expectations. Otherwise, the worker should not have been assigned to the job! In an enterprise, *coaching* is not a substitute for the education and training that the worker must have had before being assigned to the job. Instead, in an enterprise, *coaching* is a technique by which to reinforce performance expectations that are already known to the worker, but that may not have been met due to human *error*.

- In contrast, in other than an enterprise, coaching a youngster in a sport, for example, is a teaching process—teaching a youngster something that he or she does not yet know.

- To repeat, there is an important difference between reinforcing that which is already known and teaching that which is yet to be known.

- In an enterprise, if the supervising or managing *coach* learns that the worker is ignorant of the requirement, the *coaching* is immediately terminated. The *coach* recognizes that an *administrative procedure barrier(s)* has failed—specifically, the *barrier(s)* that is intended to assure that workers are *qualified* before they are assigned. This recognition should initiate a course of action that is entirely different from *coaching*.

- This will be demonstrated later in the presentation.

Coaching Objective

Proactively prevent the recurrence
of human error

- The remainder of the discussion on *coaching* describes the process in an enterprise environment—i.e., an environment in which the objective is to *prevent the recurrence* of *error* rather than an environment in which the objective is to teach

- A job would be stopped to provide *coaching* only if there were imminent danger of the occurrence of an *event*. Otherwise, almost always, *coaching* is performed immediately following the completion of the job (or shortly thereafter) such as to minimize the potential for the *recurrence of error* on the next job to be performed by the person being *coached*.

- From the perspective of the next job, *coaching* is proactive.

Coaching Functions

- Observe behavior

- Provide feedback

- Reinforce desired behavior and expectations

- Obtain commitments to correct undesired behavior

- Notice that there is nothing in the list of *coaching* functions relating to teaching.

- When a *coach* makes an *observation* of *behavior*, he or she is acquiring facts. *Observations* are *factual*.

- The *coach* provides the *observational, factual* feedback to the worker being *coached*. The feedback is non-judgmental, either in words or in body language.

- Upon being presented with the observational feedback that indicates a *non-conformance* to performance expectations, the worker should be awakened to the knowledge, cognition, skill or other *attributes* which he or she already possesses (or should possess) for the job.

- In an ideal *coaching* experience, the worker will recognize that the factual observation is different from the desired *behavior*, admit his or her *error*, and commit to future *behavior* in accordance with *behavioral* expectations.

- The *coaching* steps are described in detail on page 213 and demonstrated on pages 214–216.

Coaching versus Other Processes

- Coaching
  - Performed usually by someone close to the worker
  - Provides immediate feedback regarding behavior
  - Results in immediate behavioral change
- Other processes involving observations—e.g., audit
  - Performed by outsiders
  - Provides delayed problem identification feedback
  - Results in delayed behavioral change

- *Coaching* is often performed by a manager, supervisor, peer or subordinate who is in the same organizational chain as the worker or, if not in the same chain, in a related organizational chain. Thus, it is that the *coach* would have the required expertise addressed on the next page.

Skills of a Successful Coach

- Observation skills
- Sizing-up skills-recognizing personality strengths and weakness
- Oral communication skills
- Listening skills
- Conflict resolution skills
- Expertise

- There are courses, seminars and workshops covering the acquisition of *observation*, communication and conflict resolution skills.

- Sizing-up a worker's personality strengths and weaknesses is an important element in determining how to set the stage for the delivery of the feedback so as to be able to increase the potential for the acceptance of the feedback. Those closest to a worker have the greatest opportunity to understand his or her strengths and weaknesses and to be able to use this understanding to the benefit of the feedback.

- Obviously, oral communication skills are needed to clearly and completely describe the factual observation.

- Listening skills are needed because, often, the worker will provide information about a related issue that needs to be addressed. The approach to address this will be demonstrated in one of the role-plays presented in the next few pages.

- Conflict resolution skills are needed in the *event* that the worker's response to the observational feedback becomes confrontational. Again, the approach to address this will be demonstrated in one of the role-plays presented in the next few pages.

- The *coach* must be credible. Credibility is a function of one's expertise and the factual accuracy of the feedback. The *coach* must have expertise about the element(s) of the job for which he or she is providing feedback, not necessarily about every single element of the job being observed. However, the fewer the elements of the job for which the *coach* has expertise, the less effective the field *observation* and *coaching*.

- The *coach* should understand the job and its standards and success criteria, as well as its potential *problem* areas and difficulties.

The Seven-Step Coaching Process

1. "Break the ice".
2. Declare intent—in accordance with the "Field Observation System".
3. State the observation.
4. **Wait for a response.**
5. Assure that the response provides recognition of the desired behavior.
6. Ask for a specific solution.
7. Agree together that the solution is appropriate.

- Feedback should be given following the completion of the job, unless there is imminent danger of the loss of personal, environmental or equipment safety or the creation of a costly *defect*, in which case the observer / coach should stop the job. Otherwise, the observer / *coach* should not interrupt the job.

- The *coaching* process should start as soon after the completion of the job as is practicable, taking into consideration the need for the observer / *coach* and worker to have a private conversation.

- Basically, *breaking the ice* is setting a stage and establishing or reinforcing a relationship that will help the worker to be receptive and favorably responsive to the observation. Recall from an earlier slide, that sizing-up and understanding the worker's personality strengths and weaknesses is an important prerequisite of this first step.

- Informing the worker that the feedback about to be offered is in accordance with the *field observation and coaching system* has two benefits:

  - It further induces worker receptiveness.

  - Given that the worker has had training about the system, it alerts the worker to his or her responsibilities and expected *behavior* as the recipient of a *coaching observation*.

- Feedback should cover only something over which the worker has control. Here's an example. A worker is observed working in an area in which there is inadequate permanent lighting and the work procedure does not require the use of mobile lighting. These issues should be fed back to the Facility Maintenance and Maintenance Planning organizations, and only incidentally to the worker in the field.

- Again, recall from an earlier slide that the observation is a statement of fact without making any type of oral or body language judgment. For a discussion of the difference between *observation* and *fact* versus *assessment* and *conclusion,* see page 241.
- Stating nothing other than the observation and **waiting** for a response to the observation is the crux of the *coaching* process. There are two reasons for this.
  - It enables the observer / *coach* to determine whether or not the worker is aware of the standard, requirement or expectation. The worker should have this awareness; otherwise, his or her assignment to the job constitutes a failure of one or more *administrative procedure barriers.*
  - It gives the worker the opportunity to identify any *problems* related to performance in accordance with the standard, requirement or expectation.
- Given the forgoing reasons and given that this type of *coaching* is neither teaching nor supervising, at this point, it is appropriate for the observer / *coach* to do nothing other than to state the observation. State it and stop. Don't be out-waited; the next step is the worker's.
- The worker's response to the observation should indicate that he or she is aware of the standard, requirement or expectation. However, there can be a wide variety of worker responses and observer / *coach* reactions—best described by exemplification.
- Following is a simple situation and various scenarios, starting with Step 4, the statement of the observation. Each scenario gives a different worker response and appropriate reaction.

Situation:

- A senior calibration technician, Jack, is calibrating pressure gauges that are installed in an area of the electricity generating plant's turbine deck, near rotating equipment that produces high decibel noise. The job takes less than half an hour. The accesses to the area are guarded by signs indicating that hearing protection is required when entering the area. An observer / *coach,* Jill, a maintenance supervisor, is making an observation of Jack's work under the *field observation and coaching system.* Jack is working without hearing protection. Jack does not report administratively to Jill. Jill decides not to stop the work because she understands that Jack is not immediately imperiled. She understands that the hearing protection requirement is intended to protect workers over a long period of time.
- Jill (Step 4): "Jack, I noticed that while you were making the calibrations, you were not using hearing protection."

Scenario # 1:

- Jack: "Oh, my gosh! Of course, I should have been wearing ear-plugs. We're using the new temperature compensated pressure gauge working standards. I guess I was thinking about the new procedure, maybe even fixated on it. I just blew it." (*Lapse-based error.* Jack demonstrates he is now aware of and respects the requirement.)
- Jill: "It can happen to anyone. So what about the next time." (Jill asks for a solution.)
- Jack: "No question. I'll wear hearing protection. I won't get fixated. And thanks for the feedback." (Jill receives a solution.)
- Jill: "Sounds good to me and thank you, too, for your cooperation. Now don't forget to give my regards to Mary." (Jill agrees with the acceptability of the solution.)

Scenario # 2:

- Jack: "Oh, yeah, I know that I should be wearing ear plugs but I came into the area from the South and there are no ear plugs at this end. The ear-plug container is way at the North end and that's a ten minute walk back and forth. It's not worth it for such a short job." (*Value-based error*. Jack demonstrates his awareness of the requirement and identifies a *problem* in adhering to the requirement.)

- Jill: "That's a good point about the location of the ear plug container. I'll be sure to arrange for another ear-plug container to be placed at the South end. Also, I'm glad that you recognize the requirement. Jack, you're a senior guy. You're a leader. The other technicians look up to you. What you do sets an example. Jack, what are you going to do in the future?" (Jill addresses the ear-plug issue and asks for a solution from Jack.)

- Jack: "You're right. No question. I'll wear hearing protection. Thanks for the feedback and thanks for arranging for ear plugs to be available at this end." (Jack demonstrates his willingness to value the requirement. Jill receives a solution.)

- Jill: "You're welcome. And thank you, too, for raising the ear-plug issue and for your cooperation. Now don't forget to give my regards to Mary." (Jill agrees with the acceptability of the solution and follows through with the correction of the issue.)

Scenario # 3:

- Jack: "Heck, Jill, I thought that hearing protection is required only if you're going to be in the area for over an hour. My job takes only twenty minutes."

- Jill: "Actually, Jack, hearing protection is required at all times when you're in this area. Were you informed of the requirement?

- Jack: No. (*Knowledge-based error*.)

- Jill: "I'm sorry about your not being informed. As you may know, I'm obligated to originate a *condition report*. Please don't take this personally. The *problem* is not your *behavior*. The *problem* is that you were not informed. Your name will not be in the *condition report*. Now don't forget to give my regards to Mary." (The *coaching* process was ended because Jack did not know the requirement. In this simple case, it was easy for Jill to inform Jack of the requirement. In another, more complex case, it might not have been easy or even appropriate for Jill to inform Jack of the requirement—again, because *coaching* in an enterprise is NOT a teaching or training job.)

Scenario # 4:

- Jack: "You know, Jill, you should mind you own business. I don't work for you." (Possibly a *value-based* or *reflexive-based error*.)

- Jill: "Let me remind you, Jack, that I'm making a field observation in accordance with the *field observation and coaching system*." (Jill gives Jack another chance to react properly.)

- Jack: "Oh, you're right. I'm sorry. I'm just upset about something else and I took it out on you. Please forgive me." (Jack takes the second chance.)

- At this point the process continues in accordance with any of the other scenarios, above.

Scenario # 5:

- Jack: "You know, Jill, you should mind you own business. I don't work for you. (Possibly a *value-based* or *reflexive-based error*.)

- Jill: "Let me remind you, Jack, that I'm making a field observation in accordance with the *field observation and coaching system*." (Jill gives Jack another chance to behave properly.)

- Jack: "That's hogwash. Just leave me alone, will you?" (Jack refuses the second chance. The *coaching* process was ended because of Jack's *attitude*. Jill is to originate a *condition report[s]*. There are two *problems*—one, failure to use hearing protection and two, failure to behave in accordance with the expectations of the *field observation and coaching system*.)

- -

- When originating a *condition report*, the worker's name should not be used. Instead the full circumstances should be described, including the type of work that was done, and the location and time at which it was done, enabling the worker's identification by the responsible supervisor, but shielding the worker's identification by those who have no need to know.

- Once the worker demonstrates awareness of and compliance with the standard, requirement or expectation, there is nothing wrong with a *coach* offering tips to further enhance performance. If any such tip significantly enhances technical excellence or cost reduction, it should be addressed in a *condition report* resulting in a procedure change to incorporate the tip for the technical or cost benefit.

Feedback—Summary

- Be appropriately timely.
- Be appropriately private.
- Cover only that for which the worker has control.
- Be factual, not evaluative.
- Be specific, not general.
- Be credible and trustworthy.
- Do not impose a solution.

- -

Follow-up.

- If a commitment was given by a worker regarding future *behavior*, such as in Scenarios 1, 2 and 3 in the preceding pages, the observer / *coach* should try to follow-up by making a future observation of the same type of work performed by the same worker—with appropriate recognition of the worker's good work. In the absence of future good work, in the absence of the worker's *behavior* in accordance with his or her earlier commitment during *coaching*, there's a *problem* that has to be addressed with the worker's supervisor and it may necessitate disciplinary action.

Coaching
Special Considerations for Engineers

- How's it going?
  - Personally?
  - Professionally?
  - This particular job?
- What concerns do you have?
  - Technical?
  - Needed data?
  - Administrative?
  - Needed resources?
  - Error-inducing conditions?

- The thought processes involved in engineering and administrative work can't be observed. The output from thought processes (e.g., documents) can be observed and assessed. Therefore, an engineer / administrator can be *coached* mostly by getting him or her to respond to questions—the right questions at the right time.
- *Behavioral characteristics* of engineers and engineering supervisors: (The source of this list has been lost; therefore, the credit for it's origination is regretfully omitted.)
  - Curious
  - Creative
  - Technical
  - Confident / overconfident in narrow areas of expertise
  - Introverted
  - Insensitive to others
  - Overly sensitive, thin skinned; not comfortable with criticism, giving or receiving
  - Like the certainty of numbers and facts, and hate the soft stuff
  - Uncomfortable with ambiguity
  - Need, but hate structure
- Of course, this list is stereotypical. Nevertheless, it's good to keep these *characteristics* in mind as a prerequisite to initiating the *coaching* process.

Coaching Exercises

- The scenarios given on pages 214–216 can be used for *coaching* exercises.

Condition Reporting, Root Cause Analysis, Corrective Action, and Performance and Status Measurement System

- Outline:
  - Participant responsibilities
  - Design of the system
  - Data collection criteria
  - Standard data tables
  - Problem statement
  - Fact / observation versus conclusion / opinion
  - Operating experience
  - Initial screening of condition report
  - Problem significance
  - Criteria for requiring further action
  - Extent of problem analysis
  - Root cause analysis guidelines
  - "Apparent" versus "known" root cause analysis

- A *condition reporting, root cause analysis, corrective action, and performance and status measurement system* is of great importance for the *prevention of the recurrence of error.*

- The actions listed in the outline on the slide approximate the flow of activities or the flow of processes in the *condition report, root cause analysis, corrective action, and performance and status measurement system.*

- As noted earlier, the term *condition report* is used in lieu of *problem report* because *good practices* should be reported, not only *problems.*

- Dictionary definitions of the word *problem* are along the following lines: (a) a question proposed for solution; (b) a question, matter or situation that is perplexing.

- In the context of a single action or *behavior*, a *problem* is something that can induce an *error* or the *error,* itself. There are *four levels of error:*

  - *Level 1 Error—Failure to prevent an error that could have an intolerable effect;*
    Level 1 Error results in the failure of the 1st Level Barrier(s).

  - *Level 2 Error—Failure to perform in accordance with a requirement or expectation;*
    Level 2 Error is the initiating error.

  - *Level 3 Error—Failure to detect the Level 2 Error;*
    Level 3 Error results in the failure of the 2nd Level Barrier(s).

  - *Level 4 Error—Failure to mitigate and ameliorate the effects of the error;*
    Level 4 Error results in the failure of the 3rd Level Barrier(s).

- This is consistent with the model given on page 65.

- The *error*, itself, may be either a *non-conformance, anomaly,* or *departure from logic.*
- A *non-conformance* is a departure from a requirement.
- An *anomaly* is a departure from an expectation that is not necessarily a requirement.
- The *problem* is distinct from its *effect.*
- In summary, here's the hierarchy:
  - *Condition:*
    - *Good practice*
    - *Problem*
      - Other than an *error*, anything that creates an *undesired effect* (e.g., an act of God or nature, *malicious compliance, malicious behavior*)
      - *Error (Levels 1 through 4)*
        - *Non-conformance*
        - *Anomaly*
        - *Departure from logic*
- In statistics, there are two types of errors:
  - *Type I*—Rejecting a lot of items that is of an acceptable quality level, or rejecting a true hypothesis.
  - *Type II*—Accepting a lot that is not of an acceptable quality level, or accepting a false hypothesis.
- In the context of this Bookinar™, these Type I and II errors are not *errors.* The *sampling plan* may well have been chosen properly. The cost of the *sampling inspection*, plus, with a given probability, the cost of the Type I and II outcomes, may be substantially less than the cost of 100 percent *inspection* of each lot. In this case, there is no *error* in the choice of the *sampling plan* and there is no *error* in the *sampling plan*, itself, because it provides the outcomes in accordance with the known probabilities. It's tantamount to a good decision with a partially *undesired effect* as addressed on pages 20–21.
- Sometimes an *error* exists which is not a *non-conformance* because there is no requirement from which to depart, and which is not an anomaly because there is no management expectation from which to depart (management lacking the cognition to have established either a requirement or an expectation), but which is a departure from logic.
- For example, in the *Piper Alpha Case Study* on pages 168–174, it was noted that there was no procedure for the following: identification of each plausible type of occurrence that could threaten worker safety; for each such type of occurrence the identification of the various levels of severity; for each such level of severity the establishment of the appropriate response or action; for each such response or action, the assignment of responsibility and authority. There was no higher level requirement for such a procedure and there was no management expectation for such a procedure. The absence of such a procedure was an *error* contributing to the great magnitude of the loss. The absence of such a procedure was a departure from logic.

Condition Reporting, Root Cause Analysis, Corrective Action, and Performance and Status Measurement System (Cont'd)

- Outline (Cont'd):
  - Data collection
  - Interviewing techniques
  - Root cause analysis techniques
  - Change analysis
  - Failure mode and effects analysis
  - Hazard-barrier-effects analysis
  - Time-line analysis
  - Cause and effects analysis / Fishbone diagram
  - Probabilistic risk or safety analysis, using event and fault trees
  - Management and oversight risk tree (MORT) analysis
  - Process flow diagram / value stream diagram

Condition Reporting, Root Cause Analysis, Corrective Action, and Performance and Status Measurement System (Cont'd)

- Outline (Cont'd):
  - Human error causal factor taxonomy
  - Hardware failure modes
  - Human error root causes
  - Extent of causal factor analysis
  - Types of corrective action
  - Corrective action commitment-elements of information
  - Preventive corrective action verification
  - Preventive corrective action effectiveness
  - Reports to management

Design of the <u>CO</u>ndition <u>RE</u>port and <u>C</u>orrective <u>A</u>ction <u>T</u>racking Tool
Users of the Tool

- Condition report (CR) originator
- CR originator's supervisor
- CORECAT controller
- Actionee
- Sub-actionee

- The software tool used to track any CR and its *corrective action* status is a critical element of the overall *management system for condition reporting, root cause analysis, corrective action, and performance and status measurement.*

- For brevity, hereinafter, this tool shall be referred to as CORECAT, an acronym for **CO**ndition **RE**port and *Corrective Action Tracking.*

- CORECAT software should be robust and should be integrated with other software for other functions, such as the design engineering, construction, manufacturing, maintenance or operations functions. (In the preceding statement, see how easy it was, even for this expert presenter, to discriminate with regard to the functions with which CORECAT should interface, excluding, by example, such functions as marketing, sales, accounting, human resources, etc.) Of course, CORECAT should be considered for use in all functions and should be able to interface with the software for all functions. *Problems* / conditions exist in all functions. Why limit the use of a robust tool to only selected functions?

- In any large, high technology enterprise, the types of CORECAT users are listed in the slide.

- In a large enterprise, given the higher frequency of the occurrence of conditions, a single person may not be able to fulfill the function of CORECAT controller. The controller actually may be multiple persons acting individually or acting as a committee.

- The responsibilities of each type of CORECAT user are given in the following pages.

Design of CORECAT
CR Originator Responsibilities

- Identify any condition within the scope and threshold of the system.
- Immediately inform one's supervisor of the condition.
- Immediately inform the supervisor in whose operation the problem condition occurred.
- Immediately inform the operations supervisor if it is know or suspected that the problem condition adversely impacts continued safe operations.
- Immediately inform the appropriate supervisor if it is known or suspected that the problem condition is required to be reported to an external entity.
- Originate the CR; enter the required data into CORECAT.

- In a *EHS&Q-conscious work environment*, everyone is encouraged to identify conditions (*good practices* and *problems* as described on page 221) and to originate CRs.

- Prior to originating the CR, one may discuss the condition with one's supervisor. Supervisory feedback, for one thing, may help to hone the definition or statement of the *good practice* or *problem* condition.

- As a courtesy and, sometimes as a necessity to facilitate adjustment to an on-going process, the *problem* condition should be communicated immediately to the supervisor whose production is adversely impacted.

- Also, the *problem* condition should be communicated immediately to the operations supervisor if it is known or suspected that it necessitates an adjustment to plant operations for safety—e.g., a stoppage of operations or a reduction in operational output, such as a reduction in generation in a nuclear powered electricity generating plant.

- Similarly, the *problem* should be communicated immediately to the supervisor who has the responsibility for further reporting the *problem* condition to an external entity (e.g., the US Environmental Protection Agency, Nuclear Regulatory Commission, Food and Drug Administration, Federal Aviation Administration, a state agency, an insurer or a customer).

- The immediacy of these communications is important from the perspectives of loss minimization, safety, and regulatory compliance. There are time limits within which oral and written reports must be made to regulatory agencies.

- Of course, the CR originator and his or her supervisor may or may not be knowledgeable of the impact of a *problem* condition on the continued safety of operations or on external reportability. Fortunately, the *CORECAT* controller will or should be knowledgeable on this score.

Design of CORECAT
Supervisor Responsibilities

- Originate the CR.
- Give guidance to the CR originator.
  - Confirm the existence of the good practice or problem condition.
  - Help to define the condition.
- Assure that the communications listed on the preceding slide are made, as applicable.

- Sometimes, individual contributor workers (e.g., maintenance technicians) may not have access to the *CORECAT*. Therefore, when such a worker identifies a condition, it is the supervisor's responsibility to originate the CR.

- Sometimes, in assessing a management or technical process, or it's written procedure, guidance may be needed as to whether or not there actually exists a *good practice* or *problem* condition. Guidance may be needed to define the condition and to prepare the justification or logic for the call. This, too, is a supervisory responsibility.

- As addressed in the last bullet on page 221, the foregoing is especially the case for a *problem* condition for which there is no departure from a requirement or management expectation.

Design of CORECAT
Controller Responsibilities

- Immediately inform the operations supervisor if the problem adversely impacts continued safe operations.
- Immediately inform the appropriate supervisor if the problem is required to be reported to an external entity.
- Review the CR for clarity and completeness.
- Identify any additional information needed to clarify or complete the CR, obtain the additional information, and enter it into CORECAT.
- Assign a "significance level" to the CR and enter it into CORECAT.

- Again, the immediacy of the communications is very important.

- If the controller is a person acting as an individual, as contrasted to acting as a member of a committee, from the list of responsibilities on this and the next two slides, it's apparent that the controller must have a wide range of experience and professional abilities—*operations, environmental affairs, quality assurance, investigation* and *root cause analysis,* data analysis, *performance self-assessment, negotiating* and *interpersonal relations* experience and abilities. Wow! In large, high technology enterprises, the controller is a committee with well defined responsibilities of each member.

- If the controller is a committee, the range of abilities listed above must exist collectively and the voice of each member of the collective must be heard. (See page 187.)

- The controller should not alter any *CORECAT* entry made by the *CR* originator, regardless of its *error,* inflammatory language or illogic.

- Any information entered by the controller should be entered in a data field that is different from that used by the *CR* originator. *CORECAT* must be able to distinguish the difference between data entered by the originator and data subsequently entered by the controller.

Question: Why is it important to not alter any entry made by the *CR* originator and to be able to distinguish between data entered by the originator and any one else?

Answer: The enterprise, specifically the controller, should avoid the potential for being accused of data manipulation or data falsification. This accusation cannot be made if the *CR* originator's data entries are not altered. This is especially important in enterprises that are subject to oversight by regulatory agencies. For example, accusations of this type were made by *whistleblowers* during the construction of nuclear powered electricity generating plants in the 1970s and 1980s. Some such accusations were true; some were false.

Design of CORECAT
Controller Responsibilities (Cont'd)

- Determine whether or not the CR may be closed without further action. If so, enter the justification for the closure and the closure, itself, into CORECAT.
- Negotiate action commitments and enter them into CORECAT.
- Review actions for consistency with commitments. Negotiate additional commitments, as necessary, and enter them into CORECAT.
- Enter the code for the each identified root and contributing cause into CORECAT.
- Review for completeness of all actions. When complete, enter the closure of the CR into CORECAT.

- Basically, there are four justifications for closing a CR without further action.

  1. The CR is judged to be invalid because there is no reportable condition (no *good practice* or *problem*). The justification for the judgment is entered.

  2. A CR data entry is incorrect. The CR may be closed in favor of a new, correctly prepared CR. The CRs are cross-referenced, each containing the ID # of the other.

  3. There are duplicate CRs. An entry is made in each CR stating the duplication, cross-referencing the CR ID #s, and identifying the surviving CR.

  4. The CR is for a *problem* condition for which the effect is of insufficient *significance* to warrant any further action based on a single occurrence of the *problem*. In this case, the standard *performance measurement reports* will indicate the cumulative frequency of occurrence of the *problem*. If that frequency is high or has an upward trend, further action may be taken on the basis of this grouped data. (See pages 259–260.)

- Action commitments are negotiated, not assigned. The actionee must agree to the action to be taken. This is important from two perspectives:

  1. The actionee's resources are to be used to take the action. It's folly to think that those resources will be used for any action with which the actionee disagrees. (If a substantial disagreement cannot be resolved between the controller and the actionee, the controller always has the option of escalating the issue to the next level of management. There's nothing personal in escalation; it's the appropriate way by which to resolve a substantial difference.)

  2. The actionee has expertise. Very often, he or she recognizes the best course of action.

- The elements of a *preventive corrective action commitment* are addressed on page 356.

Design of CORECAT
Controller Responsibilities (Cont'd)

- Review the adequacy of investigations and root cause analyses.
- Review the status of actions against commitments.
- Report the absence of compliance with commitments.
- Periodically, issue performance and status measurement reports.
- Periodically, perform self-assessment of the Conditioning Reporting, Root Cause Analysis, Corrective Action, and Performance / Status Measurement System.

- Ideally, CORECAT should be designed such as to provide an immediate feedback of any action commitment for which action is not taken by the committed completion date. This would be timelier than, and in addition to, the standard status reports issued periodically.

- Given its importance, it's *good practice* to periodically perform *self-assessment* of the various processes that comprise the *condition reporting, root cause analysis, corrective action, and performance & status measurement system,* such that the complete system is *self-assessed* at least biennially—if not more frequently, if there are concerns.

- The system should be *audited* by the Quality Assurance organization at least biennially.

Design of CORECAT
Actionee Responsibilities

- As negotiated, make action commitments.
- Take actions as committed and enter them into CORECAT.
- Sub-assign actions and enter them into CORECAT.
- Review sub-assigned actions for consistency with commitments. Accept actions taken by sub-assignees and enter their acceptance into CORECAT.

- Of course, any action that is to be sub-assigned should be negotiated first, regardless of the nature of the organizational reporting relationship.
- Of course, the actionee remains responsible, even though the action is sub-assigned or delegated.

Design of the CORECAT
Capabilities of the Tool

Function with:
- Multiple controllers
- Multiple problems per CR
- Multiple actionees per problem
- Multiple action commitments per actionee
- Multiple sub-assignments per action commitment

- In a large enterprise, CORECAT must operate with multiple controllers acting as members of a controller committee. The same data may be subject to search and screening by multiple controllers simultaneously.

- CORECAT must be able to link multiple *problems* to the single CR in which these *problems* were originally reported; then link multiple assignees to each *problem* and its CR; then link multiple action commitments to each assignee, the *problem* and the CR—and do the same for sub-assignees.

Question: What would be a good starting point for the design of the CORECAT tool?

Design of CORECAT—Design Sequence

- Start with a requirements-type document.
- Design the desired standard output reports.
- Anticipate the queries.
- Identify the data elements needed to produce the standard output reports and responses to queries.
- Establish the standard data tables for the data elements needed to produce the standard output reports and responses to queries.
- Establish the code for each data entry which is to be made via a standard data table.
- Format the data elements in a logical data entry sequence.
- Design the navigation of the tool.

- As with any design project, the documentation of the requirements is essential. Make sure that each performance requirement of the *CORECAT* software, hardware and software-hardware interface is identified and defined. This presenter has identified 17 data-related terms and their definitions and 41 data quality *attributes* and their definitions.

- A *data element* is a category of *data*. For example, *date* is a *data element* and *01/27/2008* is data. *Defect type* is a *data element* and *scratch* is data.

- IF one knows what data is to be presented in the *standard performance / status measurement output reports* and what queries might be made and what data is to be presented in response to those queries,

  THEN one can determine the *data elements* for which data must be collected.

  The *CORECAT data elements* must be consistent with and support the *CORECAT* output reports. Data desired in an output report cannot be provided if it is not first collected.

- Output reports provide *grouped data*, meaning that the frequency of occurrence of something is counted and reported. Data entries can be grouped and counted only if they are *codified*. Data entries can be codified only if they are *standardized*—i.e., only if the same information is entered the same way consistently. To accomplish this, a table (or menu) providing *standard data entries* must be used for each *data element* for which data is to be grouped. Each *standardized data entry* must have a unique code. More on this later.

- Based on his or her preceding data entry, the *CORECAT* user should be presented with or navigated to the next *data element* for which a data entry would logically be made.

Question: What are the criteria for data collection?

Design of CORECAT (Cont'd)
Data Collection Criteria

- Data elements relate to a success factor or goal of the enterprise.
- Data elements are defined such as to prevent data confounding.
- Data elements have a consistent definition over time.
- Data elements and data are easy to understand.
- Data is easy to enter into CORECAT.
- Data is quantitative when appropriate.
- Data that is intended to be factual is factual.
- Factual data is sufficiently precise.
- Data cannot be manipulated.

- The data collected should be useful. If it has no use, it should not be collected. It's useful if it's important to the enterprise in (a) performing *investigations* and *root cause analyses*, (b) the assessing, or (c) providing standard output reports or responses to queries—if in one way or another it can contribute to technical excellence or cost reduction..

- The definitions of the *data elements* should be *mutually exclusive*. The purpose of *mutual exclusivity* is to make it unlikely that the same type of data will be entered at different times into two or more different fields. If that happens the data are *confounded* and the output repots and responses to queries are less meaningful and even incorrect. (See pages 344–345 for a good example of *confounding*.)

- If the definition of a *data element* changes over time, the data collected under one definition cannot logically be compared to the data collected under the other definition. As is said, the data are now apples and oranges.

- A discussion of *observation* and *fact* verses *opinion* and *conclusion* is given on page 241.

- An example of *data manipulation* is as follows: An action completion due date comes and goes without the action being completed. A new date is negotiated and entered into *CORECAT* without the ability to recognize the existence of the original date. This is somewhat opinionated, but this would be *data manipulation* allowed by the design of the tool.

- The ultimate in avoiding *data manipulation* is restricting the alteration of data originally entered.

Design of CORECAT (Cont'd)
Standard Data Tables

- Person
- Organization
- Facility
- Hardware
- Document
- Process
- Type of problem / Type of defect
- Regulatory classification
- Significance level
- Failure mode
- Problem cause
- Type of corrective action

- There's a distinct difference between a *data element* and a *standard data table*, the latter being used to provide the data entries for the former.

- For example, the *standard data table* for *Person* may be used to provide data entries for three different *data elements* or fields: a person may be the (a) *CR originator*, (b) *Actionee*, or (c) *Sub-assignee*. A single table may be used to list and codify all persons, any one of whom may be entered into any one of these three fields.

- The *standard data table* for *Organization* may be used to provide data entries for the:

  - *Problem IDing Organization*—In addition to internal organizations, this may include external organizations, such as insurance companies, regulatory agencies and customers. It's important to know the: (a) percentage of *problems* identified initially by external organizations that exist beyond the internal defenses of the enterprise; (b) percentage of *problems* and *root causes* that is self-identified by the responsible organization; (c) what organizations, and within the organizations, what processes are finding the most *problems* of the most *significance*. That bears upon the allocation of *problem detection* resources.

  - *CR Originating Organization*—This always should be an internal organization, even if the condition was initially identified by an external organization.

  - *Adversely Affected Organization*—This may be an organization other than the one responsible for the *root cause(s)*. Recall that *root causes* reside in organizations upstream of the organization that last touched the process. (See the *Therac-25, Stator Bar Removal,* and *Piper Alpha case studies*—pages 56–61, 116–121 and 168–174, respectively.)

  - *Root Cause Responsible Organization.*

  - *Actionee Organization* and *Sub-assignee's Organization.*

- Ideally, the *standard data table* for *Hardware* would be derived from the engineering generation breakdown of the hardware design. It would be the same table.
- The table for *Document* is the most difficult to develop. Here's a logic for consideration:
  - Technical document, sub-categorized by function—e.g.,
    - *Engineering Design Document*— with its sub-categories, e.g.,
      - *System Description*
      - *Component Specification*
      - Etc. (26 types of such documents have been sub-categorized by this presenter.)
    - *Procurement Document*—with its sub-categories, e.g.,
      - *Request For Proposal.*
      - *Request For Quote.*
      - *Procurement Requisition.*
      - *Purchase Order.*
    - *Manufacturing Document*, with it's sub-categories.
    - *Maintenance Document*—with its sub-categories, e.g.,
      - *Electrical Standard Maintenance Procedure.*
        - *Preventive Maintenance.*
        - *Corrective Maintenance.*
      - *I&C Standard Maintenance Procedure.*
        - *Preventive Maintenance.*
        - *Corrective Maintenance.*
      - *Civil / Structural Standard Maintenance Procedure.*
        - *Preventive Maintenance.*
        - *Corrective Maintenance.*
    - *Plant Operations Document*—with its sub-categories, e.g.,
      - *Standard Operations Procedure.*
      - *Alarm Response Procedure.*
      - *Etc.*
    - *Inspection and Test Document*—with its sub-categories, e.g.,
      - *Electrical / I&C Inspection*
        - *Receiving / Source Inspection.*
        - *Manufacturing Inspection.*
        - *Maintenance / Modification Inspection.*
      - *Mechanical Inspection*
        - *Receiving / Source Inspection.*
        - *Manufacturing Inspection.*
        - *Maintenance / Modification Inspection.*
      - *Civil / Structural Inspection*
      - *NDE / SNT-TC 1A.*
        - *Radiography.*
        - *Ultrasonics.*
        - *Magnetic Particle.*
        - *Penetrant.*
        - *Eddy Current.*
        - *Visual.*

- *Administrative Document.*
  - Sub-Categorized by Function.
    - Sub-Categorized by Designated Process Owner's Organization. (See pages 85–86.)
- *Software.*
  - Sub-Categorized by Function.
    - Sub-Categorized by Designated Process Owner' Organization.
- The *standard data table* for *Process* can be used to provide data entries for the following *data elements*: (a) *Problem IDing Process* [i.e., process used to identify the *problem*]; (b) *Problem Process* [i.e., process in which the *problem* exists]; (c) *Corrective Action Verification Process.*
- (This presenter has identified 72 standard processes that are used in high technology enterprises, with some drilling down to as many as four sub-levels.)
- *Type of Problem / Type of Defect, Significance Level, Failure Mode, Problem Cause* and *Type of Corrective Action* will be covered in subsequent pages.
- Although there are various *data elements* relating to *Date*, there is no need for a *standard data table* for it. The software should be programmed to read a date if t is entered in any conventional format or the format can be specified in the data entry field.
- Here are some *data elements* involving Date: (a) *CR Origination Date;* (b) *Condition Initial Existence Date;* (c) *Condition Found Date;* (d) *Commitment Action Due Date;* (e) *Commitment Action Extended Due Date;* (f) *CR Closure Date.*
- *Condition Found Time Of Day* may also be a *data element* of importance.

Design of CORECAT (Cont'd)
Problem Statement-Data Elements

- Hardware Item Drawing Basic #
- Hardware Item Drawing Revision #
- Hardware Item Serial #
- Plant Slot # / Machine ID # / Fabrication Station ID #
- Characteristic
- Type of Problem / Type of Defect

- - - - - - - - - - - - -

- Document Type
- Document Basic #
- Document Revision #

- - - - - - - - - - - - -

- There are only three types of things that can have the *problem*—things in which the *problem* can exist: (a) a hardware item; (b) a document; or (c) a process implementation that is not in accordance with its design document, written procedure or management expectation. Of course, in all three things a person is almost always at the root.

1. A hardware item can be *non-conforming* to its engineering design document.

2. An engineering design document, procedure or other kind of document can be *non-conforming* to a higher tier requirement or otherwise inadequate.

3. Hardware and documents may be okay and, nevertheless, a process may be implemented in violation of its written procedure requirement or management expectation.

- In the slide, the first six bullets above the line help to describe a hardware *problem*.

- Each bullet shown on the slide should be a separate *data element* with a separate field on the data entry form. For example, for the hardware item, the data entry field for the *item's drawing basic number* should be separate from the data entry field for the *item's drawing revision number*.

- If, instead of separate *data elements* or data entry fields, the *data element* or field were simply labeled *Hardware Item ID*, there would be increased potential for the omission of important elements of information. The *drawing revision, serial* or *slot number* might be omitted from the entry, or even worse.

- Separate *data elements* are required also to enable the codification of those data that are used in the preparation of *standard performance / status measurement reports* and responses to queries. For example, in the slide, the data entries for the *data elements* in blue font are obtained from standard data tables and the entries are codified. Were all the bullets lumped together as one field, this data could not be codified.

- Separate fields provide a structure that helps to assure the entry of all necessary data and the ability to codify the data needed for output reports.

- A *plant slot number* is an identification given to a specific three-axis location in the plant at which component is installed. When component of identical design has multiple applications or is installed in multiple places in a plant, the slot number is used to differentiate among the multiple installations.

- For manufacturing, one might want to know the *characteristic* containing the *defect*, and the *type of problem or type of defect* in the *characteristic* so that the frequency of their occurrence can be reported.

- An *Is / Is Not Matrix* is a tool for helping to define a *problem*. In the left-hand column, the questions regarding the *problem* are: who?, where?, when?, and how?. In the first row, the questions are: is? or is not?. In the following case, the what? of the *problem* is that security personnel are inattentive, slow to respond, and sometime drowsing or asleep.

	IS	IS NOT
WHO IS INVOLVED?	• Second shift security staff.	• First shift security staff.
WHEN DOES IT OCCUR?	• All the time. • Particularly after holidays and long periods of off duty. • During normal operation	• Limited to any specific calendar period • During off-normal operation.
WHERE DOES IT OCCUR?	• In Plant #1	• In Plant #2
HOW DOES IT OCCUR?	• Lack of activity	• Activity

- From the matrix, it's apparent that the *problem* is limited to second shift personnel in Plant # 2, particularly following holidays and long periods of off-duty. It appears to occur when nothing is going on. A brief discussion with the security staff and security supervisors at both plants indicated that the second shift supervisor at Plant # 1 is less well liked by his staff than any of the other supervisors, and that she seems to give meaningless assignments throughout the shift. Given that there are no apparent differences in physical fitness between the second shift staffs at both plants, it seems from *apparent root cause analysis*, as described on pages 271–273, that the cause is boredom among the Plant # 1 staff, exacerbated by possible lack of rest during a preceding holiday or long off-duty period.

- To make it easier for a CR to be originated and, thereby, to encourage CR origination, it may be best to have a single field in which the originator would enter the *problem statement*. In *CORECAT*, this overall *Problem Statement* field would precede the data fields on pages 237, 239 and 240 which provide the sub-elements of the *problem statement*. Subsequent to the CR originator's single textual, non-codifiable entry into the *Problem Statement* field, the controller, using the information in originator's entry and, probably, other information subsequently acquired, would make the entries into each of the fields on pages 237, 239 and 240.

238

Design of CORECAT (Cont'd)
Problem Statement—Data Elements (Cont'd)

- Type Of Process Implemented
- Process Implementation Document Basic #
- Process Implementation Document Revision #
- Process Implementation Document Step #

- -

- Requirement
- Requirement Source Document Basic #
- Requirement Source Document Revision #

- -

- As Is / As Found Condition

- Unlike all of the preceding bullets in the previous slide and unlike the first four bullets of this slide, the *data element* entitled *Requirement* gets a narrative type of data entry. The same applies to *As Is / As Found Condition*.

- It's best that the entry for Requirement be verbatim as it appears in the requirement document.

- The entry for As Is / As Found Condition should be such as to make it easy to distinguish the difference between that which is required and that which exists in the hardware, document or process implementation. The entry for As Is / As Found Condition is based on direct observation.

Question: Which data entries for the *data elements* on the preceding slide and on this slide are *fact* as contrasted to *opinion*.

Answer: All.

Design of CORECAT (Cont'd)
Problem Statement—Data Elements (Cont'd)

- Near Miss / Event Sequence Of Activities
- Near Miss / Event Timing Of Activities
- Near Miss / Event Unusual Attributes Of Activities
- Near Miss / Event Immediate Actions Taken

- -

- Actual Effects Of Problem
- Potential Effects Of Problem

- -

- Apparent Cause(s) Of Problem

- -

- Recommended Corrective Action(s)

- It's important to learn the sequence of activities that led up to a *near miss* or *event*, the timing of each activity and any unusual *attributes* of each activity. Questions along these lines will be asked during the interview process, but it's best to get this information in writing as soon as possible. (See pages 275–280.)

- It's important to learn about the immediate actions that were taken, probably for the sake of safety (*containment, recovery, escape, mitigation*). These actions might change the configuration of the equipment making it more difficult to reconstruct the *event* or *near miss*.

- Although the first four bullets of this slide are *data elements* for which the entries should be factual, it's easy to understand that, because of the nature of the information, there may be *factual errors* or *errors of omission*.

- The entries for the *data elements* listed in the last three bullets of this slide are clearly intended to be the *CR* originator's opinion. These opinions are valued because the *CR* originator has expertise on the subject of the *CR*. These opinions may contribute to the final decisions regarding *significance level*, *root* and *contributing causes*, and *preventive corrective actions*.

- The cause(s) entered by the CR originator are not from a codified *standard data table*. Rather, they are entered as text. Later, following the *root cause analysis* (*apparent* or *formal*) the controller will make entries for both *Root Cause* and *Contributing Cause* using the *Problem Cause standard data table*.

Question: What are the *attributes* that differentiate *fact* from *conclusion*?

Observation / Fact vs. Assessment / Conclusion

- Attributes of Observations / Facts:
  - Measurable by independent means and measured
  - Observed, owned, and agreed to by the "community"
- Attributes of Assessments / Conclusions:
  - Interpretation, opinion, evaluation and judgment
  - Not owned or agreed to by the "community" (It's owned by the assessor.)
  - Possibly benefiting the assessor (There's a reason for one's assessment.)
  - Based on some data, experiences and personal standard

  Source: Derived from a document originated by Frank Kane

- *Observation / Fact*-Example:

  If it is stated that the room is 72° F, using a calibrated thermometer, the temperature can be measured as 72° F (*measured by independent means*) and everyone in the room can see the thermometer reading (*observed, owned and agreed to by the community*).

- *Assessment / Conclusion*-Example:

  If it is stated that the room is cold (opinion based on the speaker's standard, who likes the room to be at least 74° F), others in the room need not agree. Some may say the room is "just right" or "warm"—based on their personal standards or preferences. Nevertheless, it's cold to the speaker.

Question: What is an *operating experience program?*

Operating Experience

Operating problem
(and good practice)
data collection and
data sharing programs

- The Institute of Nuclear Power Operations (INPO), the Department of Energy (DOE), and the Nuclear Regulatory Commission (NRC), possibly among others, have *operating experience-type (OE) programs.*
  - Utilities that own one or more nuclear powered electricity generating plants voluntarily participate in the INPO OE program.
  - Nuclear research laboratories are directed to participate in the DOE OE program.
  - Utilities that own one or more nuclear powered electricity generating plants are required by rules and regulations to participate in the NRC OE program.
- These programs work along the following lines:
  - *Problems* of specified types above a specified threshold are reported by the participating enterprise to the data collection organization (e.g., INPO, DOE, NRC) which, in turn, distributes the reports to all other participating enterprises. Periodically, the data collection organization may issue grouped data reports to all participants.
  - A specific person, e.g., an OE coordinator, in the participating enterprise is designated to receive the reports from the data collection organization. Upon its receipt, the OE coordinator determines whether or not the reported *problem* could possibly apply to the recipient enterprise. If so, the OE coordinator originates a CR on the subject. The *CORECAT* controller negotiates appropriate action commitments.
- Of course, the benefit to the participating enterprise is the opportunity to learn from and avoid the mistakes of others. Otto von Bismarck is credited with the following quotation: "Fools say that they learn by experience. I prefer to profit by others' experience".

Undesired Effect

An adverse impact on
human safety and health,
the environment,
compliance with the law,
relationship with a stakeholder,
accomplishment of a mission or function,
or economic status

- Given the completion of the processes for the (a) origination of a CR, (b) review of the CR for clarity, completeness and accuracy, and (c) review of the CR for possible stoppage or reduction of operations or production or external reportability—given the completion of these processes, the next process that comes into play in the overall *problem reporting, root cause analysis, corrective action and performance / status reporting system* is the process for determining the *significance* of the *undesired effect* of the reported *problem* condition.

- To maintain process sequential continuity, the information on this and subsequent pages through page 252 is essentially a repetition of the information on pages 25 and 28–36.

- Although there are various sets of terms for the classification of the *significance* of the *undesired effect* of the condition (for example, *critical, major* and *minor*), the terms *event, near miss, precursor* and *minor* shall be used here.

- The terms *event, near miss, precursor,* or *minor,* may also be referred to as *significance levels SL1, SL2, SL3,* or *SL4,* respectively.

Event

- Undesired effect of high significance—e.g.,
  - Fatality
  - Hospitalization
  - Non-compliance with a law
  - Reportable to a stakeholder
  - Discomfort in a relationship with a stakeholder
  - Loss of certain types of missions
  - Loss of $X or more—directly or indirectly
- Failure of all barriers
- One or more root causes

- An *event* is an occurrence for which the *undesired effect* is of *high significance*. This definition is from the perspective of this Bookinar™—from an *EHS&Q* perspective. From a lay perspective, an *event* is a happening, an occurrence, either adverse or not, especially of some importance, but not necessarily of importance.

- The enterprise establishes the criteria for what constitutes high *significance*.

- In the developed world, an occurrence that results in a human *fatality* (an obviously *undesired effect* of high *significance*) is always classified as an *event*.

- Continuing from the perspective of the developed world, almost always, an occurrence that results in a person's overnight *hospitalization* (another obviously *undesired effect* of high *significance*) will be classified as an *event*.

- Many enterprises will classify an occurrence as an *event* if the *undesired effect* is a *non-compliance with a law* or if the occurrence is *reportable* to a regulatory agency, insurer, client or customer—or even to stockholders or a community interest group.

- For example, if an accident results in an injury that is reportable in accordance with OSHA rules and regulations, the accident is classified as an *event*.

- Here's another example. If an accident results in an oil spill that is above deminimus and that is reportable in accordance with US EPA or state environmental regulatory agency rules and regulations, the accident is classified as an *event*.

- The classification of an occurrence based on the degree of *discomfort in a relationship with a stakeholder* may be considered on a case-by-case basis. Often, for "political" reasons, occurrences that yield discomfort with a stakeholder are classified at a higher *level of significance* than would be the case if a stakeholder were not affected.

- Another criterion for an occurrence to be classified as an *event* is the *loss of a pre-identified type of mission or function* that is of such high importance that there is no need to estimate its dollar loss for the purpose of classification.

- For example, at a power plant, if the *undesired effect* is the unintended stoppage of electricity generation, a forced outage, the occurrence would be classified as an *event*.

- Notice that the first six criteria are not quantified. The final criterion for the classification of an occurrence as an *event* is *loss of a pre-established number of dollar or more*.

- An *event* is the result of:
  - *The failure of all barriers that should have prevented the error which activated the hazard (Level 1 barriers)*; or
  - *The failure of all barriers that should have detected the error which activated the hazard (Level 1 barriers)*; or
  - *The failure of all barriers that should have mitigated and ameliorated the undesired effects of the occurrence (Level 1 barriers)*; or
  - The failure of a combination of these *barriers*.

- A non-existent but needed *barrier* constitutes a failed *barrier*. An existing *barrier* that is poorly designed or that is poorly implemented constitutes a failed barrier.

- An *investigation* and formal *root cause analysis* should be performed for an *event*. However, if an *event* or a similar *error* or occurrence does not have the potential to recur, would it make sense to spend the resources for *investigation, root cause analysis* and *preventive corrective action?*.

- With proper *investigation* and *root cause analysis*, almost always, more than a single *root cause* will be identified for the *event*.

Question: What is a *near miss*?

Near Miss

- Undesired physical effect of moderate or minor adverse significance or no undesired physical effect
- Sometimes, a highly significant political effect
- Unacceptably high likelihood of becoming an "event"
- Failure of one or more barriers, with only one or relatively few barriers not failing
- One or more root causes

- A *near miss* is an occurrence for which the undesired physical effect may be moderate or *minor* or for which there may be no undesired physical effect.

- From time to time, a *near miss* is reported by the public news media, particularly a *near miss* in the airline industry that has high public visibility. For example, it's reported that airplanes have narrowly averted a collision on a runway. In such cases, the political adverse effect is significant.

- Unfortunately, for other industries for which there is not high public visibility, but for which there is relatively high public and employee *risk*, *near misses* are not reported by the public news media—e.g., in the petrochemical industry.

- For a *near miss*, there is a high likelihood of a future, similar occurrence becoming an *event*.

- For a *near miss*, although one or more *barriers* failed, at least one or, possibly, a relatively few *barriers* did not fail.

- The success of the one or relatively few *barriers* is what distinguishes a *near miss* from an *event* in which all *barriers* have failed.

- Almost always there are multiple *root causes* for a *near miss*, just as there are multiple *root causes* for an *event*.

- *Investigation* and formal *root cause analysis* should be performed for a *near miss*.

Question: What is a *precursor*?

Precursor

- Undesired effect of minor significance
- Failure of a single barrier or relatively few barriers, with more barriers not failing
- Single root cause or relatively few root causes

- A *precursor* is an occurrence for which the *undesired effect* is of relatively low *significance*.
- The differences between a *precursor* and a *near miss* are that:
  1. For the former, the worst undesired physical effect is the loss of a relatively small amount of money and there is no adverse political effect, whereas for the latter, the worst undesired physical effect is greater and there can be a very adverse political effect.
  2. For the former, there are fewer *barrier* failures than for the latter. From the *barrier* failure perspective, the difference between the former and latter is a matter of the relative number of *barrier* failures.
  3. Similarly, for the former, there are fewer *root causes* than for latter. Again, the difference is a matter of the relative number.
- *Apparent root cause analysis* should be performed for *precursors*. (See page 271.)
- The frequency of *events* will be reduced if good *apparent root cause analyses* are performed for *precursors*.

Minor

- Trivial undesired effect
- "Track and trend"

- An *error*, or the occurrence caused by the *error* that is classified as *minor* has trivial *undesired effects*.

- A *minor* occurrence is barely above the threshold for reporting into the *CORECAT*.

- For a single *minor* occurrence, the only *corrective action* may be to fix the thing that has the *problem*. There is no analysis as to the *problem* cause. It's not worth it.

- However, with a robust *CORECAT*, the frequency of each type of *minor* occurrence is accounted.

- Therefore, the action for this type of occurrence is sometimes referred to as *track and trend*.

- If the frequency of *minor* occurrences rises to a level at which the cost of the occurrences in the aggregate becomes significant, of course, additional action should be taken.

Exercise—Event? Near Miss? Precursor?

- A young, agile employee descending a flight of stairs, holding the handrail, slips on a patch of ice on a step, does not fall, and does not incur any injury.

- A young, agile employee descending a flight of stairs, not holding the handrail, slips on a patch of ice on a step, falls, latently grasps the handrail to stop the fall, and incurs a slightly pulled muscle.

- An older, less agile and less physically fit employee descending a flight of stairs, not holding the handrail, slips on a patch of ice on a step, tries to but fails to grasp the handrail, falls, and breaks his hip.

- The first bullet is a *precursor*, the second is a *near miss*, and the third is an *event*.
- For the *precursor*:
  - First, there was an *procedure barrier* failure. The procedure for removing ice from the stairwell failed. It's not known whether the procedure failed due to its poor design or due to its poor implementation.
  - Second, there was an *equipment barrier* failure. The slip prevention tread on the stairwell failed because it was covered with ice which, in turn, was due to the *procedure barrier* failure. Frequently, *procedure barrier* failures yield *equipment barrier* failures.
  - Also, there may have been a *human barrier* failure of inattention.
  - The *barriers* that held are:
    - The *administrative training procedure barrier* through which the employee had been trained to hold the handrail;
    - The *human barrier* of the employee's compliance with his or her training;
    - The *human barrier* of physical agility;
    - The *human barrier* of muscle tonus.
  - This is a *precursor* because there was minimal or no *undesired effect* and because multiple *barriers* held. However, to be conservative, this *precursor* could be upgraded to a *near miss*, given the fact that *human barriers* constituted the large majority of the *barriers* that held, and given the large amount of variation in the effectiveness of *human barriers*. Unfortunately, this type of upgrade doesn't happen as often as it should.

- For the *near miss*, the *human barriers* of agility and reflexes, enabling the handrail to be grasped, are the only *barriers* that held.
- Of course, for the *event*, none of the *barriers* held.

Question: Given that *errors* or occurrences resulting from *error* are classified based on their *significance*, what is meant by *significance*?

Significance

Significance = Risk + Urgency
where:

- **Risk** = (Severity of the undesired effect) X (Probability of recurrence)
- **Urgency** = Extent of the **window of opportunity** in which to fix the root and contributing causes of the barrier failures

- Usually, *significance* is categorized as a *significance level* using a number or alphabetic character. For example, an *event* would be categorized as *Significance Level 1 (SL1)*; a *near miss* as *SL2*; a *precursor* as *SL3*; a *minor* occurrence as *SL4*.

- Referring back to page 28, if any one of the first six criteria is met, the occurrence is classified as an *event, SL1*. In this case there is no need to apply the formula on this slide.

- However, unlike the others, the seventh criterion, dollars, is quantifiable.

- The dollar loss is the *severity of the undesired effect of the occurrence*. It can be multiplied by the *probability of the recurrence*. The product is the *risk*.

- Recognize that this probability has a time period associated with it.

- For example, if the loss is $1,000,000 and the *probability of the recurrence* in the next twelve months is 0.25, the *risk* for the next twelve months is $250,000.

- If $250,000 exceeds the pre-established threshold for classification as an *event*, the occurrence would be classified as an *event, SL1*. Conversely, if $250,000 is less than the pre-established threshold for *SL1* but more than the threshold for *SL2*, the occurrence would be classified as *SL2*, and so on.

- The *SL* classification is made so as to indicate the level of effort to be expended for *investigation* and *root cause analysis*.

- For any *SL1* involving any of the first six criteria on page 28, certainly there would be the highest level of effort—*investigation* and formal *root cause analysis* leading to the cost effective elimination or correction of the *root* and *contributing causes* of the *barrier* failures.

- For any *SL1* that involves only a dollar loss, it's conceivable that the *risk* could be transferred by the acquisition of insurance. It's further conceivable that the enterprise would combine *investigation* and *root cause analysis* with the acquisition of insurance.

- For any *SL2*, especially for a *near miss* involving human health and safety and environmental protection, the highest-level effort also should be used to determine the *root* and *contributing causes* of the *barrier* failures—again, *investigation* and formal *root cause analysis*. For any *SL2* that does not involve human health and safety and environmental protection, given a limit on resources, *apparent root cause analysis* may be used to determine *root* and *contributing causes*. (See page 271.)

- For *SL3*, *apparent root cause analysis* should be used.

- For *SL4*, there is no need for analysis because the *risk* is tolerated.

- In addition to: (a) eliminating *risk* by the elimination and correction of *root* and *contributing causes*, (b) transferring *risk* by the acquisition of insurance; and (c) tolerating *risk*-(d) *risk* can be compensated for—e.g., a fire watch can be established during welding activities.

- The other element of *significance* is *urgency*, the window of opportunity within which to identify and eliminate or correct the *root* and *contributing causes*.

- For example, assume that occurrences in Process A and in Process B each have a *risk* of $1,000,000. Further assume that Process A is scheduled to be performed again within a week and that Process B is scheduled to be performed again not sooner than six months from now. Addressing the *root* and *contributing causes* for Process A is far more urgent than addressing them for Process B.

- The added *urgency* for the occurrence in Process A increases the *significance* of the occurrence in Process A compared to the *significance* of the occurrence in Process B.

- Of course, this *urgency* must be taken into consideration when establishing the schedule for the *investigation*, the *root cause analysis*, and *preventive corrective actions*.

Criteria for Requiring Further Action

- Significance level of the individual occurrence of the problem
- Adverse trend of the frequency of repeated occurrences of the problem
- Unacceptable frequency of repeated occurrences of the problem, regardless of the absence of an adverse trend

- Now that the *significance level* of a *problem* has been established, the processes for action kick into the overall *problem reporting, root cause analysis, corrective action and performance / status reporting system.*

- A *problem* was defined on page 221. When a single occurrence of a *problem* imposes an intolerable or unacceptable *risk* going forward, further action should be taken. Otherwise, a single occurrence of a *problem* may not warrant further action.

- However, over time, the frequency of occurrence of a *problem* (or its *root cause*) may have an adverse trend, the slope of which, when considering the cumulative loss, may warrant further action.

- Even in the absence of an adverse trend, the frequency of occurrence may have an absolute value that, when considering the cumulative loss, also may warrant further action.

- It's the responsibility of the *CR* controller and the manager of the adversely impacted organization to identify cases in which the trend or absolute value of the frequency of *problem* occurrence warrants further action and, in such cases, to originate a *CR* for the cumulative *problem*. (See next page.)

- Sometimes, even in the absence of an adverse trend or high absolute value of the frequency of occurrence, cumulative data may indicate the need for action. For example, it's obvious that additional action should have been taken but was not taken in the case of a pipe failure following numerous years of CRs indicating rust, for which the dispositions were "clean and paint". In the absence of cumulative data, prior CRs were not recognized. Those making the dispositions thought that there remained plenty of wall thickness *margin*. Ultimately the pipe had a through-wall leak. Without cumulative data it was difficult to estimate the point at which it would have been prudent to make wall thickness measurements.

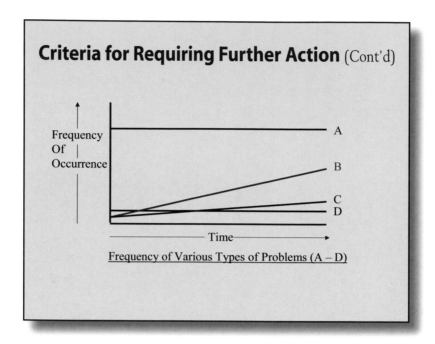

Criteria for Requiring Further Action (Cont'd)

Frequency of Various Types of Problems (A – D)

- Given the expectation of the continuation of the frequency patterns for *problems* represented by Lines *A* and *B*, action would be necessary even if the loss from the individual occurrences were only moderate. Possibly, action would be necessary even if the loss from an individual occurrence were low, if the cumulative loss were high.

- Certainly, there should be close monitoring of the frequency of the *problem* represented by Line C. Possibly, additional action should be taken, again depending upon the value of the cumulative loss.

- It's not likely that action would be taken for the type of *problem* represented by Line *D*, except in two types of cases.

- Were the market to demand close to zero *defects*, because of the pressures of competition and because the *defectives* couldn't be inspected out, action would be necessary. This type of situation might apply for parts fabricated for computer chips or for the assembly of the chips, themselves. But, basically, in this case, although the dollar loss for fabricated *defectives* is very small, the potential exists for a large dollar loss if customer dissatisfaction results in the loss of a contract.

- There's an economic principle relating to investment that goes along the following lines. The first dollar should be invested in that which yields the highest rate of return, the second dollar should be invested in that which yields the next highest rate of return, and so on, to the extent that investment dollars are available. The last available dollar may be invested even for a return of a penny (assuming reasonable assurance of the return). Under this principle, for the situation represented by Line D, given the availability of investment dollars for such a low level of return, action might be taken. (Highly unlikely.)

Extent of Problem Analysis

- The reported problem in the primarily affected process
- Similar types of problems in the primarily affected process
- The reported problem in similar types of processes
- Similar types of problems in similar types of processes

Primary Process Similar Problems	Primary Process Reported Problem
Similar Processes Reported Problem	Similar Processes Similar Problems

- *Reported problem* means the *problem* that was identified and entered initially into the CORECAT tool. *Primary process* means the process (or equipment) in which the reported *problem* was initially found.

- An initial action negotiated with an actionee might be the performance of an *extent of problem analysis*, also referred to as *extent of condition analysis*, to determine whether:

  - Any other *problem* that is similar to the reported *problem* also exists in the primary process, as represented by the cell in blue font;

  - The reported *problem* exists elsewhere, in any other process that is different from but similar to the primary process, as represented by the cell in red font;

  - Any other *problem* that is similar to the reported *problem* also exists in a process that is similar to the primary process, as represented by the cell in green font.

- There is no preferred method by which to perform extent of *problem* analysis but here are a couple of suggestions:

  - The analyst must recognize the nature and *attributes* of the reported *problem* and have the management and technical expertise to identify these same or similar *attributes* in the same or similar processes. For example, if the *problem* existed in a particular part of a process characterized by certain *attributes*, the analyst would look for other processes in which these same *attributes* apply.

  - Data would be collected by the review of documentation for each similar process, the interview of persons working in these processes and the real-time observation of these processes.

- The performance of *extent of problem analysis* is usually limited to occurrences that are classified as *events* and *near misses*. However, the principle can be applied on a abbreviated scale to *precursors*.

Question: What are the benefits of correcting the causes of *problems* found by *extent of problem analysis?*

Answer:

- *Extent of problem analysis* helps to *prevent the recurrence* of the reported *problem* and the occurrence of similar *problems,* and the losses associated with any *recurrence or similar occurrence.*

- The cost of correcting the *root* and *contributing causes* of the reported and similar *problems* at one time is substantially less than the cost of correcting the causes sequentially.

- *Extent of problem analysis* helps to avoid customer and regulatory agency dissatisfaction that would exist were the reported *problem* to recur elsewhere or were a similar *problem* to occur. The perception would be that the *preventive corrective action* (pages 351–352) had an unduly narrow span of vision. There would be little tolerance for the *recurrence of the reported problem* in a different process or product or for the occurrence of a similar *problem.*

Root Cause Analysis

Data acquired by investigation
subjected to established analytical processes,
to identify the things and behaviors
that need to be changed
such as to prevent or
minimize the probability of
the recurrence of error.

- *Investigation* and *root cause analysis* are separate processes.

- *Investigation* involves five categories of data collection techniques: (a) document review [e.g., review of design documents, procedures, records]; (b) interview; (c) on-line, real-time observation of the process; (d) *inspection, testing* and laboratory analysis; (e) specialized techniques, such as *statistically designed experiments*, engineering analyses and modeling.

- The effectiveness of the analysis is limited by the effectiveness of the *investigation*—the extent to which the *investigative* data is meaningful, complete and accurate.

- The *established analytical processes* may be any of those described in this Bookinar™ (e.g., starting on page 281, *change analysis, failure mode and effects analysis, hazard-barrier-effects analysis, time-line analysis, cause and effects analysis*, among others).

- For *SL1* or *SL2*, very often, multiple *root cause analysis* techniques are used.

- There are two elements of the established *root cause analysis* technique: (a) a logical and disciplined arrangement and display of the data; (b) a logical and disciplined analysis applied to the data.

- **Absent the identification of the causes of *human error*, the analysis is missing the *root*.**

- There are four levels of *human error:*

    1. *The first level of error is the failure to establish a barrier(s) to prevent an initiating error, when such a barrier is warranted.* Sometimes, *prevention* cannot be accomplished, or cannot be accomplished economically, or sometimes the consequence of *error* is negligible. In such cases, the absence of the *barrier* would not constitute an *error.* Sometimes a *barrier* can only partially effective, less than 100 percent effective, either because of technical limitations or cost benefit considerations. Again, in such cases, to the extent that the *barrier* achieves its expected effectiveness, there is no *error.*

    2. *The second level of error is the initiating error*—i.e., the *error* that may directly actuate the *hazard* or the *error* that may lying in wait for an *initiating action* to actuate the *hazard.*

    3. *The third level of error is the failure to establish a barrier(s) to detect the initiating error or to detect the hazard actuated by the error.*

    4. *The fourth level of error is the failure to establish a barrier(s) to mitigate and ameliorate the effects of the hazard.*

Causal Factor

Any error that
yields an occurrence
that
results in an undesired effect
or that
exacerbates of the level of severity of an undesired effect

- A *causal factor* can be at any level in the hierarchy of causes—from *direct cause* to *root cause*. (See pages 260–262.)

- At the lowest level, at the root, a *causal factor* can be the ultimate cause of a specific type of *human error*. Ultimate in this context means after the answers to the *why?* questions have been received to exhaustion. (See page 266.)

- At a higher level, above the root, a *causal factor* may be inadequate procedure design or inadequate equipment design, or a *non-conformance* to a design.

- At the highest, a *causal factor* may be the *direct cause*—either the *initiating error* or the *initiating action*.

Direct Cause

Any initiating error

or

any initiating action
that immediately precedes the occurrence
that yields the undesired effect

- The *direct cause* can be one of two types:
  1. A *behavior* that constitutes a *human error*—e.g., the operator repositions a valve in violation of the approved procedure, the *initiating error*, immediately resulting in the occurrence;
  2. A *behavior* that does not constitute a *human error*—e.g., the operator repositions the valve in accordance with the approved procedure, the *initiating action*, immediately resulting in the occurrence. In this case the *initiating error* is in the procedure preparation, review and approval process; or

     A part or component fails in operation, the *initiating action*. In this case, if there was an appropriate decision to *run to failure*, there was no *initiating error*. Otherwise, the *initiating error* is in the design of the item, design of its application, design of its maintenance or conformance to design.
- Note that the *direct cause* may be either an *initiating error* or an *initiating action*. (See page 23.)

Contributing Cause

Any deficiency or error that
increases the likelihood of the occurrence
that yields the undesired effect
but that, by itself,
cannot cause the occurrence,
or any deficiency or error that
exacerbates the level of significance of the undesired effect

- A deficiency in a hardware item or in a document may result in an occurrence. A *human error* may result in an occurrence. Sometimes, however, the *human error* is not the result of a deficiency in the human—e.g., *skill-based* and *lapse-based error* need not be the result of human deficiency. (See pages 44–52.)

- A *contributing cause* can be either of two types:

  - It can increase the likelihood of the occurrence.

  - It can exacerbate the *level of significance* of the *undesired effect*.

- In performing *root cause analysis*, it's important to also identify *contributing causes*.

- The *contributing causes* for one occurrence (e.g., an *event*) may be a *root cause* for a different occurrence (e.g., another subsequent *event*).

Root Cause

Any deficiency or error,
which when eliminated or corrected,
prevents
or
reduces the probability of
a repetition of the occurrence
that yields the undesired effect

- Only a human deficiency can be the *root cause* of any *near miss* or *event*. By definition, a *near miss* or *event* occurs in the absence or ineffectiveness of appropriate *barriers*, and *human error* caused by human deficiencies are at the *root* of such absence or ineffectiveness.

- The *root cause* is identified by asking and getting answers to the question *why?* in accordance with criteria listed on page 266.

- An intermediate cause (as contrasted to an ultimate cause) of a *error* is not a *root cause*.

- The thing that has the *problem* is not a *root cause*. For example, an inadequacy in a procedure is not a *root cause*, such as step for which the required action is incompatible with human capability. However, this inadequacy is not a *root cause*. What caused the inadequacy? Why? Why? It's a *human error* of one of the types described starting on page 44. And then *why?*, *why?* some more to find the *root causes*.

- Sometimes, *prevention* cannot be accomplished or cannot be accomplished economically. Sometimes, a reduction in the *probability of recurrence* of the *error* or a reduction in the *significance* of its *undesired effect* is the best that can be done.

Root Cause Analysis
Administrative Guidelines

- Designate an owner of the problem.
- Define of the problem completely and specifically.
- Get speedy access to eye witness data.
- Establishment the investigation and analysis team.
- Prepare and issue the team's charter.
- Prepare and issue the plan.
- Maintain high standards of discipline and proof.

- These guidelines apply to *investigations* and *root cause analyses* performed for *events* and *near misses*.
- Very often, initially, the owner of the *problem* is the manager of the organization adversely affected by the *problem*. The owner may be the actionee who accepts a commitment to perform the *extent of problem analysis*.
- Of course, the actionee for any *root* or *contributing cause* should be the manager of the organization responsible for the existence of the cause.
- In the case of an accident, speedy access to eye witnesses is important for a few reasons. It may help to:
  - Better define the *problem*.
  - Better understand the initiating and other causes of the *problem*.
  - Avoid the loss of information and misinformation, due to memory loss over time.
  - Avoid the loss of data due to collusion, for whatever reason.
- To get speedy access to the data, the *investigation* and *root cause analysis* team should be established as soon as possible. The *attributes* of the team are described on pages 268–269.
- The team's charter should be issued as soon as possible. The charter should (a) identify the team members, (b) state the *problem*, (c) state the scope of the team's work, (d) state the objectives of the team's effort, e) authorize the team to do its work, and, (f) essentially, direct the managers of the involved organizations to support the team's work. Therefore, the issuer of the charter must be at a high enough level in the organization to have the authority to give such direction. Even with this direction, different managers may have different priorities.

- The plan should describe (a) the responsibilities of each team member with regard to the data to be collected, (b) the data source[s], (c) the data collection method[s], (d) the tools and techniques to be use for *root cause analysis*, and (e) the report preparation, review and issuance—with appropriate schedule information.

Root Cause Analysis
Administrative Guidelines (Cont'd)

Perform root cause analysis for events,
near misses AND precursors.
If root cause analysis is not performed for precursors,
the frequency of occurrence of events and near misses
will increase.

- This is not to say that the same level of effort should be applied for the *root cause analysis* of a *precursor* as should be applied for the analysis of an *event* or *near miss*. For a *precursor*, a much lesser level of effort should be applied—specifically, using the technique of *apparent root cause analysis* as described on pages 271–273.

Root Cause Analysis
Administrative Guidelines (Cont'd)

- Ask "Why"?—5 times.

- **Ask "Why"?—to the point at which the answer is one of the causal factors in the *Human Error Causal Factor Taxonomy.***

- Ask "Why"?—to the point at which the answer goes out of your control.

- Ask "Why"?—to the point at which the answer does not add value.

- The rule of thumb of asking *Why?* five times is merely a shorthand way of saying that *why?* should be asked to the point at which answers are out of the control of the enterprise or of no value. It could be any number of times.

- Here's an example. Recall from the *Stator Bar Removal Case Study*, starting on page 116, that one of the *barrier* failures was the lack of an administrative procedure requiring engineering analysis of any maintenance process in which there are significant forces, stored energy and loads, such as in the stator bar removal process. Given that this was among a number of causes of the accident, the *root cause analyst* would ask *why?* such a procedure was lacking.

- Was it because the Maintenance Department supervisor or manager did not recognize the need for an engineering analysis? Did the supervisor lack the cognitive ability to recognize this need—i.e., make a *cognition-based error of omission?* If so, why did he or she lack this cognitive ability?

- Was it because the Engineering Department supervisor or manager failed to arrange for the issuance of a higher level, enterprise-wide procedure requiring that the *owner* of any process in which there are significant forces, stored energy and loads be required to seek an analysis of that process from the Engineering Department? Did the Engineering Department supervisor or manager lack the foresight or cognitive ability to recognize the need for this higher-level procedure—i.e., did he or she make a *cognition-based error of omission?* If so, why did he or she lack this cognitive ability?

- It's understood that "significant forces..." is ill-defined. However, at least it will raise the question in the process owner's mind and a decision can be made on a process-by-process basis.

Root Cause Analysis
Administrative Guidelines (Cont'd)

As a root cause analyst,
one is responsible for identifying
the causes to be considered for correction.
One is *not* responsible
for determining the feasibility of
any such corrections.

- The root cause analyst should not be constrained by the possibility that a cause may not be economically correctible.

- The analyst should not be constrained by the possibility that management may assign a low priority to the correction of the cause.

- Although the analyst has the expertise in the process or item for which the *problem* causes are being analyzed, the analyst may not have the expertise with which to decide on the type of correction for a given cause and the cost of that correction. Furthermore, the analyst should not usurp that role, which is management's.

- It's acceptable for a person to be an analyst and, later, to participate in the *corrective action* decision process. However, while that person performs as an analyst, he or she should focus on causes and not allow there to be other constraining conditions.

Root Cause Analysis
Administrative Guidelines (Cont'd)
Needs of the Analyst / Team

- Knowledge and cognitive ability
  - Administrative processes
  - Product
  - Technical processes
- Ability to perform investigation; ability to use data collection techniques
- Ability to use root cause analysis techniques (analytical ability)
- Objectivity

- When a team is performing a *root cause analysis*, it is not necessary for each member of the team to possess each of these *attributes*, other than objectivity, an *attribute* that should be possessed by analysts universally.

- For example, if a team member is expert in the use of *root cause analysis* techniques and his or her contribution is to facilitate the use of these techniques, he or she need not necessarily have expertise in the process or product in question or in data collection techniques. Of course, a person with this limited expertise would not be expected to and would not be assigned to analyze the process or product or to collect data.

- Similarly, a team member who has expertise in the process or product need not necessarily have expertise in the use of *root cause analysis* techniques provided, of course, that this team member takes guidance from others who do have expertise in the application of *root cause analysis* techniques.

- One of the ways by which to try to assure the objectivity of an individual analyst or analytical team is to assign analysts who are *independent*, as described in the next page. However, sometimes, in order to have a requisite level of technical expertise on some relatively unique subject, it may be necessary to have a team member who is not *independent*. Nevertheless, such a team member would strive for objectivity by:

  - Open mindedness;
  - *Questioning attitude*;
  - Freedom from fear.

Question: What are the *attributes* of *independence*?

Root Cause Analysis
Administrative Guidelines (Cont'd)
Independence

- Absence of responsibility for earlier decisions
- Absence of an organizational reporting relationship to those who are or were responsible for earlier decisions
- Equivalency of knowledge and cognitive ability

- In addition to open mindedness, a *questioning attitude* and freedom from fear, *independence* is an important *attribute* for the attainment of objectivity.

- One is *independent* if one has the three *attributes* listed in the slide.

- Many, many years ago, prior to quality assurance and quality engineering maturing as professions, chief inspectors sometimes were promoted to the roles of Quality Assurance (QA) Managers or Quality Engineering (QE) Managers. To demonstrate their *independence* to regulators and customers, these new QA / QE Managers were organized to report to the top-level officer of the enterprise or facility. It was impressive to see that the QA / QE Manager had a solid line reporting relationship to the top guy (*guy* in those days).

In their new roles, the QA / QE Managers were responsible for recommending quality-related *attributes* for incorporation into the management or business systems and for identifying quality-related deficiencies in the management / business systems. The new QA / QE Managers were the best of the best among inspectors. However, there was no way for some of them to achieve *independence* truly. Simply, they lacked the cognitive ability and tools with which to recognize the quality-related management / business system needs and issues and with which to "sell" the needed system improvements and corrections.

Recall that *evaluation* is the highest level of Benjamin Bloom's six *levels of cognition*. (See page 45.) Today, recognizing their evaluation responsibilities, quality, safety and environmental managers are among the most capable and well rounded with regard to management / business systems.

Root Cause Analysis
Administrative Guidelines (Cont'd)
Cause of Events

Events occur due to
human error
in the:

- Design of the management systems or in the conformance to the design of the management systems—management systems that govern the design of the product;
- Design of the product (i.e., the item or service) or in the conformance to the design of the product;
- Design of the technical processes or in the conformance to the design of the technical processes—processes that convert the product design into the product.

- Recall also that *events* and *near misses* occur due to *human error* at four levels:

1. *Error in failing to provide a barrier(s) [Level 1 Barrier(s)] for the prevention of initiating error;*

2. *Error that activates the hazard, an initiating error* (sometimes in conjunction with an *initiating action*);

3. *Error in failing to provide a barrier(s) [Level 2 Barrier(s)] for the detection the initiating error or for the detection of the hazard activated by the initiating error or initiating action;*

4. *Error in failing to provide a barrier(s) [Level 3 Barrier(s)] to mitigate and ameliorate the undesired effects of the hazard.*

- Notice above, the *three levels of barriers.*
- (See pages 65–66.)

Apparent Root Cause Analysis vs. Formal Root Cause Analysis

- Apparent root cause
  - A root cause identified by means of logic applied to existing data and to inexpensively acquired new data that is reasonably qualified, verified and validated

- Known root cause
  - A root cause identified by means of:
    - Use of a formal root cause analysis technique (e.g. hazard-barrier-effects analysis)
    or
    - Compelling logic applied to sufficient qualified, verified and validated data

- *Apparent root cause analysis* should be performed for *problems* that are classified as *precursors*. The idea is to limit the amount of expenditure but, nevertheless, on a best-efforts basis, to identify the *root cause(s)* of the *problem*.

- There are four reasons for performing apparent root cause analyses for *precursors*:

  1. Resources are insufficient to enable the use of formal *root cause analysis* techniques considering the frequency of occurrence of *precursors*.

  2. The *significance* of a single *precursor* does not warrant the use of formal *root cause analysis* techniques. However, if the frequency of a given type of *precursor* rises to an intolerable level or the trend of the frequency indicates a rise to an intolerable level, formal *root cause analysis* may be needed.

  3. Some analysis should be done for a *precursor*, lest the *problem* cause(s) go totally undefined and uncorrected, which could lead ultimately to an *event*.

  4. The *apparent root cause analysis* technique is almost always cost-beneficial.

- A *root cause* identified using *apparent root cause analysis* is an *apparent root cause*. A *root cause* identified using a *formal root cause analysis* technique is a *known root cause*.

- *Apparent* simply means that, given the substantially reduced level of analytical effort, there is no assurance that the identified cause(s) is truly the *root cause(s)*. That's why the result of *apparent root cause analysis* may be limited to the correction of a *thing that has the problem*—e.g., the correction of a procedure. It's left at that, rather that ascertaining the reason for the procedural inadequacy to begin with and the reason for not having *detected* the procedural inadequacy sooner.

- It's unnecessary to spend resources for formal *root cause analysis* when QVVd data is sufficient and when the logic applied to the data is so compelling as to yield the *known root cause(s)*.

Apparent Root Cause Analysis vs Formal Root Cause (Cont'd)

Apparent Root Cause Analysis	Formal Root Cause Analysis
Performed for precursors. Used frequently.	Performed for events and near misses. Used rarely.
Performed by applying logic to existing and easily acquired additional data.	Performed with extensive investigation and formal root cause analysis techniques.
Performed by many people who need not have training in formal investigation and root cause analysis techniques.	Performed by a few persons who have training in formal investigation and root cause analysis techniques.
Performed by "self" and others.	Performed largely by "outsiders".

• In addition, as noted on the preceding page, the causes identified by *apparent root cause analysis* can be referred to as *apparent root causes* and the causes identified by *formal root cause analysis* can be referred to as *known root causes*.

Question: What are the techniques used for data collection?

Investigation Techniques
Sources of Data

- Interview
- Document analysis—e.g., procedures, design documents, design analysis documents, procurement documents, software, records
- On line, real time observation
- Laboratory analysis
- Specialized techniques—e.g., statistically designed experiments for analysis of variance, engineering analyses, modeling.

- Following an *event* or *near miss*, the purpose of data collection is to enable *formal root cause analysis*. The analysis is of the data. Good data, the better the chance of good *root cause analysis*. Poor data, no chance.
- These are the five categories of data collection techniques.
- Distinguishing facts from conclusions is one of the most difficult things to do in the data collection process, particularly with regard to data from interview and document analysis.
- For example, in interviewing, some questions should evoke a *factual* responses. However, a response may not be *factual* because of the respondent's memory loss, bias or fear. Or, for example, in reviewing a document, an item of information therein may be described as *factual*. However, the original QVVing of that *fact* may have lacked sufficient rigor.
- Courses are available for improving *observation* skills.
- A tally sheet may be used to record the frequency of observations that fall into each different category.
- A *spatial diagram* may be used to record the frequency of observations that fall within different spatial limits. For example, an outline of the human body may be drawn and each bodily injury may be plotted on the outline to show the frequency of injuries that occur to each part of the body. Or a layout drawing might be used to plot the frequency of reports of foul odors in each area.
- Laboratory analysis is used to determine *failure modes* as distinguished from causes.
- There are dozens of books on statistically designed experimentation for analysis of variance.

Question: What should be done immediately following an accident?

Investigation Techniques (Cont'd)
Immediately Following The Event

- Preserve the scene.
  - Rope off the area.
  - Prevent any inappropriate change.
  - Appropriate the products.
- Videotape. (Video critical tasks as they are being performed.)
- Hold those at the scene for written descriptions of eye witness accounts of the event / near miss, and / or for interviewing.
- Prepare for interviewing.
- Interview as soon as practical-those at the scene and others, as necessary.

- Of course, the primary actions are to give first aid and comfort to the injured and to avoid any further escalation of the *undesired effects*. With sufficient resources to work in parallel, the actions listed on the slide should be taken.

- Some steps of a process may be videotaped continuously because of their inherent danger or potential for financial loss.

- The immediate response to an *event* and the control of the *event* scene are analogous to the immediate response to a physical crime and the control of the crime scene.

- Specially trained individuals should be assigned and on call to respond, even though they may not be assigned to carry on the *investigation*. Otherwise, valuable time will be lost.

- The materials necessary to facilitate the immediate response and to enable control of the scene should be readily available—e.g., a camera, materials with which to cordon off the affected area, materials with which to collect samples, safety equipment. Without the ready availability of these materials, valuable time will be lost.

- A written procedure should describe the responsibilities of plant personnel to preserve the scene pending the arrival of the first responders—of course, preservation being exclusive of that which is necessary for safety and *mitigation*. Otherwise, the tendency will be to restore the situation to normal as quickly as possible and valuable information will be lost.

- The last three bullets on the screen are the most difficult. While it's important to interview people as soon as possible, it's also important to interview them separately, with the appropriate preamble and setting—as addressed on the next page. It might be best to immediately get a written statement from each eyewitness before interviewing him or her.

Question: What are the factors to be considered in the interviewing process?

Interviewing Techniques
Interview Preparedness Checklist

- Interview time
- Interview place
- Interview environment
- Questions:
  - Sequence
  - Types
  - Generality versus specificity
  - Final question
- Fact vs. opinion
- Note taking
- Clarifications
- Summaries

- Prior to the occurrence of an *event*, the interviewing process should be established and procedurally documented. If it is not, following an *event*, valuable time and, consequently, valuable data will be lost or interviewing *errors* will be made or both.

- Of course, interviewing *error* may result in the withholding of data or in the acquisition of false data or both.

- The place at which the interview is conducted should be private and unobservable by others who are to be interviewed subsequently. Others, given the opportunity to observe, even without hearing, will *read into* the interviewee's body language and the amount of time spent in the interview.

- The interviewee should be informed and, hopefully, convinced that:

  - The purpose of the interview is to acquire data that will help in the analysis to determine the *root* and *contributing causes* of the *event*, and that will help to get these causes corrected such as to *prevent* a repetition of the *event* or of a similar *event*.

  - The purpose stated immediately above is the only purpose.

  - While the interviewer's notes will link the interviewee with the information that he or she provides, this link will not be shared with anyone other than the *investigation* and *root cause analysis* team unless it is absolutely necessary for the *prevention of the recurrence* of the *event* or of a similar *event*.

  - There will be no repercussion from the admission of *error* or from the identification of *error* in the performance of another. The response to *error* is understanding and learning—e.g., by removing *error-inducing conditions* and helping one to improve oneself—not blame. (Of course, this rings hollow if prior actions have been to the contrary.)

276

- The sequence of the questions and the types of questions will be covered in the next few pages.

- It's *good practice* to go from general to specific. Starting with specific may limit the information received.

- At transition points in the interview (also covered in the next few pages) and at the end of the interview it's *good practice* to ask very open-ended question along the following lines:

  What else can you tell me about this phase?

  What else can you tell me about this event?

  Who were the other eye witnesses?

  Who else should I talk to?

  This gives the interviewee the opportunity to add information that might not have been addressed by earlier questions or that he or she might have forgotten to mention in response to earlier questions. Also, it may lead the interviewer to prospective interviewees who had not been identified previously.

- Some questions are intended to evoke factual responses and some are intended to evoke the opinions. The difference between fact and opinion is addressed on page 243.

- The notes of the interview should clearly distinguish between fact and opinion. The notes should indicate the level of confidence that the interviewee has in his or her response, particularly with regard to a response that is intended to be factual.

- Sometimes, in addition to the interviewer, there is a note-taker. The benefit of a separate note-taker is that it enables the interviewer to concentrate on the interview, itself, allowing it to flow more smoothly with less interruption. The potential *risk* is that the interview may proceed too quickly for the note-taker to get it all and get it right.

- Either way, at any time during the interview, it's appropriate to ask for clarification, if necessary.

- Either way, at transition points in the interview, the notes should be read to the interviewee and the interviewee should be asked to verify their accuracy and to add any additional information that may have been omitted.

Interviewing Techniques (Cont'd)
Interview Questions

- Event:
  - What happened? What did you see and hear? What caused you to be aware of the event?
- Conditions Leading to the Event:
  - What conditions existed immediately prior to the event—with regard to each of the six Ms?
  - What parameter values, if any, did you noticed immediately prior to the event? What values were unusual? What caused these unusual values?
  - What changes of state, if any, did you notice immediately prior to the event—e.g., relay repositioning, alarms, etc? How did these changes of state come into being?
  - When did various activities or events occur? In what sequence? At what times?

- W. Edwards Deming: "If you don't know how to ask the right questions (the right way, at the right time, of the right person), you discover nothing." (Presenter's parenthesis.)

Question: In the questions on this slide and on the next two slides, what are the *attributes* in common?

Answer: The questions are open-ended and are arranged in a logical sequence, transitioning from one phase of the occurrence or *event* to the next.

- With an open-ended question, the interviewee must use his or her terms (not the interviewer's terms) and must think more broadly. The response to an open-ended question usually yields more information than a response to a closed-end question.

- Each of the primary bullets on the slide represents a phase of the interview. A transition point exists at the conclusion of the responses to the indented bullets, prior to entering a new phase. For example, there may be six transition points, each at the end of a phase shown in this and the following two slides:
  - The occurrence or *event*, itself;
  - The conditions leading to the occurrence / *event*;
  - The effects of the occurrence / *event*;
  - *Recovery* from the occurrence / *event*;
  - Apparent causes of the occurrence / *event*;
  - Recommended *corrective actions*.

- Even the most experienced interviewers use a checklist of questions as given on this and the next two slides, or something similar.

Investigation Techniques (Cont'd)
Interview Questions (Cont'd)

- Effects:
  - What happened after each activity / event?
  - What unusual sensations, if any, did you have? Odors? Heat? Moisture? Etc?
  - Which of these unusual sensations existed before the event? When? What caused these unusual sensations?
  - What happened during and after your unusual sensations?
- Recovery
  - What help was available to you? When was it available? What could be done to improve the "help"?
  - What communications were ongoing? How clear and audible were the communications? What caused any lack of clarity or audibility?

- Although not shown on the slides, the reader is reminded that at the conclusion of each phase of the interview, it's *good practice* for the interviewer or note taker to read the notes verbatim and to ask the interviewee to provide any corrections or additions necessary to make the notes accurate and complete. For example, ask: *What should be changed or added to these notes to make them accurate and complete?* Don't ask: *Are these notes accurate and complete?*

- Obviously, these questions are for an *event* involving the failure of hardware. A similar set of questions should be prepared for an administrative *event* that does not necessarily involve the hardware failure.

Investigation Techniques (Cont'd)
Interview Questions (Cont'd)

- Apparent Causes:
  - What procedures were used?
  - How clear and accurate were the procedures? Was it necessary to take steps outside the procedures? What steps? Why?

- Corrective Recommendations:
  - What lessons did you learn from this event?
  - What do you think caused the event?
  - What would you do to correct these causes?

- Closure:
  - What else about this event can you tell me?
  - Who were the other eye witnesses to the event?
  - Who else should I talk to?

- Notice the question: *Who were the other eye witnesses to the event?* That's a very important question because sometimes, as stated earlier, immediately following the *event*, it may be hard to corral and identify all of the eye witnesses.

- Also, notice the last question: *Who else should I talk to?* It may well be appropriate to interview persons who were not eye witnesses. The response to this question may identify prospective interviewees who were not previously identified.

Root Cause Analysis Techniques

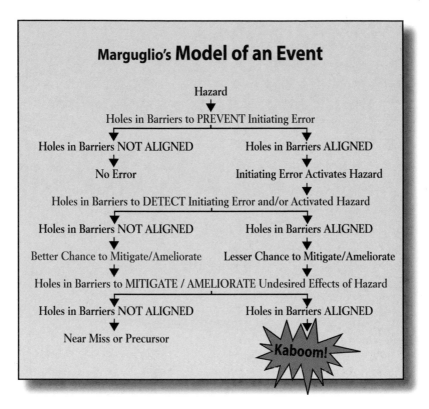

- This model shows *three levels of barriers* (in red font):

  1. First level—the barrier(s) to prevent an initiating error that can activate a hazard.

  2. Second level—the barrier(s) to detect the error and / or the actuation of the hazard.

  3. Third level—the barrier(s) to mitigate and ameliorate the undesired effects of the hazard.

- An example of a *second-level barrier* is a building smoke detection system with an alarm. An example of *third-level barriers* are the building's fire suppression system and evacuation plan and evacuation drills in accordance with the plan.

- For some *events*, such as for a catastrophic bridge collapse, there are no *second-*and *third-level barriers* to give *warning* or to lessen the *significance* of the *event*. This statement is based on *in-service inspection* being categorized as a *first-level* (*error / failure prevention*) *barrier*.

- For a manufacturing setting, the *first-level barrier(s)* is to *prevent* a *defect*. The *second-level barrier(s)* is to *detect* the *defect* on a timely basis. The *third-level barrier* is, for example, to *prevent* shipment of *defective* product or, if shipped, to provide for the immediate notification to the purchaser, replacement of *defective* product, analysis as to the *root cause* of the *first-and second-level barrier* breakdowns, and communication to the customer of the *corrective action to prevent recurrence* of the shipment of *defective* product.

- This model shows *four levels of error:*

  1. *First level—the error in failing to have an effective first-level barrier(s) to the initiating error;*

  2. *Second level—the initiating error;*

  3. *Third level—the error in failing to have an effective second-level barrier for detection of the initiating error or for the detection of the hazard activated by the initiating error;*

  4. *Fourth level—the error in failing to have an effective third-level barrier for the mitigation and amelioration of the undesired effects of the hazard.*

- Failure to have an effective *barrier* may be due to *error* in the design of the *barrier* or *error* in the implementation of the design.

- Of course, failure to have an effective *barrier* does not constitute *error* when there is no technical or economic basis for the *barrier*. The establishment of a *barrier* in the absence of its need, itself, constitutes an *initiating error*.

- Sooner or later there will be an *initiating error*.

- Here are examples demonstrating the difference between an *initiating action* and an *initiating error*.

  - If an operator repositions a valve in accordance with an approved operating procedure, and if the result is an occurrence with an undesired significant effect, the operator did not make the *initiating action*, not the *initiating error*. The *initiating error* occurred either in the design of the hardware system or in the preparation of the operating procedure. There should have been *first-* and *second-level barriers* to *prevent* and *detect*, respectively, any *error* in the hardware system design or in the procedure preparation. In addition, given the potential *significance* of the *undesired effect* and the potential for the failure of the *first two levels of barriers*, there should have been a *third-level barrier(s)* to lessen the *significance* of the *undesired effect*.

  - If an operator repositions a valve in violation of the approved operating procedure, this *direct cause* of the *undesired effect* is the *initiating error*.

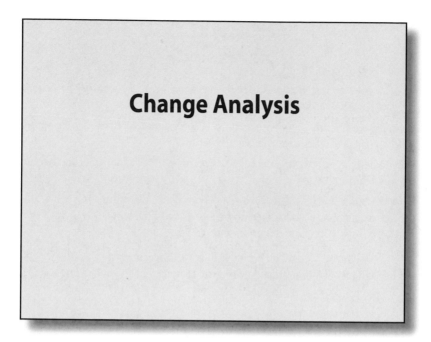

Change Analysis

- Following the *investigation* of the *event* or *near miss* (including document review, interview, real-time on-line observation, laboratory analysis and any special experimentation, analysis, testing or modeling) it's time to apply one or more of the *root cause analysis* techniques.

- Use *change analysis* if the *problem* exists in one among many ostensibly identical processes.

- For example, *change analysis* may be used if a *problem* exists in one manufacturing line but does not exist in other lines, all producing the same model-numbered item. Or, for example, *change analysis* may be used if a *problem* exists in an airline's process at one airport and does not exist in ostensibly the same process at other airports.

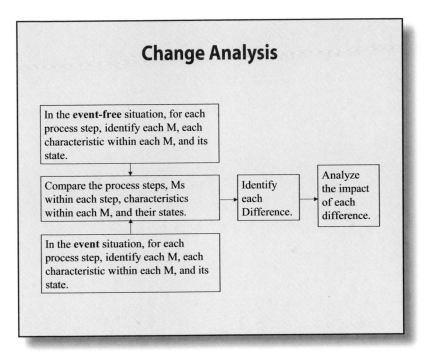

- Aside from having subject matter expertise, the most difficult aspect is following the analytical technique, step-by-step. The technique is tedious but not difficult to understand. If the technique is not followed, if discipline is not maintained, the analysis may be flawed.

Change Analysis (Cont'd)
Analytical Process

1. What is the step?
2. What are the six Ms in the step?
3. What are the characteristics in each M?
4. What is the state of each characteristic in the success situation?
5. What is the state of the characteristic in the failure situation?
6. Is there a difference between steps, Ms, characteristics or their states?
7. Is the difference a root or contributing cause of the event or near miss? Could the difference be a potential root or contributing cause of a future event or near miss?
8. If so, how?

- For both the *problematic* and *problem-free* processes, identify each step.

- Within each step, identify each of the six *M*s (machine, material, method, man, mother-nature [natural {and man made} environment], and measurement).

- For each *M*, identify each *characteristic*—either functional, dimensional, or chemical.

- For each *characteristic*, identify its state. For example, the state of a functional *characteristic* in the *problem-free* process may be 240 volts ± 1% whereas it may be 240 volts ± 5% in the *problematic* process. Or, for example, the state of a dimensional *characteristic* in the *problem-free* process may be 1.000" ± .001" whereas it may be 1.000" ± .005" in the *problematic* process. Or, for example, the state of the chemistry for a material in the *problem-free* process may be 1.0% carbon whereas it may be 5.0% carbon in the *problematic* process.

- For the *problem-free* and *problematic* processes, identify each difference in a step, *M*, *characteristic* or its state. Identify all differences, not only those that appear to be significant.

- It's best practice to not *truncate* the analysis—i.e., to not disregard any step or difference that logically has no bearing on the *event* at hand. Such a step or difference may well bear upon a potential future *event*. How embarrassing would it be to have another *event* in the same process, even for entirely different *root causes*? How difficult would it be to explain that to one's management, a regulator, client or customer, or jury?

- In analyzing a difference that has no logical bearing on the *event* at hand, it's very possible that the *event-free* situation is incorrect or undesired and that the *event* situation is correct or desired.

- The point is: If there should not be a difference, why is there a difference?

Change Analysis (Cont'd)
Analytical Process

9. Was the difference a design inadequacy? If so:
   a. What was the nature of the inadequacy?
   b. Why did the barrier for prevention of the design inadequacy fail? Why?
   c. Why did the barrier for timely detection of the inadequacy fail? Why?
   d. Why did the barrier for mitigation fail? Why?
10. Was the difference a non-conformance to design? If so:
   a. What was the nature of the non-conformance ?
   b. Why did the barrier for prevention of the non-conformance fail? Why?
   c. Why did the barrier for timely detection of the non-conformance fail? Why?
   d. Why did the barrier for mitigation fail? Why?

- The *a* through *d* type questions are standard in that they apply universally, regardless of the *root cause analysis* technique being used.
- The *b* through *d* type questions are based on the model on page 65.
- In *b* through *d*, the *why?* question must be asked repeatedly until the answer indicates a *human error causal factor.* Then additional *whys? Should* be asked until the answer:

1. Indicates additional *human error causal factors* in persons other than the last person to touch the process; or

2. Is in things beyond one's control; or

3. Contributes little or no value.

If the *why?* question is not asked to that point, the *root cause* will not been identified.

Aside from Change Analysis, it is best to use the following root cause analysis techniques concurrent with the design of the:

- Administrative processes;
- Hardware;
- Technical process.

- The *root cause analysis* techniques to be covered hereafter should be used, as appropriate, in conjunction with the design of the administrative processes, hardware and technical processes. The objective is to identify the design *problems* BEFORE they materialized into an *event*. Why wait for the *event* to identify the design *problems*?

- Remember, any of these (administrative processes, hardware and technical processes) can be a product or a part of a product, or they can be used to create the product.

Failure Mode and Effects Analysis

- A *failure mode* is the way by which a *characteristic* no longer meets its requirement. (See pages 344–346.)

- From this presenter's experience, it's preferable to use *failure mode and effects analysis* for components and parts and to use other techniques for administrative and technical processes.

- *Failure mode and effects analysis* may be used during the design of the component or part or subsequent to its failure. For components containing *critical characteristics* (pages 26–27), the former is preferable. It's certainly less expensive.

- In the design phase, *failure mode and effects analysis* is used mostly to determine the component or part *characteristic's* potential *mode of failure* and the effects of such failure.

- Following the failure of the component or part, this technique is used to determine the causes of the failure.

Failure Mode and Effects Analysis Analytical Process—During Design

1. Identify each design characteristic of the component or part (item).
2. For each characteristic, identify the failure modes for the item's storage, shipping, operational application, and maintenance.
3. For each failure mode identify the undesired effect.
4. If the effect is tolerable, whichever is most economical, either:
   a. Live with the effect.
   b. Change the design to eliminate the failure mode or compensate for it.
5. If the effect is intolerable, whichever is most economical, either:
   a. Change the design to eliminate the failure mode.
   b. If the design cannot be changed to eliminate / compensate for the failure mode, establish a barrier(s) to lessen the effect to a tolerable level.
6. If neither 5a nor 5b can be achieved, redesign the item "from scratch".

- A *failure mode* is the way by which a *characteristic* no longer meets its requirement. (See pages 344–346.)

- For step 2, one must postulate not only the credible *modes of failure* that might be applicable during the operation of the item, but also the modes of failure that might be applicable during storage, shipping and maintenance of the item. For example, the *failure mode* for a *characteristic* of an item when it is stored in a unventilated warehouse in an equatorial zone may be considerably different from the *failure mode* of that *characteristic* when it is installed in an air conditioned system operating in the equatorial zone.

- For step 2, one may need to postulate the credible *failure modes* not only for normal operations, but for off-normal operations following an accident. The item may have a *mitigating* function and, therefore, may be required to continue it's operation following an accident. The item may be subject to greater stresses and more adverse environments following an accident.

- These decisions may differ depending on the level in the supplier-user chain. For example:
  - The supplier of a component may accept a 0.01 failure rate for a given *failure mode*.
  - The supplier of the sub-system in which the component is applied may need a 0.0001 failure rate, achievable only by designing the sub-system with two components in active parallel.

- The user of the system in which the sub-system is applied may be unable to tolerate any failure whatsoever and, therefore, may design the system with three subsystems in active parallel. In addition, the user may establish requirements for the immediate *corrective maintenance* of any failed subsystem and for the immediate cessation of operations at any time that there is only one subsystem operational.

- In an ideal situation, the designer of the component will understand the way by which the component affects the function of the host next higher assembly into which the component will be assembled. Of course, this ideal situation may be achievable only when the component is of a specialty design for one or a few customers. The ideal situation becomes far less achievable for a component which is sold to a mass market.

- The reader should learn the process of *commercial grade item dedication*. This is a process by which to assure that an item produced under a lesser quality assurance (QA) or quality control (QC) standard may be installed in a host next higher assembly that is required to comply with a higher qa or qc standard. This process is beyond the scope of this Bookinar™ but, basically, the dedication process is accomplished by one or a combination of the following techniques:

  - Purchaser's increased *audit* or *surveillance* of the supplier's QA / QC processes;

  - Purchaser's increased *in-process* and *final inspection* and *test* of the component at the supplier's facility;

  - Purchaser's increased *receipt* and *installation inspection* and *test* of the component at the purchaser's facility;

  - Purchaser's analysis of the application of the component.

  Rarely, if ever, are techniques 1 and 4 used solely.

- In making a determination of the *level of criticality* of a component's *characteristic*—i.e., the *significance* or tolerability of the *undesired effect* of the *characteristic's* functional failure—credit should not be taken for redundancy in the application of the component. Redundancy should not reduce the *level of criticality*. That would defeat the purpose of the *critical* designation to begin with. (See pages 26–27.)

- If a component from an original equipment manufacturer (OEM) is no longer available as a spare item, and if a new, hopefully equivalent component is needed as a replacement item, the FMEA should be performed for the new replacement item to assure it's functional equivalency and to assure that the design of the new replacement item doesn't introduce a *failure mode* that did not exist in the component from the OEM.

- The active parallel designs and the administrative maintenance and operational constraints constitute added *barriers*.

Failure Mode and Effects Analysis
Analytical Process—After the Event

1. What is the failed component or part (item)?
2. Is the failure the primary failure or a secondary failure?
3. For the primary failure, what characteristic of the item failed?
4. In what mode did the characteristic fail?
5. How did the failure mode result in the event? What was the failure mechanism and the degradation influence?
6. What is the design feature to prevent the failure mode or to detect and mitigate / ameliorate the undesired effect of the failure?
7. Is the design feature adequate?
   a. If not, go to Step 8.
   b. If so, what is the fabrication, assembly, storage, shipping, installation, or maintenance non-conformance that led to the failure? Go to Step 9.

- A secondary failure is one that occurs as a result of an earlier failure, the primary failure. It's best to address the primary failure rather than the secondary failure.

- In addition to the *failure mode*, the *failure mechanism* and the *degradation influences* must be determined. For example:

  - The *failure mode* might be the sticking of a switch contact.

  - The *failure mechanism* might be that a foreign material got lodged beneath the contact.

  - The *degradation influences* might be that the pendent which contains the switch is used in dusty environment.

Given that a dusty environment is the intended use environment, the *root cause analysis* certainly would address the question of why dust was able to infiltrate the pendant such as to be able to lodge beneath the contact.

(See page 346.)

Failure Mode and Effects Analysis (Cont'd)
Analytical Process—After the Event

8. If there was a design inadequacy:
   a. What was the nature of the inadequacy?
   b. Why did the barrier for prevention of the design inadequacy fail? Why?
   c. Why did the barrier for timely detection of the inadequacy fail? Why?
   d. Why did the barrier for mitigation fail? Why?
9. If there a was a non-conformance to design:
   a. What was the nature of the non-conformance?
   b. Why did the barrier for prevention of the non-conformance fail? Why?
   c. Why did the barrier for timely detection of the non-conformance fail? Why?
   d. Why did the barrier for mitigation fail? Why?

- Notice that the *a* through *d* questions are the same as those on page 287 for Change Analysis.

- Again, in *b* through *d*, the *why?* question must asked repeatedly until the answer indicates a *human error causal factor*. Then additional *whys?* Should be asked until the answer:

  1. Indicates additional *human error causal factors* in persons other than the last person to touch the process; or

  2. Is in things beyond one's control; or

  3. Contributes little or no benefit..

  If the *why?* question is not asked to that point, the *root cause* will not been identified.

- Again, aside from having subject matter expertise, the most difficult aspect of this technique, as with other *root cause analysis* techniques, is following the thought process, step-by-step. The process is tedious but not difficult to understand. If the process is not followed, if discipline is not maintained, the analysis may be flawed.

Hazard-Barrier-Effects Analysis

- A *hazard* is anything in a hardware item or process that can lead to an *undesired effect*.

- Recall that a *hazard* must be viewed from a broad perspective. A *hazard* is not only something that can impart a danger to human safety and health. It is something that can lead to *non-compliance* with the law, reportability to a regulatory agency or client / customer, loss of a good relationship with a stakeholder, loss of a mission, or dollar loss.

- Recall that a *barrier* is anything that:

  1. Prevents or helps to prevent an initiating error;

  2. Detects or helps to detect the error or the hazard activated by the error; or

  3. Mitigates / ameliorates or helps to mitigate / ameliorate the severity of the hazard's undesired effect. (See pages 65–66.)

- *Hazard-barrier-effects analysis* may be used during the design of a process or component.

- From this presenter's perspective, *hazard-barrier-effects analysis* is preferable for analyzing a process, and *failure mode and effects analysis* is preferable for analyzing a component.

- It's best to use this technique in the design phase, rather than to wait until the process has failed, especially if there are hazards, which if activated by *error*, would yield effects that are intolerable.

Hazard-Barrier-Effects Analysis (Cont'd)

- Apply to the initial design of a process or to a failed process.
- Any of the six Ms can be or can have the potential to become hazardous.
- Any of the six Ms can be the source or recipient of the hazard.
- The hazard may be natural or man-made.
- Error can activate the hazard or allow the hazard to be undetected or to have an undesired effect.
- There should be administrative process, technical process, equipment and human barriers to:
  1. Prevent the occurrence of error that can activate the hazard;
  2. Detect the occurrence of error or the activation of the hazard;
  3. Prevent the hazard from having a significant undesired effect.
- Barriers should be well designed, provided to users and used consistently.

- Again, the six *Ms* are machine, material, method, man, mother-nature and man-made environment, and measurement.
- It's important to recognize that any *M* may have the potential for a *hazard* under different conditions. As a most simple example, a dry stair with slip retardant material would not impose a "slip" *hazard* (a "trip" *hazard*, yes, but not a "slip *hazard*"). However, under wet or icy conditions, the stair does impose a "slip" *hazard*.
- This is another way of saying that two or more *Ms* interacting in given states can impose a *hazard*. For example, a statistically designed experiment may demonstrate that the interaction of two variables in given states results in a much higher probability for the creation of a *defect* in a *characteristic* of a product.
- Any *M* can be the source of a *hazard* or the recipient of a *hazard*. Both conditions must be considered. For example, a man can be the source of a shock *hazard* by failing to *tag-out* or electrically isolate a component before performing maintenance on the component, and the man can be the recipient of the shock *hazard*. Or, for example, a machine can be the source of *hazard* to a man and the recipient of a *hazard* (e.g., an environmental *hazard* such as high temperature) that may cause its (the machine's) failure.
- If the design of a process imposes a man-made *hazard*, the obvious initial response is to try to redesign the process to eliminate the *hazard*. That's a *first-level barrier*. If that can't be done or can't be done economically, a limited *first-level barrier* (to try *prevent* the *initiating error*) and the other *two levels of barriers* need to be established.
- Given a well-designed process, there should be compliance with the process, including its *barriers*.

Hazard-Barrier-Effects Analysis (Cont'd)
Analytical Process

1. What is each task in the process?

2. What are the six Ms in each task?

3. For each M, what is the hazard(s)?

4. For each hazard, what are the administrative process, technical process, equipment or human barriers that should be in place? *The absence of a barrier is a failed barrier.*

5. Is the design of the barrier(s) adequate? *An inadequately designed barrier is a failed barrier.*

6. Was the barrier communicated to the process implementer? *A non-communicated barrier is a failed barrier.*

Hazard-Barrier-Effects Analysis (Cont'd)
Analytical Process (Cont'd)

7. Was the communication adequate? *An inadequately communicated barrier is a failed barrier?*

8. Was the barrier was used? *An unused barrier is a failed barrier.*

9. Was the barrier used correctly and consistently? *An incorrectly or inconsistently used barrier is a failed barrier.*

10. Which of the barrier failures were root and contributing causes of the undesired effect?

11. Which of the failed barriers failed because of barrier design inadequacy?

12. Which of the failed barriers failed because of non-conformance to barrier design?

Hazard-Barrier-Effects Analysis (Cont'd)
Analytical Process (Cont'd)

13. If there was a design inadequacy:
    a. What was the nature of the inadequacy?
    b. Why did the barrier for prevention of the design inadequacy fail? *Why?*
    c. Why did the barrier for timely detection of the inadequacy fail? *Why?*
    d. Why did the barrier for mitigation fail? *Why?*

14. If there was a non-conformance to design:
    a. What was the nature of the non-conformance?
    b. Why did the barrier for prevention of the non-conformance fail? *Why?*
    c. Why did the barrier for timely detection of the non-conformance fail? *Why?*
    d. Why did the barrier for mitigation fail? *Why?*

- The *a* through *d* questions are the same for the analytical techniques described earlier.

- Remember the instruction about the *why?* questions. (See page 287.)

Case Study
Stator Bar Removal

<u>Assignment</u> – Using the hazard-barrier-effects analytical thought process and the standard questions, identify the:

- Failed barriers
  - Categorize each failed barrier as to its type – i.e., administrative process, technical process, equipment or human.
  - Determine whether the failed barrier was due to inadequate design or non-conformance to design.
  - Using postulated scenarios and the *Human Error Causal Factor Taxonomy*, determine the possible human error causal factors for each failed barrier.
- Error-inducing conditions and error-likely situations.
- Non-conservative decisions.

Case Study – Stator Bar Removal

A member of a generator stator rewind crew was injured during the process of removing a stator bar from the stator of a generator.

Written Procedure:

Presenter's Note: The following steps constitute the body of the written procedure in toto. Anything not stated in the following steps did not exist in the written procedure.

1. Lift the turbine end of a stator bar out of its slot using a chain hoist.

2. Insert a glass fiber wedge (4' long and 1 ½' wide) half way or 2' under the stator bar. The weight and return flexing force of the bar holds the wedge in place.

3. Using another hoist, an air driven mechanical winch or "tugger", with a wire rope, attach a sling to the end of the rope.

4. Wrap the sling around the notch in the back of the wedge.

5. Increase tension with the tugger, such that the wedge is pulled toward the tugger, underneath the bar, raising the bar out of its slot.

6. When the bar is sufficiently out of its slot, remove the bar by hand.

7. Remove the wedge by hand.

8. Repeat Steps 1-7 for each stator bar.

Case Study – Stator Bar Removal (Cont'd)

Photograph # 1—Crew-Member Holding Wedge

Photograph # 2—Tugger

Case Study – Stator Bar Removal (Cont'd)

Problem:

The stator is designed with slide ripple springs that are used to retain the stator bar in its slot. The ripple springs are positioned between the edge of the bar and the wall of the slot. As the wedge is slid under the stator bar, the leading edge of the wedge has a tendency to "capture" the side ripple springs. If enough springs are captured, the wedge becomes jammed in the slot. This occurs a minimum of 10 times and a maximum of 15 times per stator. When this occurs, the stuck wedge is removed by hammering it up and out with a mallet sufficiently to create "grip points" enabling the manual removal of the wedge.

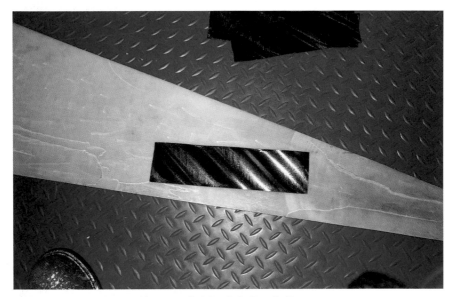

Photograph # 3—Side Ripple Spring

Accident Scenario:

For this stator bar, Step 1 of the procedure was accomplished by (a) attaching a sling to the overhead hoist chain, (b) using a prying tool to raise one end of the stator bar, (c) putting the loop end of the sling around the raised end of the stator bar, and (d) pulling down on one end of the hoist chain such as to raise the other end of the chain, with its attached sling, thus raising the end of the stator bar – readying it for insertion of the wedge.

Per Step 2, the wedge was inserted.

Per Step 3, one end of a sling was attached to the end of the tugger wire rope

Per Step 4, the other loop end of the sling was looped around the notch at the back of the wedge.

Per Step 5, (a) tension was applied to the tugger rope and to the sling causing the wedge to traverse in the slot, raising the stator bar sufficiently out of the slot, (b) tension was released from the tugger rope / sling, and (c) the sling was removed from the slot in the wedge.

Case Study – Stator Bar Removal (Cont'd)

Accident Scenario (Cont'd):

Per Step 6, the stator bar was manually removed.

However, per Step 7, the wedge could not be removed, not even by hammering. It had captured enough ripple springs to cause it to jam in the slot. It was decided to use the tugger to remove the wedge. The loop end of the sling was re-inserted into the wedge's slot. The slack was taken up and the rope / sling was tensioned thinking that the wedge would pivot up and out of the slot sufficiently to create "grip points" for its manual removal.

The wedge did not budge. More tension was applied until the tugger's air motor was heard to strain. A "stop" hand signal was given to the tugger operator. At that instant, the wedge became free of the slot, rotated up and out of the slot, pivoting along the jammed leading edge. There was enough force to snap the tip of the wedge. The broken wedge became airborne, tumbling end-over-end toward a crew-member.

The crew-member was standing about 15' from the original position of the wedge, not in a direct line between the wedge and the winch. The airborne, tumbling, broken wedge struck the crew-member in his chest and in the lower part of his face. The crew-member collapsed upon impact. His injuries were bruising of the chest and sternum and lacerations of his lower face. (He was lucky.)

This Stator Bar Removal Procedure had been used for about 70 stator jobs. For this stator, bar 143 of 144 was in the process of removal when the accident occurred

Assignment Completion:

- In presenting this seminar live, it's interesting to compare case study results using the earlier *brainstorming* approach, on pages 116-121, with the results using *hazard-barrier-effects analysis* here. In the live situation, the results using brainstorming are far less complete than the results using *hazard-barrier-effects analysis.*

- Blank templates with which to complete a large part of the assignment are provided on the next two pages.

- Remember to use discipline and to do the analysis by the numbers.

- Template # 1 should be completed before starting to work on Template # 2.

- A *task* in this context, is not necessarily a *step* as written in a procedure. For example, *Stator Bar Removal Procedure Step # 1* reads as follows: "Lift the turbine end of a stator bar out of its slot using a chain hoist." However, as described on the preceding page, there are four different tasks involved in this one procedure step (tasks which may not necessarily be described in the written procedure if they constitute *skill of the trade*).

- If one were to analyze on the basis of the procedure, step-by-step, instead of on the basis of the actual work, task-by-task, one would miss hazards. For example, in raising the end of the stator bar [Item (b) in Step 1], the bar imposes a "pinch" *hazard.* No big deal, but it illustrates the point.

Template # 1—Hazard-Barrier-Effects Analysis

Task Sequence ID Number: _____
Description of Task: _____
_____
_____
_____

Task Sequence ID Number: _____
Description of Task: _____
_____
_____
_____

Task Sequence ID Number: _____
Description of Task: _____
_____
_____
_____

Task Sequence ID Number: _____
Description of Task: _____
_____
_____
_____

Task Sequence ID Number: _____
Description of Task: _____
_____
_____
_____

Task Sequence ID Number: _____
Description of Task: _____
_____
_____
_____

Task Sequence ID Number: _____
Description of Task: _____
_____
_____
_____

Task Sequence ID Number: _____
Description of Task: _____
_____
_____
_____

Template # 2—Hazard-Barrier-Effects Analysis

Task Sequence ID Number: _____

M 1—Machine Hazard: _____

LEVEL 1 BARRIER FAILURE: _____
  Design Failure: _____
  Nature of Failure: _____
  Why L 1 Barrier Failure: _____
  Why L 1 Barrier Failure: _____
  Why L 1 Barrier Failure: _____
  Why L 1 Barrier Failure: _____
  Why L 1 Barrier Failure: _____
  Human Error Causal Factor: _____
  Implementation Failure: _____
  Nature of Failure: _____
  Why L 1 Barrier Failure: _____
  Why L 1 Barrier Failure: _____
  Why L 1 Barrier Failure: _____
  Why L 1 Barrier Failure: _____
  Why L 1 Barrier Failure: _____
  Human Error Causal Factor: _____

LEVEL 2 BARRIER FAILURE: _____
  Design Failure: _____
  Nature of Failure: _____
  Why L 2 Barrier Failure: _____
  Why L 2 Barrier Failure: _____
  Why L 2 Barrier Failure: _____
  Why L 2 Barrier Failure: _____
  Why L 2 Barrier Failure: _____
  Human Error Causal Factor: _____
  Implementation Failure: _____
  Nature of Failure: _____
  Why L 2 Barrier Failure: _____
  Why L 2 Barrier Failure: _____
  Why L 2 Barrier Failure: _____
  Why L 2 Barrier Failure: _____
  Why L 2 Barrier Failure: _____
  Human Error Causal Factor: _____

LEVEL 3 BARRIER FAILURE: _____
  Design Failure: _____
  Nature of Failure: _____
  Why L 3 Barrier Failure: _____
  Why L 3 Barrier Failure: _____
  Why L 3 Barrier Failure: _____
  Why L 3 Barrier Failure: _____
  Why L 3 Barrier Failure: _____
  Human Error Causal Factor: _____
  Implementation Failure: _____
  Nature of Failure: _____
  Why L 3 Barrier Failure: _____
  Why L 3 Barrier Failure: _____
  Why L 3 Barrier Failure: _____
  Why L 3 Barrier Failure: _____
  Why L 3 Barrier Failure: _____
  Human Error Causal Factor: _____

Template # 2—Hazard-Barrier-Effects Analysis

Task Sequence ID Number:	N.
M 1—Machine Hazard:	Energy in tugger line. The greater the distance between the tugger and the wedge, the greater the range and speed of the tugger rope whiplash should the rope become disengaged from the wedge.
LEVEL 1 BARRIER FAILURE:	Technical Procedure—"Stator Bar Removal".
Design Failure:	Yes, technical procedure failure.
Nature of Failure:	Tugger was too far away from wedge.
Why L 1 Barrier Failure:	Procedure does not specify the maximum distance allowed between tugger and wedge.
Why L 1 Barrier Failure:	Designer of the stator bar removal process and Maintenance Supervisor were unaware of the hazard. *Why L 1 Barrier Failure:* Designer and Maintenance Supervisor have not been trained as how to recognize hazards. (Knowledge-based error)
Why L 1 Barrier Failure:	This type of training is not a prerequisite for the job of a Maintenance Process Designer or Supervisor.
Why L 1 Barrier Failure:	Maintenance Manager believes that this training is unnecessary for a Process Designer or Supervisor. (Cognition-or value-based error)
Why L 1 Barrier Failure:	When interviewed, it was apparent that the Maintenance Manager doesn't fully understand the objectives and learning outcomes of \"hazard-barrier-effects" analysis education and doesn't think there's value added in this type of education.
Human Error Causal Factor:	Designer—Knowledge-based error. Maintenance Supervisor—Knowledge-based error. Maintenance Manager—Cognition-and value-based errors.
Implementation Failure:	Not Applicable.
LEVEL 2 BARRIER FAILURE:	Administrative Procedure for "Review of Maintenance Technical Procedures".
Design Failure:	Yes, administrative procedure failure.
Nature of Failure:	Procedure does not provide adequate criteria for safety and quality review of maintenance technical procedures.
Why L 2 Barrier Failure:	Designer of the maintenance technical procedure review process, Maintenance Supervisors, and Maintenance Manager are not aware of the criteria for adequate safety and quality review.
Human Error Causal Factor:	All—Knowledge-or cognition-based errors.
Implementation Failure:	Not Applicable.
LEVEL 3 BARRIER FAILURE:	Technical Procedure—"Stator Bar Removal".
Design Failure:	Yes, technical procedure failure.
Nature of Failure:	Procedure does not specify the establishment of a non-safety zone and the set-up of a cordon to prohibit access to the non-safety zone.
Why L 3 Barrier Failure:	Same as above.
Human Error Causal Factor:	Same as above.

(For the tugger hazard described above, there is also an equipment barrier failure (e.g., failure to have a device to limit motor RPM) and human barrier failures (e.g., failure of the injured crew-member to recognize the tugger's hazard, and to stand out of harm's way, and failure of crew leader and other crew members to recognize the hazard and to act in accordance with the principle of mutual accountability for safety.) [See pages 120–121.]

Time-line Analysis

- *Time-line analysis* is used when it is suspected that activities spanning a relatively long period of time have caused or contributed to the *event* or *near miss*.

- For the techniques covered earlier, processes were analyzed. For this technique, activities, not processes, are analyzed. Any one of the activities may involve one or more processes, but the depth of the analysis is only to the activity level, not to the detailed process level.

Time-line Analysis
Analytical Process

1. What is the activity?
2. Was there a problem in the performance of the activity?
3. What was the nature of the problem?
4. Could the problem have caused the event or near miss, or have exacerbated the undesired effect? Could the problem be the cause of a future event or near miss, or exacerbate the undesired effect?
5. Was the problem due to a design inadequacy? Of an administrative process? Of a technical process? Of an equipment?
6. Was the problem due to non-conformance to design?

- For each activity in sequence, from the first, *A1*, to the last, *An*, a determination is made as to whether or not there was a *problem* in the performance of the *activity*. The *problem* can exist in an item of hardware, in a process, or in a man (man's incorrect implementation of a process), or in some combination of the three, and the *problem* can be with any one or more of the *three levels of barriers*. (See pages 220–221 for a discussion of the meaning of the word *problem*.)

- Recall the earlier discussion relating to the *truncation* of an analysis. It's not *good practice* to *truncate* an analysis.

- For the analytical techniques previously covered, the discipline was in addressing each process step and each *M* within each step, or in addressing each hardware *design characteristic* and each *failure mode* within each *characteristic*. For *time-line analysis*, the discipline is in addressing each activity—not missing any activity—and addressing the activity at a reasonable level of specificity.

- For example, for *time-line analysis*, it would be inappropriate to breakdown the *pre-job briefing* activity into its elements. Also, it would be inappropriate to engulf the *pre-job briefing* activity into the larger context of the *maintenance* activity. Cutting it neither too fine nor too coarse is a skill developed with practice.

- For any activity for which performance is deemed to be *problematic*, the root cause analyst or analytical team may decide to perform additional analysis of the process(es) or equipment, associated with that activity. For example, from *time-line analysis*, if it were learned belatedly that:
  - A disassembly had been performed and, thereafter, a reassembly had been performed incorrectly, the disassembly and reassembly processes might be subjected to *hazard-barrier-effects analysis*.
  - An equipment had failed, the equipment might be subjected to *failure mode and effects analysis*.
- For the following case study, again two templates are provided on pages 313 and 316.
- Again, identify the activities and complete Template # 1, before starting on Template # 2.
- In completing Template # 1, it's important also to identify activities that were not performed, but that should have been performed. For example, in the *Generator Rotor Hoist Case Study* that follows shortly, there was no engineering analysis to determine the minimum hoist capacity, with *margin*, required to make the hoist. There was no rationale to assume that a hoist that was used for previous jobs is acceptable for the generator rotor hoist.
- For the *Generator Rotor Hoist Case Study*, a completed Template # 1 is provided on pages 314–315, and an example of the completion of Template # 2 is provided on page 317.

Time-line Analysis
The Standard Questions

7. If there was a design inadequacy:
   a. What was the nature of the inadequacy?
   b. Why did the barrier for prevention of the design inadequacy fail? *Why?*
   c. Why did the barrier for timely detection of the inadequacy fail? *Why?*
   d. Why did the barrier for mitigation fail? *Why?*
8. If there a was non-conformance to design:
   a. What was the nature of the non-conformance?
   b. Why did the barrier for prevention of the non-conformance fail? *Why?*
   c. Why did the barrier for timely detection of the non-conformance fail? *Why?*
   d. Why did the barrier for mitigation fail? *Why?*

- Again, the *a* through *d* questions are the same.

- Again, remember the practice for *whys?*.

- *Time-line analysis* may be viewed as an *opening technique* because for any one activity in which there is an equipment or process failure, it may be necessary to also perform *failure mode and effects analysis* or *hazard-barrier-effects analysis* or both, or other analyses, as well.

Case Study—Generator Rotor Hoist

Assignment—Using the time-line analysis thought process and the standard questions, identify the:
- Failed barriers
  - Categorize each failed barrier as to its type—i.e., administrative process, technical process, equipment or human.
  - Determine whether the failed barrier was due to inadequate design or non-conformance to design.
  - Using postulated scenarios and the *Human Error Causal Factor Taxonomy*, determine the possible human error causal factors for each failed barrier.
- Error-inducing conditions and error-likely situations
- Non-conservative decisions

Case Study—Generator Rotor Hoist

Presenter's Note: Everything that was done in this case and that is pertinent to this case study is described in this scenario. If something is not in the scenario, it was not done.

Scenario:
- Periodically, the Power Generation Company (PGCo) rented a specific hoist from a Rental Company (RCo).
- In anticipation of the need to move the rotor core into the generator housing, the PGCo rented the hoist once again. In addition to the "boilerplate" clauses (e.g., insurance clause), the Purchase Order (PO) for the rental identified the model and serial number of the hoist, delivery and return dates, and rental price. These were the PO requirements in toto.
- On May 20, the hoist was delivered, one week in advance of the scheduled date for the move. A *qualified* operator, from a Design and Construction Services Company (D&CSCo) under contract to the PGCo, functionally tested the hoist upon its receipt. Ostensibly, the test at least included the movement the hook up and down, in response to the depression of the "up" and "down" buttons on the pendant. The test results were acceptable. The hoist was moved to a staging area near the generator.
- On May 24, on the day shift, a PGCo Maintenance supervisor directed a technician from an Electrical Contracting Company (ECCo), under contract to the PGCo, to remove the power feed-line from the hoist and to install it on a heater. The power feed-line was hard wired to the hoist. The power feed-line was 3-phase, 480 volts. The technician did as he was directed.

Case Study—Generator Rotor Hoist (Cont'd)

- On May 25, on the second shift, a PGCo maintenance supervisor directed an ECCo technician to replace the power feed-line—i.e., to re-connected it to the hoist. This was classified as "emergent" work. The technician replaced the feed-line.

- On May 26, on the day shift, the turbine-generator project manager directed that the hoist be functionally tested. The technicians functionally tested the hoist, and declared it to be operable. However, it was noted that there was a phase reversal and that the "up" limit switch (the switch to use to stop the upward or rightward movement in an emergency) was wired to perform as the "down" limit switch, and vice-versa. "Up" was down and "down" was up.

- The crane and hoist operators selected to make the rotor move were *qualified* and *certified* for the function.

- A diagram of the rigging and hoisting set-up is given on the next page.

- On May 27, during the *pre-job brief*, the D&CSCo supervisor in charge of the move, noted only the location of the emergency switches—the "up" and "down" limit switches.

- On May 27, when the rotor was moved approximately 10 feet into the housing, the pendent failed. The "up" switch remained energized. Given the pendent failure and given that, for the limit switch, "down" was really "up", the operator was unable to stop the movement of the rotor into the housing. The movement continued until the rotor made contact with and became wedged in the housing. The force of the pull caused the catastrophic failure of the anchor lug weld. This caused a recoil motion in the chain. The recoiling chain struck a crew-member who was stationed inside the housing.

- *Post-event failure mode and effects analysis* indicated that the "up" contact on the pendant was in a degraded condition and that it was stuck due to the presence of a foreign object.

Case Study—Generator Rotor Hoist (Cont'd)

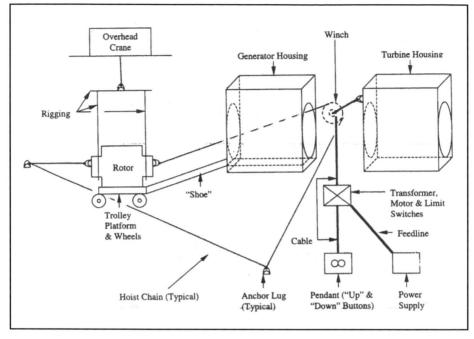

Schematic

Template # 1—Time-Line Analysis

Activity Sequence ID Number: _____
Description of Activity: _____
_____
_____
_____

Activity Sequence ID Number: _____
Description of Activity: _____
_____
_____
_____

Activity Sequence ID Number: _____
Description of Activity: _____
_____
_____
_____

Activity Sequence ID Number: _____
Description of Activity: _____
_____
_____
_____

Activity Sequence ID Number: _____
Description of Activity: _____
_____
_____
_____

Activity Sequence ID Number: _____
Description of Activity: _____
_____
_____
_____

Activity Sequence ID Number: _____
Description of Activity: _____
_____
_____
_____

Activity Sequence ID Number: _____
Description of Activity: _____
_____
_____
_____

Template # 1—Time-Line Analysis

Activity Sequence ID #: 1
Description of Activity: Engineering analysis to determine the load capacity required for the rental hoist. (Problem. Not done.)

Activity Sequence ID #: 2 (April 19)
Description of Activity: Issuance of purchase order (PO) for rental hoist. (Problem. No quality-related requirements in PO—e.g., lack or requirements by which to assure appropriate in-service inspection and load testing of hoist prior to its delivery.)

Activity Sequence ID #: 3 (May 20)
Description of Activity: Delivery of the rental hoist.

Activity Sequence ID #: 4 (May 20)
Description of Activity: Functional test of the rental hoist upon receipt. (Problem. No test procedure. No documentation of test results to indicate functions tested.)

Activity Sequence ID #: 5 (May 20)
Description of Activity: Movement of hoist to staging area.

Activity Sequence ID #: 6 (May 24)
Description of Activity: Direction given to remove power feed-line from hoist. (Problem. No authority to modify rental property.)

Activity Sequence ID #: 7 (May 24)
Description of Activity: Removal of power feed-line from hoist. (Problem. No maintenance procedure. Nothing done to help to assure that feed-line, when replaced, will be wired properly.)

Activity Sequence ID #: 8 (May 25)
Description of Activity: Replacement of power feed-line. (Problem. No maintenance procedure. Ultimately, it will be determined that replacement was done incorrectly.)

Activity Sequence ID #: 9 (May 26)
Description of Activity: Direction given to functionally test hoist.

Activity Sequence ID #: 10 (May 26)
Description of Activity: Functional test of hoist. (Problem. No test procedure. No documentation of test results to indicate functions tested. Test failure. Reversal of phases—"up" limit switch is wired as "down" and vice versa.)

314

Template # 1—Time-Line Analysis

Activity Sequence ID #: 11
Description of Activity: Declaration of hoist operability, noting reversal of phases—"up" limit switch is wired as "down" and vice versa. (Problem. Unacceptable condition is accepted.)

Activity Sequence ID #: 12 (May 27)
Description of Activity: Performance of pre-job briefing. (Problem. Phase reversal not noted in briefing.)

Activity Sequence ID #: 13 (May 27)
Description of Activity: Rotor moved.

Activity Sequence ID #: 14 (May 27)
Description of Activity: Pendant up switch fails. (Problem.)

Activity Sequence ID #: 15 (May 27)
Description of Activity: Operator cannot stop hoist. (Problem.)

Activity Sequence ID #: 16 (May 27)
Description of Activity: Rotor wedges in housing. (Problem.)

Activity Sequence ID #: 17 (May 27)
Description of Activity: Anchor bolt fails. (Problem.)

Activity Sequence ID #: 18 (May 27)
Description of Activity: Hoist chain recoils. (This is not a problem because it is a secondary failure.)

Activity Sequence ID #: 19 (May 27)
Description of Activity: Crew-member is struck by recoiling chain. (This is not a problem because the crew-member was standing in the proper location in order to guide the rotor into place.)

Template # 2—Time-Line Analysis

Failed Activity ID Sequence Number: _____
- *Describe the Failed Activity:*_____
_____

- *Could Failed Activity Have Caused or Contributed to the Event / Near Miss? Yes ___ No ___*
- *What Kind of Barrier Failed? Admin Proc? ____ Tech Proc? ____ Equip? ____ Human? ___*
- *Identify the Failed Barrier:* _____
- *Is the Barrier Failure Due to Inadequate Design ____ or Non-conformance to Design ____?*
- *Describe the Inadequacy of the Barrier Design Failure:* _____
_____
_____

  - *Why Not Prevented?* _____
_____

  - *Human Error Causal Factor:* _____
  - *Why Not Detected?* _____
_____

  - *Human Error Causal Factor:* _____
  - *Why Hazard Not Mitigated?* _____
_____

  - *Human Error Causal Factor:* _____
- *Describe the Non-conformance to the Barrier Design:* _____
_____

  - *Why Not Prevented?* _____
_____

  - *Human Error Causal Factor:* _____
  - *Why Not Detected?* _____
_____

  - *Human Error Causal Factor:* _____
  - *Why Hazard Not Mitigated?* _____
_____

  - *Human Error Causal Factor:* _____

Template # 2—Time-Line Analysis

Failed Activity ID Sequence Number: 7

- *Describe the Failed Activity:*

Removal of power feed-line from hoist. (May 24)

- *Could Failed Activity Have Caused or Contributed to the Event / Near Miss?* Yes
- *What Kind of Barrier Failed?* Administrative procedure
- *Identify the Failed Barrier:*

Administrative Maintenance Procedure 20, Revision 6, "Preparation and Use of Technical Maintenance Procedures"

- *Is the Barrier Failure Due to Inadequate Design or Non-conformance to Design?* Both
- *Describe the Inadequacy of the Barrier Design Failure:*

Procedure 20, Revision 6, does not require that, upon disassembly, wires / cables and terminals are to be matched marked or color coded, to facilitate the correctness of the reassembly.

  - *Why Not Prevented?*

  During interviews, the procedure originator and reviewers stated that did not recognize the need for such a requirement.

  - *Human Error Causal Factor:*

  Cognition-based error. **Why did not the procedure preparer and reviewer have this cognitive ability? This question must be answered.**

  - *Why Hazard Not Mitigated?* Not applicable.

- *Describe the Non-conformance to the Barrier Design:*

In violation of Leasing Agreement, the leased hoist was modified without permission.

  - *Why Not Prevented?*

  During interview, the Maintenance supervisor stated that even in the absence of procedural guidance, he was aware of the absence of authority to remove the feed-line from the hoist. Furthermore, he stated that he did it for expediency, recognizing that the hoist was scheduled for the next day. Lastly, he stated that he didn't think that his lack of authorization was significant because the feed-line was to be replaced immediately.

  - *Human Error Causal Factor:*

  1. Value-based error in that the supervisor didn't think that the lack of authorization was applicable because the modification was only temporary.

  2. Error-inducing condition-based because the supervisor did not have a readily available power line for his other job—the absence of this power line constituting an error-inducing condition for this hoist. (For the other job, the *unavailability* of a power line may be due a different set of human error *causal factors*.)

  - **Is supervisor's value-based error indicative of a general disregard for authority and conformance to expectations? This question must be answered.**

Cause and Effects Analysis
Fishbone Diagram

- *Cause and effects analysis* or a *fishbone diagram* is used mostly to determine the cause of failure of a process.

- The *fishbone diagram* was originated by Kaoru Ishikawa (deceased) who greatly influenced the development of quality management systems at Japan's Kawasaki shipyards. Therefore, a *fishbone diagram* is also referred to as an *Ishikawa diagram*.

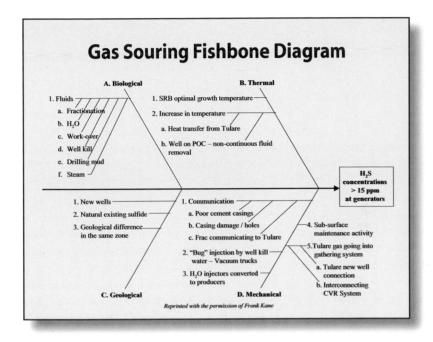

- The diagram is referred to as *fishbone* because the lines of the diagram resemble the bones of a fish.

- In the diagram on this slide, the *undesired effect* is shown to the extreme right hand side of the spinal column, at the head of the fish. The *undesired effect* is a concentration of hydrogen sulfide greater than 15 parts per million. The possible causes of this high level of concentration are shown in the bones attached to the spinal column.

- The causes that are of a similar nature, or that are related, are grouped together. In this diagram, these causes are grouped into biological, thermal, geological and mechanical categories. When similar or related causes are placed into groupings, the fishbone / *Ishikawa diagram* is further referred to as an *affinity diagram*.

- In an *affinity diagram*, the causes are determined by *brainstorming*, which is in contrast to working through a process *step-by-step*, and within each step, *M-by-M*. Brainstorming may not be as thorough.

- This diagram only shows the primary and secondary levels of possible causes for the undesired concentration. Of course, the *root causes* must be determined. For example, for bone *D.1.a* (mechanical / communication / poor cement casings) data would have to be collected to determine whether or not poor cement casings are contributing to the effect. If so, the *root causes* would have to be determined using additional brainstorming or, better still, using one of the previously described *root cause analysis* techniques, such as *hazard-barrier-effects analysis*.

- To determine *root causes*, in asking the *whys?*, additional levels of *cause* bones will need to be added to the diagram—with each additional level being a bone oriented in a different direction. The result can be visually daunting, even when a computer application is used to draw the diagram.

- For the answer to each *why?*, one must ask the standard questions as given on page 287. (There is no need to repeat those questions on this page.)

- Another concern is that the diagram does not foster the recognition of causal relationships. For example, temperature plays a controlling role in both the sulfur isotopic fractionation and amounts of hydrogen sulfide generation during thermochemical sulfate reduction. This diagram does not show the interaction between temperature and sulfur isotopic fractionation.

- Regardless of the concerns, the *fishbone / Ishikawa diagram* is a very popular *root cause analysis* tool in the manufacturing and chemical process industries, especially with the advent of software with which to draw the diagram. In this case, the tool was used for a gas extraction operation.

- An *affinity fishbone / Ishikawa diagram* is another *opening technique* because for any one bone in which there is an equipment or process failure, it may be necessary to also perform *failure mode and effects analysis* or *hazard-barrier-effects analysis* or both, or other analyses, as well.

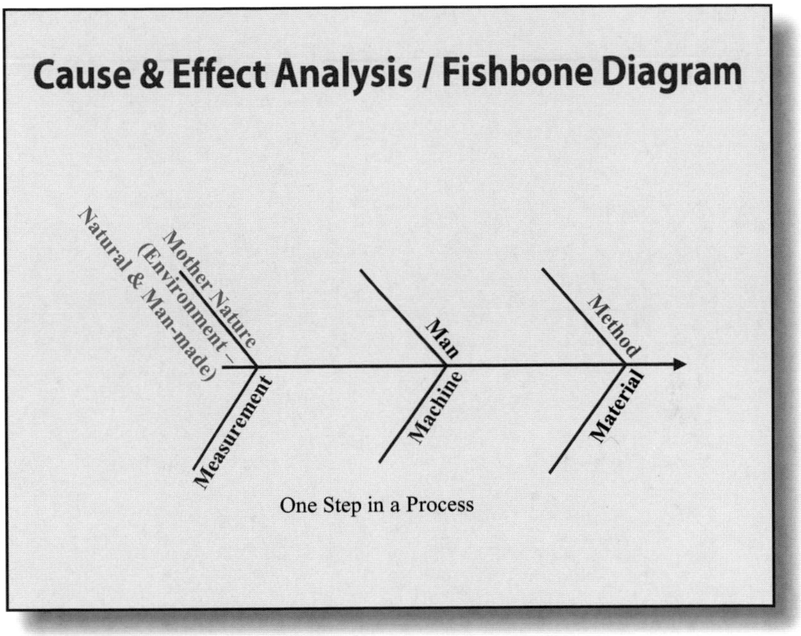
Cause & Effect Analysis / Fishbone Diagram
Mother Nature
(Environment –
Natural & Man-made)
Man
Method
Measurement
Machine
Material
One Step in a Process

- The *fishbone diagram* for a process may be organized by *step-by-step* in the process and, within each step, by *M-by-M*. When done this way, the technique is very similar to the *hazard-barrier-effects analysis* technique, except for the way in which the data are presented—in a diagram as contrasted to in a table.
- There is a significant difference in scope between the diagram on the previous slide and the diagram on this slide. The diagram in the previous slide is for a rather complex operation involving many processes. The diagram in this slide is for a single process only—for example, possibly for the cement casing placement process (*D.1.a*).
- One might use an *affinity diagram* of the type shown in the previous slide for the initial, overall view of an operation, and then use the *step-by-step, M-by-M, fishbone diagram* of the type shown in this slide for each process in the operation.
- For an application to a specific process, the approach used in this slide is more thorough than the brainstorming approach used in the previous slide—only because there is rigor and discipline in analyzing a process on a *step-by-step, M-by-M* basis compared to analyzing a process by brainstorming.

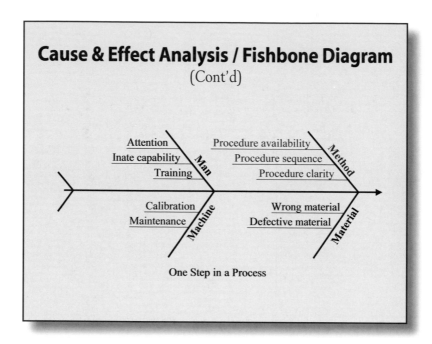

- This slide is merely to demonstrate how additional bones may be added to the previous slide.
- A couple of first level *M* bones have been omitted because of space limitations.
- Of course, in this diagram, in reality, there would be many more second and subsequent level bones on each primary bone.

Probabilistic Risk / Safety Analysis Using Event and Fault Trees

- Sometimes *probabilistic risk analysis, probabilistic risk assessment (PRA), probabilistic safety analysis,* and *probabilistic safety assessment (PSA)* all mean the same thing.

- Unfortunately, for *PRA / PSA* there are lots of variations in the terms used.

- *PRA / PSA* should be used concurrent with or upon completion of the design of a complex set of systems. It's used to demonstrate the safety of the complex when the *precautionary principle* is or should be in effect—i.e., when it must or should be proven that the complex is safe before it is offered for use. (See page 158.)

- Following an *event, PRA / PSA* can be used to identify the weakest links in the complex and the possible ways by which the event could have occurred. If the *PRA / PSA* does not already exist, valuable time will be lost.

- Of course, there's always the possibility that the *PRA / PSA* is incorrect because the initial analysis was flawed or because it was not maintained to be consistent with subsequent design changes to systems in the complex.

Probabilistic Risk Analysis (PRA) / Probabilistic Safety Analysis (PSA)

- Basic questions:
  - What can occur?
  - How likely is the occurrence?
  - What are the undesired effects of the occurrence?
  - Should the occurrence be prevented?
  - Can the occurrence be prevented?
  - Should the undesired effects of the occurrence be mitigated and ameliorated?
  - Can the undesired effects of the occurrence be mitigated and ameliorated?

- Basically, this slide lists the questions that are desired to be answered using *PRA / PSA*.

PRA / PSA (Cont'd)

- PRA / PSA tools:
  - Event tree
  - System model—represented by a fault tree
  - Statistical analysis

- An *event tree* links together systems. An *event tree* is a structure that is used to determine:
  - Interfaces among the systems;
  - What *end states / ultimate effects* will result if there is a challenge to a system, such as an *initiating [undesired] occurrence* as defined on the next page.
- In the design phase, if an *initiating [undesired] occurrence* were postulated, an *event tree* could be used to determine how the systems would behave in response to that occurrence, and what *end states* or ultimate effects could possibly result.
- A *fault tree* links together the subsystems, modules and components in a system. A *fault tree* is a structure that is used to determine:
  - Interfaces among the subsystems, modules and components of the system;
  - How a given system failure can occur;
  - Potential for a given system failure to result from a single component failure;
  - Probability of failure of the system.
- In the design phase, if a given system failure were postulated, a *fault tree* could be used determine how that system failure could come about (if at all) as a result of subsystem, module or component failure(s). Also, (in the opposite direction) if a given component failure were postulated, a *fault tree* could be used to determine the resulting system failure (if any).
- An *event tree* describes WHAT possible *end states* / ultimate effects may result when systems are challenged by an *initiating [undesired] occurrence*, whereas a *fault tree* describes HOW a system can fail.

PRA / PSA (Cont'd)
Event Tree Terminology

- **Initiating Occurrence**—A perturbation challenging the plant systems. The value used for an *initiating occurrence* is "frequency of occurrence per period".
- **Top Response**—The *success* or *failure* of the initial system in response to the *initiating occurrence*, or the *success* or *failure* of a subsequent system in response to the functional performance of the immediately preceding system.
- **Sequence**—A complete path through the event tree, from the initial *top response* to the final *top response*. A *sequence* is quantified by multiplying the frequency of the *initiating occurrence* by the probability of success or failure of each *top response* in the *sequence*.
- **End State**—The final effect for a given *sequence*. The final effect can be desired or undesired. If the undesired effect is significantly adverse, the *end state* could be an "event".

- In some industries, an *initiating occurrence* is referred to as an *initiating event*. In these same industries, the term *event* has a conflicting definition, it being an *undesired effect* of the greatest adverse consequence or of the highest adverse *significance*. (See pages 26–29.)

- In these same industries, a *top response* is referred to as a *top event*, resulting in the same conflict of terminology.

- Since identical *end states* may result from many different sequences, identical end states are usually combined together or *binned*, resulting in a smaller number of final unique *end states*.

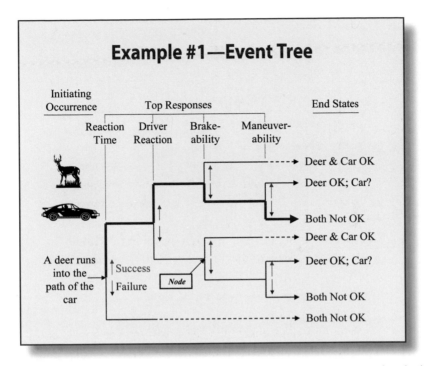

- This slides provides a simple example of an *event tree*. The tree is only as good as the logic of the *top responses*. For the sake of illustration, each of the top responses can be viewed as a system.
- In this tree, an arrow pointing upward represents a successful response; an arrow pointing downward represents a failed response.
- The point at which a response occurs is called a *node*.
- The *initiating occurrence* is the running of a deer into the path of a moving car.
- The analysis is limited to determining the *end states* of the deer and the car—not the *end states* of the driver or of any other persons or property that might be affected. That would require a more complex *event tree*.
- Working through a single *sequence*, shown by the bold, blue lines, if there is sufficient reaction time, there is success. If the driver reacts by depressing the brake pedal within the allowable time, there is success. If the brakes do not operate or are not effective because the roadway is wet, there is failure. (In a more sophisticated tree, the operation of the brakes and the condition of the road would be two separate systems, each with their own *nodes*.) If there is not sufficient time for the driver to maneuver the car there is failure. In this *sequence*, the deer strikes the car. Both are not okay. (Notice the assignment of responsibility—i.e., the deer striking the car rather than the car striking the deer, which may bear upon the insurance coverage. Ha, ha..)
- If, at the initial *node*, there is insufficient reaction time, the subsequent system *top responses* are not applicable. The second and subsequent *nodes* are *bypassed*, as represented by the lowest, longest dotted line. In this case, both the deer and the car are not okay.

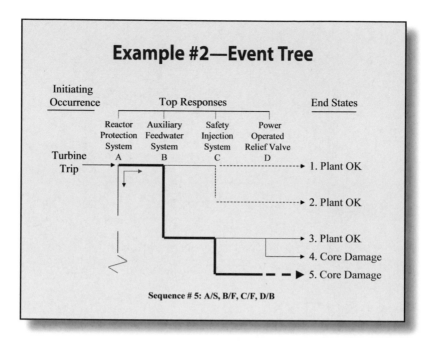

Example #2—Event Tree

Initiating Occurrence — Top Responses — End States

Reactor Protection System A	Auxiliary Feedwater System B	Safety Injection System C	Power Operated Relief Valve D	

Turbine Trip

1. Plant OK

2. Plant OK

3. Plant OK

4. Core Damage

5. Core Damage

Sequence # 5: A/S, B/F, C/F, D/B

- In this example, the *event tree* is drawn such that success is to the right, rather than up as in the previous example. Failure is down and then to the right.

- This *event tree* is *truncated* in the interest of conserving space. Failure of System A is not shown.

- The *initiating occurrence* is a turbine trip in a nuclear powered electricity generating plant. The turbine trip, itself, is an *event*, which as will be seen, can lead to even a more significant *ultimate event*.

- In this case, the turbine trip is challenging the operation of the reactor.

- *Sequence # 5* is as follows: *A*, Success; *B*, Failure; *C*, Failure; *D*, Bypass. In this sequence, when the turbine trips, the Reactor Protection System functions properly, Aux Feedwater fails, Safety Injection fails, and the operation of the Power Operated Relief Valve would make no difference one way or the other (bypassed). The result of this *sequence* is damage to the Reactor Core.

- In the preceding example and in this example, the *event tree* does its job by presenting all of the possible *end states*.

- It must then be decided whether or not an *end state* can be tolerated. In large part, that depends on the probability of success or failure of each of the *top response systems*.

- To determine the probability of the success or failure of each of the *top response systems*, the *fault tree* comes into use.

System Model

- Logical relationships of the components in a Top Response system
- Relationships represented by a *"Fault Tree"*, using *"Boolean Logic"*
  - *"AND"* Gate
  - *"OR"* Gate

- Describes the ability of the system to respond to a fault
- Ability quantified using statistical probability

- To review:
  - An *event tree* describes what possible end states / ultimate effects can result in response to an *initiating occurrence*.
  - A *fault tree* describes how a given system failure / *top response* can occur, or how a given component failure can result in a system failure / *top response*.
- A *fault tree* uses *Boolean logic*, a binary logic, represented by logic gates, the most frequently used being *AND* and *OR gates*.
- An *AND gate* is used if a given response can occur only when all of the conditions are satisfied. An *OR gate* is used if a given response can occur when any one of the conditions is satisfied.

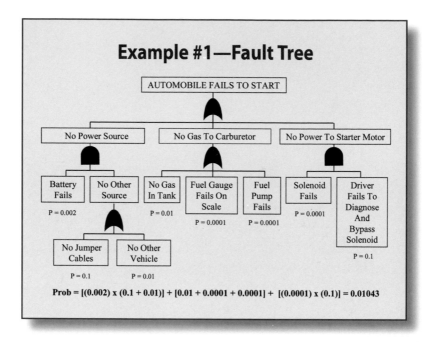

- In this example of a *fault tree*, the postulated *top response* [undesired] is that the automobile fails to start. The purpose of the tree is to determine the ways by which, or HOW the automobile can fail to start and to determine the probability of such failure.

- Again, the quality of the tree depends on the logic of the relationships drawn in the tree, the completeness of the conditions and the correctness of the logic gates. If any significant condition is omitted or if the wrong kind of logic gate is used, the tree can be misleading.

- For the purpose of exemplification, assume this tree to be logical.

- Any one of three conditions (No Power Source, No Gas To Carburetor *or* No Power To Starter Motor) can cause the automobile to fail to start. Following the No Power Source branch, the absence of power can be attributable to the failure of the battery *and* the *unavailability* of any other source of power. The No Other Source (of power) can be attributed to the *unavailability* of jumper cables *or* the *unavailability* of another vehicle from which to get a jump-start.

- At the end of each branch (the lowest level) the *probability of occurrence* of each condition has been determined. The overall probability that the automobile will fail to start can be calculated from the probabilities of the occurrence of these lowest-level conditions.

- The probability for Battery Fails is 0.002.

- The probability for No Jumper Cables is 0.1, and a probability for No Other Vehicle is 0.01. Either one of these two conditions can yield No Other Source; therefore, an *or gate* is used and the probability for No Other Source is (0.1 + 0.01).

- For No Power Source, both Battery Fails and No Other Source are conditions that must exist. Therefore an *AND gate* is used and the probability for No Power Source is 0.002 multiplied by (0.1 + 0.01). And so on, for each other branch.

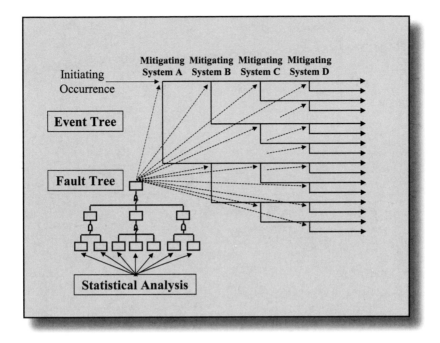

- Assume that the *fault tree* in the preceding slide were for the failure of *Mitigating System A* instead of for the failure of an automobile to start. The probability of failure determined from the *fault tree* would be applied in the *event tree* to the *node* for *Mitigating System A*.

- Similarly, the probability of failure derived from the *fault tree* for *Mitigating System B* would be applied in the *event tree* to the *nodes* for that *mitigating system*.

- And so on, for each *mitigating system* in the *event tree*. Thus, the probability of any *end state* can be determined. For example,

  - IF:
    - The number of *initiating occurrences* per year = 2.
    - *Top responses* (*Mitigating Systems A, B, C and D*) are independent of one another.
    - Failure probabilities for *top responses* are $A = 0.05$, $B = 0.2$, $C = 0.01$, and $D = 0.03$.
  - THEN:
    - For a single *initiating occurrence*, the probability of a given undesired *end state*, or ultimate *undesired effect*, for which there are no *bypasses* can be calculated as $0.05 \times 0.2 \times 0.01 \times 0.03 = 0.000003$. For the year, it would be twice that, or 0.000006.

- In the design phase, if the probability of an undesired *end state* is unacceptably high, the *event* and *fault trees* would help the designers to identify the most effective opportunities for reducing that probability.

- After the fact of an *event*, an actual undesired *end state*, the trees would help to identify the cause(s) and possible *preventive corrective actions*.

- Imagine the time that would be lost in having to prepare these *trees* subsequent to an *event*.

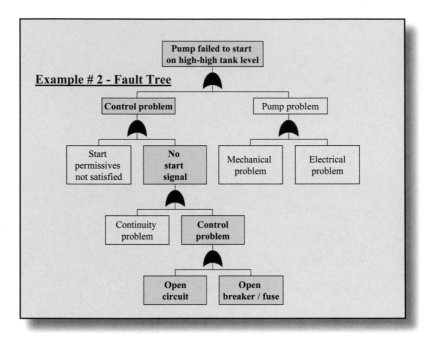

- A *fault tree* also can be used to identify how a single component or part failure can lead to a *top response*.
- In the *fault tree* on this slide, an open circuit or open breaker leads to the failure to pump fluid out of a vessel which is at it maximum storage capacity.
- If this *fault tree* were available during the design phase, there's a good chance that this design would have been altered to eliminate the *single failure paths* to the loss of the pumping function (represented in the *tree* by the string of uninterrupted *OR gates*).

- -

- *PRA / PSA* and *event* and *fault trees* have been addressed here at an intermediate level. One source of more advanced information is the *Fault Tree Handbook, NUREG-0492*, published by the United States Nuclear Regulatory Commission.

Management Oversight and Risk Tree

- The *Management Oversight and Risk Tree (MORT)* technique was developed in the mid 1970s at the Department of Energy (DOE) Idaho Nuclear Laboratory (at that time, called the Idaho National Engineering Laboratory).

- The *MORT* chart and accompanying MORT Reference (user's manual) are in the public domain and are available from DOE. (At least one consulting company has revised the MORT documentation and has laid claim to the copyright of the revised documentation.)

- The chart is printed on 24" x 36" blueprint paper. The items and sub-items in the chart are depicted as in an enterprise's personnel organization chart. The items / sub-items in each branch of the chart constitute possible causes of a *problem*. Basically, the chart constitutes a checklist of possible causes of a *problem*, with the causes organized into various administrative and technical branches.

- In using MORT, one would review each branch of the chart to determine whether or not each item / sub-item in the branch has the potential for being a *root* or *contributing cause* of the *problem*. If so, data would be acquired with which to make a determination regarding the impact of the item / sub-item. In the near-final analysis, the chart would be annotated with various colors to identify (a) the items / sub-items that are *causal factors*, (b) those that are not, and (c) those for which still additional data must be acquired in order to make the determination regarding their impact.

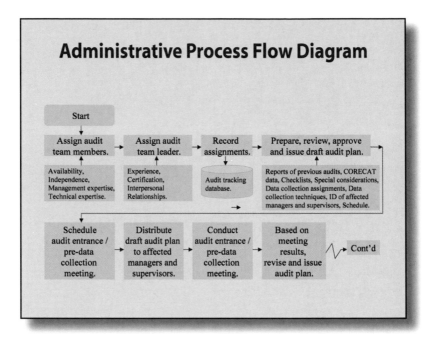

- This slide shows a *process flow diagram* for the performance of a single internal *quality audit*. The diagram excludes the process for establishing the overall *audit* program for a given *audit* cycle. The diagram is *truncated* in consideration of space limitations.

- A process flow diagram is a tool used for the design of the process to begin with. If the *flow diagram* is unavailable at the time of an *event* or *near miss*, the diagram may be created as a tool used for *root cause analysis*.

- For example, assume that *significant problems* were going *undetected* by *audit*, but were being *detected* later by a higher level oversight group or by the customer, client, community or regulatory agency. A diagram like the one on the slide might be used to identify areas that should be analyzed to determine the *root* and *contributing causes* for the *problem*.

- Team member assignment, team leader assignment, plan preparation / review / approval, and identification of right people to attend the entrance meeting would be areas of interest to *investigate* for possible causes of the *problem*. The *audit* tracking database and the scheduling of meetings probably would be of little interest for this kind of *problem*.

- Certainly, one might be able to identify these areas of interest without the *process flow diagram*, but it provides a level of discipline and rigor with which to help to assure that all of the appropriate areas of interest are considered.

- The *process flow diagram* may not provide the specificity needed for the *root cause analysis*. If *audit plan* could be an area of interest and *data collection techniques* a sub-area of interest, the analyst would have to evaluate the specifics (or lack thereof) in the written procedure and in actual practice.

- Also, analysis of the *process flow diagram* makes it so much easier to identify voids or inadequacies in the process, which may be *root* or *contributing causes* of the *problem*.

- For the sake of completion, the remainder of the process flow is given below in tabular form.
- Collecting the *audit* data
  - *Program-based* versus *performance-based* versus *results-based* data
  - *Benchmarking*
  - *Operating experience*
  - *Interviews*
  - Real time *observations*
  - Records
  - Reports
  - Status of resolution of prior issues
  - Data *sampling*
  - Specialized data collection techniques
- Analyzing *audit* data
  - *Facts* versus *conclusions*
  - Veracity of the *facts*
  - Addressing factual disagreement
  - *Pulling the string*
  - *Rolling-up* related condition
  - Analyzing *audit* data on a facility-wide basis—e.g., *common cause analysis*
- Reporting results during the *audit*
- Conducting the exit / post-data analysis meeting
- Preparing and issuing the written *audit report*
  - Structure
  - *Problem significance*
  - *Problem* ownership
  - Timeliness
- Entering *problems* into the CORECAT tool

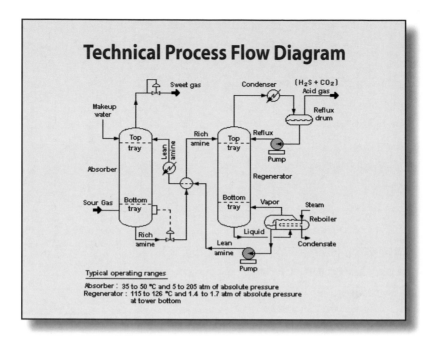

- This slide shows a *technical process flow diagram*.

- The advantages of a technical *process flow diagram* are the same as those described on the preceding page for an administrative *process flow diagram*.

- In this case, if there were a *problem* with acid gas, the diagram would help to identify areas from which data should be collected to determine the source of the *problem*.

- Of course, it takes expertise to prepare either kind of *process flow diagram*—administrative process or technical process.

- The terms *process flow diagram*, *process map* and *process flow chart* seem to this presenter to be a synonyms.

- A *process flow diagram* also can be used to identify the elements or steps of the process that contribute the highest value toward the attainment of the objectives of the process. In identifying the high value elements, the intent here is to provide additional assurance of the quality of the design of these elements and their consistent implementation.

- The next five pages provide a *process flow diagram* converted to a tabular format, for the creation, distribution and application of biosolids. This is at a somewhat coarse or general level. For example, for marine operations, notice that the procedures for the control of spills and for the reporting of spills to the environmental regulatory agency are not listed singularly but may be included in the "etc" line item. Also, test procedures are omitted from the table.

- One major objective of the *process flow table* is to determine the extent to which each process, sub-process or process element is adequately covered by documented administrative and technical procedures.

Value Chain Category	Critical Control Points (CCP)	Responsible Organization	Document(s) for the Operational Control of the CCP	Related Test Procedure(s)
Pretreatment	Users Classified As "Significant Industrial Users"	Pollution Prevention & Monitoring Division	• Sewage use ordinances and regulations. • Procedure XXX— Processing permit applications, issuing permits, inspecting against permit requirements and enforcing permit requirements. • Permits, themselves. • Etc.	
	Users Classified As "Industrial Users"	Pollution Prevention & Monitoring Division	• Sewage use ordinances and regulations. • Procedure XXX— Inspecting against requirements and enforcing requirements. • Etc.	
	Septage Hauler	Pollution Prevention & Monitoring Division	• Sewage use ordinances and regulations. • Procedure XXX— Processing permit applications, issuing permits, inspecting against permit requirements and enforcing permit requirements. • Permits, themselves. • Etc.	
WWTP Liquid Processes	Headworks— Influent	Process Engineering Section & Operations Division (Plant Operators)	• Procedure XXX— Monitoring influent. • Etc.	
	Headworks— Bar Screens	Process Engineering Section & Operations Division (Plant Operators)	• Procedure XXX—Bar screen operation • Procedure XXX— Inspection and maintenance of bar screen equipment • Etc.	

Value Chain Category	Critical Control Points (CCP)	Responsible Organization	Document(s) for the Operational Control of the CCP	Related Test Procedure(s)
WWTP Liquid Processes (Continued)	Headworks—Grit Basins	Process Engineering Section & Operations Division (Plant Operators)	• Procedure XXX—Grit basin operation • Procedure XXX—Inspection and maintenance of grit basin equipment. • Etc.	
	Primary Clarifiers	Process Engineering Section & Operations Division (Plant Operators)	• Procedure XXX—Primary clarifier operation • Procedure XXX—Inspection and maintenance of primary clarifier equipment. • Etc.	
	Secondary Clarifiers	Process Engineering Section & Operations Division (Plant Operators)	• Procedure XXX—Secondary clarifier operation • Procedure XXX—Inspection and maintenance of secondary clarifier equipment. • Etc.	
	Grease Processing	Process Engineering Section & Operations Division (Plant Operators)	• Procedure XXX—Grease processing operations • Procedure XXX—Inspection and maintenance of grease processing equipment. • Etc.	
Stabilization Processes	Solids Thickening	Process Engineering Section & Operations Division (Plant Operators)	• Procedure XXX—Solids thickening operations • Procedure XXX—Inspection and maintenance of solids thickening equipment. • Etc.	

Value Chain Category	Critical Control Points (CCP)	Responsible Organization	Document(s) for the Operational Control of the CCP	Related Test Procedure(s)
Stabilization Processes (Continued)	Solids Holding Tanks	Process Engineering Section & Operations Division (Plant Operators)	• Procedure XXX—Solids holding tank operations • Procedure XXX—Inspection and maintenance of solids holding tank equipment. • Etc.	
	Anaerobic Digesters	Process Engineering Section & Operations Division (Plant Operators)	• Procedure XXX—Anaerobic operations • Procedure XXX—Inspection and maintenance of anaerobic digesters. •Etc.	
Conditioning & Dewatering	Solids Processing / Dewatering	Process Engineering Section & Operations Division (Plant Operators)	• Procedure XXX—Solids conditioning operations • Procedure XXX—Inspection and maintenance of solids conditioning equipment. • Procedure XXX—Centrifuge operations • Procedure XXX—Inspection and maintenance of centrifuge equipment. •Etc.	
	Ferric	Process Engineering Section & Operations Division (Plant Operators)	• Procedure XXX—Application of ferric chloride • Etc.	

Value Chain Category	Critical Control Points (CCP)	Responsible Organization	Document(s) for the Operational Control of the CCP	Related Test Procedure(s)
WWTP Odor Control	WWTP	Process Engineering Section & Operations Division (Plant Operators)	• Procedure XXX—Odor monitoring and control • Procedure XXX—Processing odor complaints • Procedure XXX—Inspection and maintenance of odor control equipment. • Etc.	
Biosolids Transport	Piping	Collections Facilities Operations Division	• Procedure XXX—Inspection and maintenance of piping. • Etc.	
	Barges	Marine Section	• Barge operations ordinances and regulations • Procedure XXX—Loading, routing and operation of barges • Procedure XXX—Inspection and maintanance of barges • Etc.	
	Trucks	Biosolids Management Section, Plant Operators & Contractors	• Procedure XXX—Distribution of biosolids to contractors. • Procedure XXX—Loading and routing of contractor trucks. • Truck operations ordinances and regulations • Contracts XXX—Requirements applicable to the Contractors • Contractor Procedure XXX—Loading, routing and operation of Contractor trucks. • Contractor Procedure XXX—Inspection and maintenance of Contractor trucks. • Etc.	

Value Chain Category	Critical Control Points (CCP)	Responsible Organization	Document(s) for the Operational Control of the CCP	Related Test Procedure(s)
Biosolids Final Disposition	Direct land application Pellitization Composting Land application	Biosolids Management Section & Contractors	• Ditto, all of the immediately above. • Ordinances and regulations applicable to biosolids land applications. • Contractor Procedures XXX—Maintenance of permits • Contractor Procedures XXX—Additional processing operations, particularly for conditioning and dewatering operations, and for inspection of dewatering equipment. • Etc.	

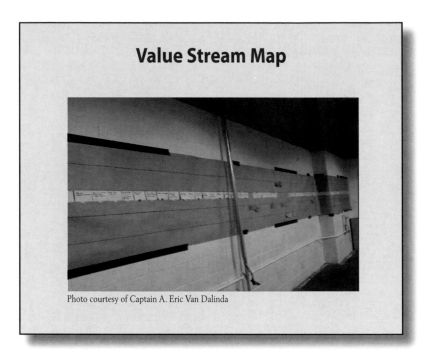

Value Stream Map

Photo courtesy of Captain A. Eric Van Dalinda

- If the problem is that a process is too time consuming or too costly, the problem may be solved by the analysis of a value stream map.
- A value stream map is a flow diagram of each task in the process to the level of the greatest detail for the task.
- Each task is analyzed as to its value to the process by asking the following questions:
  - Is the task required by law (e.g., by regulatory agency rule or regulation)?
  - Is the task required by a customer?
  - Does the task provide a technical benefit?
  - Does the task provide a cost benefit?
- If there is not at least one "yes" among the answers to the questions, the value of the task is suspect and it may be deleted from the process.
- Also, each task is analyzed from the perspective of whether or not it can be performed with equal or better technical excellence with less resources—particularly less time.
- The slide is a photograph of a typical value stream map. The map can cover many walls.

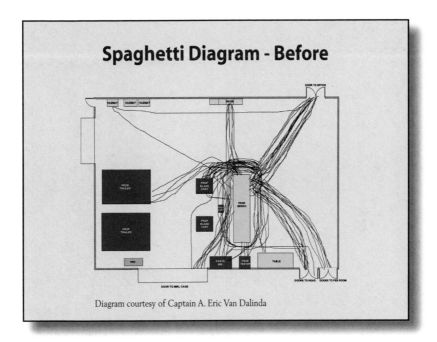

Diagram courtesy of Captain A. Eric Van Dalinda

- In addition, as part of the value stream analysis, the movement of people machines, material and parts can be flowed-diagramed by means of a continuous lines showing the movement.

- This type of flow diagram is known as a "spaghetti diagram".

- The diagram in the slide represents the movement of people before changes were made to the process.

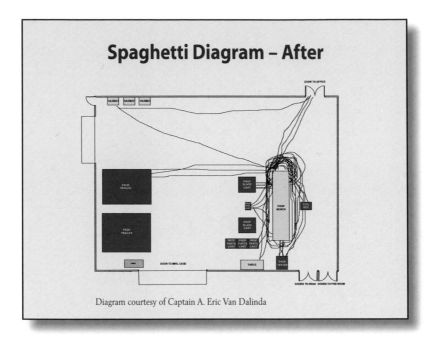

Diagram courtesy of Captain A. Eric Van Dalinda

- The diagram in the slide represents the movement of people after changes were made to the process—obviously, a significant reduction in movement and corresponding saving in time.

These Techniques Are Used To:

- Identify administrative process, technical process and equipment (and possibly human) design weaknesses so as to facilitate the establishment of barriers by which to:
  - Prevent hazards from being actuated by human error;
  - Detect error or actuated hazards;
  - Mitigate and ameliorate the undesired effects of these hazards.
- Identify root and contributing causes of undesired effects (e.g., events) so as to facilitate the correction or elimination of their causes in order to prevent or significantly reduce the probability of the recurrence of these undesired effects.

- These techniques are used to *prevent* losses—of life, injury, health, environmental protection, trust in relationships, and money. These techniques are used also to gain market advantage.

- When used in the design phase (i.e., design of the administrative process, technical processes and equipment) these techniques are proactive.

- When used following the occurrence of an *undesired effect*, the techniques are reactive.

- It doesn't make any difference whether the equipment (a) is the product or a part of the product, or (b) is used to create the product. In either case, the equipment must provide *barriers* to *error*.

- It doesn't make any difference whether the process (a) is the product or a part of the product, or (b) is used to create the product. In either case, the process must provide *barriers* to *error*.

Question: What are some common *errors* in the performance of formal *root cause analysis*?

Common Errors in Formal Root Cause Analysis

- **Failing to adhere to the discipline of the technique**
- Using unqualified personnel to perform the analysis
- Speculating as to a root cause
- Accepting a symptom or failure mode as a root cause
- Limiting the analysis to the identification of a single root cause
- Accepting an immediately preceding occurrence as a root cause
- Assuming that a correlation between two things constitutes a cause and effect relationship
- **Failing to identify the human error root cause(s)**

- These *errors* are not in any order of significance or frequency of occurrence. However, by the use of bold font, it's apparent which are thought to be the most significant.

Question: What are some other types of *error* in the performance of formal *root cause analysis?*

Answer:

- Accepting an opinion or conclusion as an observation or fact.
- Using inflammatory, prejudicial language in the *root cause analysis report*—language that can contribute to additional financial loss.
- Omitting causes based on the *belief* that their correction is not feasible.
- Unnecessarily *truncating* the analysis.

346

Failure Modes vs. Failure Causes

- The table on the next page was obtained from an industry operating experience (OE) program. (See page 242.) Purportedly, this table provides a list of *failure causes* for civil / mechanical / structural and electrical / electronic equipment failures. The purpose of this table is to enable participants in the OE program to standardize the identification of the causes of their equipment failures.

- Unfortunately, however, the table intermingles (a) *failure causes*, (b) *failure modes* and (c) *things that have the failure*, that are neither causes nor modes. There should be separate standardized tables for each of these three different *data elements* or data fields. Combining these three types of data into a single *data element* / data field results in the data being confounded. (See page 233.)

- A *failure mode* is the way or manner in which a failure occurs. A failure cause is the reason for the failure occurrence.

- From this table, following are examples of the intermixing that yields data confounding.

  - *Abnormal Wear(out)* [*Code AH*], and *Binding/sticking* [*Code BK*] are *failure modes*. These are not *failure causes*. The reason for the wear-out or binding is not indicated.

  - *Particulate Contamination* [*Code AC*] is a *failure cause*. Binding or sticking is a possible *mode* of failure resulting from particulate contamination.

  - *Bearing Failure* [*Code BS*] is neither a *failure cause* nor a *failure mode*. The bearing is the *thing that has the failure*. Seizure would be a *failure mode* and, in a separate field, Bearing would be identified as the *thing that has the failure* (the seizure).

- The most major point of the foregoing is that in the performance of *root cause analysis*, be sure to identify causes and not settle merely for *modes*.

Confounding-Failure Modes, Failure Causes and Things That Have The Problem

Civil/Mechanical/Structural	Electrical/Electronic
AA. Wrong Part	AA. Wrong Part
AB. Foreign Material / Foreign Substance	AL. Setpoint Drift
AC. Particulate Contamination	AP. Defective Connection
AD. Normal Wear	AQ. Abnormal Stress
AE. Lubrication Problem	AR. Insulation Breakdown
AF. Welding Process	AS. Shorted / grounded
AG. Abnormal Stress	AT. Open Circuit
AH. Abnormal Wear	AU. Contact Degradation
AJ. Incorrect Material	AW. Circuit Defective
AK. Valve Seat Condition	AX. Burned / Burned Out
AL. Setpoint Drift	AY. Electrical Overload
AV. Loose Parts	AZ. Material Defect
AZ. Material Defect	BE. Dirty
BB. Damage	BH. Out of Calibration
BC. Out of Adjustment	BL. Aging / Cycle Fatigue
BD. Aging / Cycle Fatigue	BP. Environmental Condition
BE. Dirty	BT. Software
BF. Flow Obstruction	BV. Circuit Card
BG. Corrosion	BX. Other
BK. Binding / Sticking	
BM. Interference	
BP. Environmental Condition	
BR. Gasket / O-ring / Seal Failure	
BS. Bearing Failure	

Scenario of an Equipment Failure

Root Causes (Whys)	Root Causes (Whys)	
Cause (Why)	Degradation Influences	Main Feed Pump 2A shaft journal bearing **loses lubrication**.
Cause (Why)	Degradation Mechanism	Main Feed Pump 2A shaft journal bearing **thermally expands**.
Failure Mode	Failure Mode or Failure Mechanism	Main Feed Pump 2A shaft journal bearing **seizes**.
Intermediate Effect	Intermediate Effect	Steam Generator 2A **loses flow** from Main Feed Pump 2A.
Intermediate Effect	Intermediate Effect	Steam Generator 2A **steam level gets low**.
Ultimate Effect	Ultimate Effect	Reactor **trips**.

- The right-most column of the table in this slide provides a sequence of conditions that lead to a nuclear reactor trip. The left-most column provides the terminology for each of the conditions in the sequence. The center column provides alternative terminology for the conditions in the sequence—for those who would prefer more sophisticated terminology.

- In the center column, notice that *Degradation Influences* is limited to the physical condition of lost lubrication. Possibly a leakage condition could be a still lower level *degradation influence*. Possibly administrative conditions could be still lower degradation influences. The terminology in the left-most column appears to be simpler and easier to implement with no loss of data.

- The main point is that a distinction must always be made between *failure mode* and *failure cause*. The way by which the bearing failed is seizure. By any other names, all of the earlier conditions are causes.

Physical Items Failure Because of:

- Design deficiency
- Construction, installation, assembly or fabrication deficiency
- Handling, storage or shipping deficiency
- Application deficiency
- Preventive maintenance deficiency
- Operations deficiency
- Run-to-failure

- *Design deficiency*—Design is inadequate, including design for the item's *manufacturability / constructability*, handling / storage, application, *preventive maintenance* (which also includes *reliability centered maintenance*), and operations.
- *Construction, installation, assembly or fabrication deficiency*—Item is not made in accordance with it design requirements.
- *Handling, storage, or shipping deficiency*—Item is not handled, stored or shipped in accordance with its design requirements.
- *Application deficiency*—Item is misapplied, i.e., item is applied: (a) for a purpose for which it was not intended; (b) in an environment for which it was not designed; or (c) under load conditions for which it was not designed.
- *Preventive maintenance deficiency*—*Preventive maintenance* is not performed in accordance with *preventive maintenance* design requirements, including requirement for performance monitoring.
- *Operations deficiency*—Item is operated beyond it design parameters during *testing* or operations.
- *Run-to-failure*—Item is operated beyond its life expectancy. (This may be a good or bad decision or it may be due to ignorance of the component's life expectancy—a decision by default.)

Marguglio's Taxonomy of Human Error Causal Factors

Knowledge-based – **Error based on behavior:**	**Lacking receipt of the knowledge of the requirement, expectation or need**
Cognition-based – **Error based on behavior:**	**Lacking ability to process the knowledge (memorize, understand, apply, analyze, synthesize or evaluate the requirement, expectation or need)**
Value-based or Belief-based – **Error based on behavior:**	**Lacking acceptance of the requirement, expectation or need**
Error-Inducing Condition / **Error-Likely Situation-based –** **Error based on behavior:**	**Lacking recognition of the error-inducing condition / error-likely situation or lacking appropriate behavior to counteract the condition / situation**
Reflexive-based / Reactive-based – **Error based on behavior:**	**Lacking conservative judgment in making an immediate response to a stimulus**
Skill based – **Error based on behavior:**	**Lacking manual dexterity**
Lapse-based – **Error based on behavior:**	**Lacking attention**

- Except for good decisions to *run to failure*, physical item failures are caused by human failures of the types given in the taxonomy.

Question: Recalling to mind *extent of problem analysis*, what is meant by *extent of cause analysis?*

Extent of Cause Analysis

- The root and contributing causes in the primarily affected process
- Similar types of causes in the primarily affected process
- The root and contributing causes in similar types of processes
- Similar types of causes in similar types of processes

Primary Process Similar Causes	Primary Process R / C Causes
Similar Processes R / C Causes	Similar Processes Similar Causes

- On pages 255–256, it was noted that prior to the performance of *root cause analysis*, it's a good practice to perform *extent of problem analysis*. The purpose of *extent of problem analysis* is to identify the scope of the existence of the *problem*.

- *Extent of cause analysis* applies the same principle in reverse.

- The final step in any *root cause analysis*, should be the determination of the extent to which the *root* and *contributing causes* (the primary causes) may exist elsewhere—beyond their existence in the initially reported failed process (the primary process) or failed equipment.

Question: What are the benefits correcting causes identified by extent of cause analysis?

Answer:

- *Extent of cause analysis* helps to *prevent* the same and similar causes from continuing to exist and, possibly, even festering and ultimately resulting in an additional failure or *event*.

- *Extent of cause analysis* helps to avoid customer and regulatory agency dissatisfaction that would exist were a cause, identified by *root cause analysis*, allowed to exist elsewhere and ultimately result in a new *event*. Again, the perception would be that the *preventive corrective action* process has an unduly narrow span of vision. There would be little tolerance for any new *event* resulting from previously identified causes.

Corrective Action

- Having performed *root cause analysis* to identify *root* and *contributing causes*, and having performed extent of cause analysis, the next steps are the acquisition of commitments for *corrective action*, its performance, and the verification of its effectiveness—as will be covered in the following pages.

Question: What are the various types of *corrective action*?

Types of Corrective Action

Fix the thing that is broken	*Hardware / Document / Human corrective action* (human implementation of a process)
Fix the effect	*Ameliorative corrective action*
Fix the causes	*Preventive corrective action*
Fix to the process **temporarily**, pending the completion of preventive corrective action	*Compensatory corrective action*

- For each undesired occurrence, the four types of *corrective action* shown in this slide must be considered.

- For example:

  - A device fails within a short time of its initial operation. The function of the device is to measure the amount of pollutant in a fluid being discharged to a body of water at a given outfall, to compare the amount of pollutant to the allowable limit, and to signal the shutdown of the outfall if the pollutant exceeds the allowable limit. The failure results in the discharge of a pollutant beyond the allowable limit.

  - The *root causes* of the failure are determined to be:

    - The design of the device is inadequate. The device cannot withstand its operational environment—i.e., the device lacks *environmental qualification* and does not *fail safe*;

    - The Engineering Department administrative procedure is not sufficiently specific as to the requirements for *environmental qualification* and analytical methods by which to evaluate the *quality of design*;

    - Engineering managers, supervisors and individual contributors lacked either knowledge or cognitive abilities regarding *environmental qualification* and design analysis techniques.

    - (Additional analysis is ongoing to determine why the Engineering Department staff lacked the knowledge or cognitive abilities regarding equipment *environmental qualification*. *Corrective action* on this score is not a part of this example.)

- Example (Cont'd)
  - The *corrective actions* are as follows:
    - *Hardware corrective action*: The failed device is replaced with one of identical design. Usually, this type of action is not recorded and tracked in the *CORECAT* tool. Rather, it's addressed in the *corrective maintenance* tool.
    - *Ameliorative corrective action*: The discharged pollutant is removed from the water body.
  - *Preventive corrective actions*:
    1. The Engineering staff is trained regarding *environmental qualification*.
    2. The Engineering Administrative Procedure is corrected.
    3. A design modification is released for the installation of a new, *environmentally qualified* device. The new device is of a specialty design, required to be tested to verify its *environmental qualification*. The fabrication and testing of the new device, (one for testing and one for actual installation) and subsequent delivery from the supplier, will take three months.
  - *Compensatory corrective actions*: Pending the delivery and installation of the new, *environmentally qualified* device, to allow the plant to continue to operate with environmental safety:
    1. A lesser design modification is released requiring the existing device (the non-*environmentally qualified* device) to be installed in series, such that if either device measures pollutant beyond allowable, the shutdown signal will be generated.
    2. The Maintenance organization is officially instructed to immediately replace either device in series should one fail, such as to retain the safety of redundancy.

Preventive Corrective Action Objectives

- Get the greatest return on investment from preventive corrective actions.
- Institutionalize the fixes to the root and contributing causes.
- Avoid solution-created problems.
- Perform in accordance with action commitments.

- The next two pages provide guidance on how to achieve the objective of the *greatest return on investment (ROI)* from *preventive corrective actions*.
- By *institutionalizing* a fix, it's being made the norm.
- Fixes are *institutionalized* by officially releasing the revised design document for the hardware design correction, or by officially issuing the revised written policy or written procedure for the process design correction, or by officially issuing a revision for the correction of any other type of document (e.g., purchase order, software application [a special type of procedure], training document, financial report).
- Fixes to human *root* and *contributing causes* are *institutionalized* by acquiring consistent correct *behavior* going forward—for example, by (a) imparting additional knowledge or cognition, (b) improving *attitude* such as to value and accept requirements, (c) promoting *behavior* to *counteract error-inducing conditions*, (d) promoting thought processes and *behavior* that lead to conservative decisions, and (e) eliminating the causes of inattentiveness. Sometimes, as a last resort, fixes to human *root* and *contributing causes* are *institutionalized* by personnel reassignment or release.
- In the absence of *institutionalization*, *problem* causes will recur. Conditions will revert to those that existed prior to the correction.

Preventive Corrective Action Decision Rules

- Human safety and health benefit
- Environmental benefit
- Political benefit
- $ benefit exceeds $ cost
  - Cut the estimated benefit in half
  - Double the estimated cost

- When human safety and health are involved, the *preventive corrective action* should be taken regardless of its cost.
- When there are environmental and political benefits, generally, this presenter recommends that the *preventive corrective action* be taken unless the cost outrageously exceeds the benefit.
- Of course, funds always should be available for *preventive corrective action* addressing human safety and health *problems*, and for environmental and political *problems* with the constraint given in the preceding bullet.
- Sometimes, in one's fervor, the estimate of the benefit may be exaggerated and the estimate of the cost may be understated, leading to the acceptance of a *preventive corrective action* project that results in an actual loss. It's *good practice* for the project sponsor, the one from whose account the expenses will be charged, to carefully scrutinize these estimates.
- One of the best tools for choosing among various *preventive corrective action* options is a *decision matrix*. The reader is referred to Nancy R. Tague's *The Quality Toolbox, Second Edition*, ASQ Quality Press, 2004, pages 219–223—an excellent book.

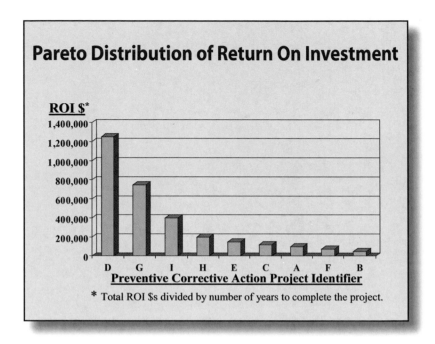

Pareto Distribution of Return On Investment

ROI $*

* Total ROI $s divided by number of years to complete the project.

- For *preventive corrective action* projects for which there are dollar benefits only, as contrasted to unquantifiable human safety and health, environmental and political benefits, it's also *good practice* to create a *Pareto chart* by which to array the projects in their order of greatest to least dollar ROI.

- In the chart on the slide, the total ROI for each project is converted to a per annum return.

- In an ideal situation, money would be available to complete all of the projects for which there is a return. However, if not, certainly projects would be funded in the approximate sequence of the amount of their annualized return—*approximate* because subsequent to starting one project, certainly another project could arise with a higher return.

- A *Pareto chart* is named for Vilfredo Pareto (1848–1923) who become known mostly for his writings on the mal-distribution of wealth, indicating that a small percentage of the populace had a disproportionately large percentage of the wealth.

- In addition to wealth, mal-distribution applies to many other things. For example, a small number of types of *defects* or a small number of types of *problems* account for a disproportionately large percentage of the waste in an enterprise. Dr Joseph Juran, referred to this small number as the *vital few* and urged that priority be given to eliminate the causes of the *vital few*.

- This principle of mal-distribution has been popularized and morphed into the *80/20 rule*—80 percent of something is attributable to 20 percent of something. Of course, for any given actual situation, the numbers can vary substantially—e.g., 70/30 or 90/10.

Question: What are the elements of information needed for a *corrective action commitment*?

Elements of a Corrective Action Commitment

- What is to be done?

- Why does it correct the cause?

- How is it to be institutionalized?

- Who is responsible for doing it?

- When is it to be completed?

- If the completion date is far off, what are the mileposts along the way toward completion, and what is the schedule for the completion of each milepost?

- When is it to be effective?

- Earlier, it was noted that each *data element* for a *problem statements* should be collected and recorded in separate field in the *CORECAT* tool. Similarly, each *data element* for a *corrective action commitment* also should be collected and recorded in a separate field. In the absence of a separate fields, there's an increased chance that a *data element* will be missed and that the commitment will be flawed.

- A *milepost* is an action that must be completed to demonstrate a significant change or significant progress in the state of a project.

- As for any project to be performed over an extended period, mileposts are required to enable the project manager to assess progress, and to improve the opportunity to recover the overall schedule if any single milepost is not met. It's unacceptable to arrive at the date committed for completion of the project, only to learn that there has been no progress or minimal progress and that actual completion is long into the future.

- Sometimes, the date on which the *preventive corrective action* is to become fully effective will lag the date on which the action is to be completed. In such a case, it's *good practice* to have both dates in the commitment. For example, there may be a commitment to complete a cost reduction design change for a procured item by January 15. There may be a commitment to complete a corresponding purchase order change by January 31. However, thereafter, there may still be old items in the supplier's pipeline for which scrappage would be uneconomical. It would be well to know when the old items will be completely out of the supplier's pipeline.

Verification of the Effectiveness of Preventive Corrective Action

- Performance metric
- Statistical process control chart
- "t" and similar tests
- Problem on–problem off test
- Hardware inspection and test
- Audit, surveillance or performance self-assessment

- The best way to verify that a *preventive corrective action* has been effective is by measurement, using a *performance metric*. For example, the measurement might be the frequency with which a given *problem* occurred prior to the *preventive corrective action* compared to the frequency with which the same *problem* occurs (hopefully zero) subsequent to the *preventive corrective action*.

- A *statistical process control chart*, as shown on the next page, is a special type of *performance metric*.

- *Statistical "t"* and similar tests can be used to determine whether there is a statistically significant difference between the measures before the *preventive corrective action* and the measures after the *preventive corrective action*.

- Sometimes a *test* can be devised to demonstrate that certain measures or conditions turn on the *problem* and corrected measures or conditions turns off the *problem*—a *problem on-problem off test*.

- *Inspection* or *test* results before the action compared to the results after the action will indicate the effectiveness of the action.

- Timely *audit, surveillance* and *performance self-assessment* can be used to verify that the action committed to be taken was, in fact, taken.

- The worst way by which to verify the effective of the *preventive corrective action* is to compare the rates of customer returns or complaints before to the rates after the *preventive corrective action*. Don't let the customer be the verifier of the effectiveness of the action.

- Of course, the *CORECAT* tool must provide for the recording of the individual and organization responsible for the verification, the technique to be used for the verification, the verification completion date, and the verification result.

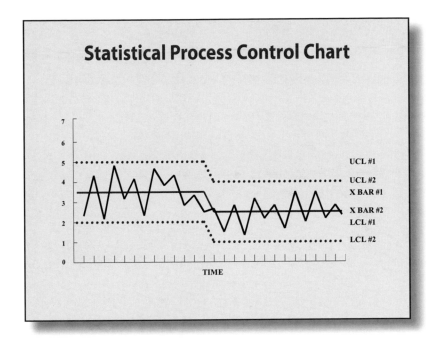

- In the chart on the slide, the *arithmetic mean (X Bar)* of the measures for the given parameter reduced favorably from approximately 3.5 (X BAR #1) to approximately 2.5 (X BAR # 2). Based on the large number of the sequential measures now falling below the original X BAR #1, it's almost certain that the process improvement action was effective.

Conditions Yielding
Ineffective Preventive Corrective Action

- The problem is wrongly defined; the wrong problem is addressed.
- Causal factor analysis is not performed.
- Causal factor analysis is inaccurate.
- Causal factor analysis is superficial.
- Action does not address the cause of the problem.
- Action is not adequately implemented.
- Verification of the effectiveness of the action is, itself, ineffective.
- Implemented action is not rigorously sustained.

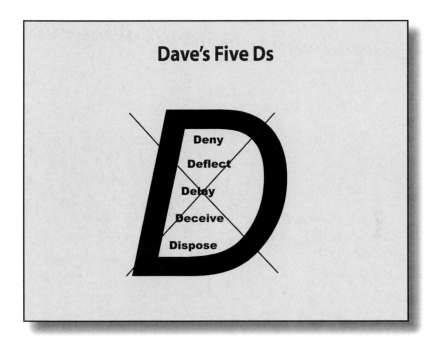

- The following story is fictitious:
  - Dave has exceptionally high intelligence. He has a master's degree in a technical field. He has a cutting wit. He has the potential to become an officer in the large enterprise at which he is employed.
  - Unfortunately, Dave is having difficulty in negotiating adequate *corrective action commitments*. In addition, progress against the negotiated *commitments* is poor.
  - Possibly to vent his frustration, he created an icon of his *five Ds*, sans the red X, and mounted this icon on the wall of his office space.
  - Dave's public, iconoclastic display of his dissatisfaction labels him a pariah among his peers and superiors and threatens his progress in the enterprise.
  - It's best for Dave to work more prudently, on a case-by-case basis, until he has the position and power to exorcise the *five Ds*. This would not be hypocritical; it would be practical. Dave should remove the icon.
- Anyone responsible for negotiating and tracking progress against *corrective action commitments* should be aware of the possibility that a *problem* owner may behave in accordance with one or more of the *five Ds*.
- In an enterprise with a *EHS&Q-conscious work environment*, five D-behavior is rare.

Reports to Management
Performance Indicators

- *Quantitative performance indicators (PIs)*, *performance metrics*, and *performance measures* are terms that mean the same thing. The term PI will be used here.

- The next few pages provide examples of PI reports that should be available from the *CORECAT* tool. If the tool is incapable of providing such reports, the robustness of its design should be questioned.

- There should be an owner for each PI who is responsible for the following:

  - Plotting the measures for the PI over time;

  - Analyzing the measures for the PI over time, such as to identify adverse trends in the measures;

  - Establishing a goal for each PI—a measure that is desired to be consistently attained;

  - Establishing an action threshold for each PI—a point at which a *condition* is required to be entered into the *CORECAT* tool in order to start the process for determining the cause(s) for the performance degradation.

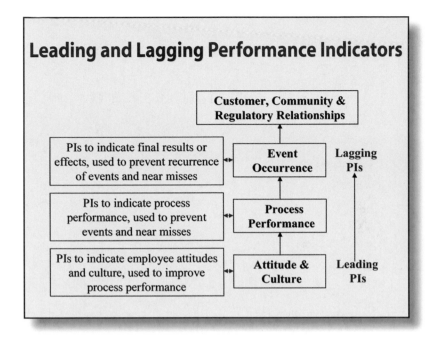

- Normally, the measures of a given *PI* are viewed over time with the purpose being to determine if and when there is a need for *intervention* in the given area of interest or process. If the *PI* doesn't provide data that would indicate the need for *intervention*, the PI is worthless. As noted on the previous page, the point of *intervention*, the action threshold, should be previously established.

- In economics there are *leading* and *lagging PIs*. For example, an upward trend in the number of applications for unemployment benefits is a *leading indicator* of the trend in the amount of disposable income or of the trend in the level of consumer spending. At some point, an upward trend in unemployment benefits applications, possibly in conjunction with other adverse trends, would indicate the need for *intervention* by the Fed.

- If the enterprise *CORECAT* tool is properly designed and implemented, as described on pages 231–236, it can produce *leading and lagging PI reports*.

- Trends in *PIs* measuring employee *attitudes* and *culture* are good indicators of the *quality of the design* and *quality of conformance to design*—quality of implementation of processes.

- Trends in *PIs* measuring process performance are good indicators of the potential for the occurrence of a *near miss* and *event*. If the trends in these *leading process PIs* are adverse, *intervention* with *corrective action* possibly can avoid a *near miss* or *event*.

- Absent leading process *PIs* or their analysis, the *near miss* or *event*, itself, will be the only indicator of the need for *corrective action*—obviously, an indicator that is too late to avoid the further *undesired effect* of customer, community and regulatory agency loss of confidence in the enterprise.

Question: What are the types of PIs that indicate the health status of employee *attitudes?*

Leading PIs—Attitudes and Culture

- Reportable industrial accidents
- Chemical exposures
- Foreign material intrusions
- Grievances
- Allegations to regulators
- Overtime
- Absenteeism
- Turn-over

- The key is to use the measures of the frequencies of these indicators in combination with one another. The result of an analysis of the frequencies for any one indicator, by itself, has less definitive meaning than the result of analyses of the frequencies for all of the indicators.

- For example, the meaning of an adverse trend in the rate of accidents in combination with adverse trends in the rates of overtime, absenteeism and turn-over is different than the meaning of an adverse trend in accidents while overtime, absenteeism and turn-over are stable or declining.

- The following few pages provide a sample of the types of reports with which to assess cultural state and process performance. These types of reports should be obtainable from a robustly designed *CORECAT* tool.

Leading PIs—Culture

REPORTING ORG	# OF PROBLEMS REPORTED	
	This Period	Cumulative – Most Recent N Periods
A	#	#
B	#	#
N	#	#
Total - All Orgs	#	#

- This slide shows the number of *problems* reported, sorted by reporting organization—for a given single period and for a given number of periods cumulatively.

- A *statistically significant difference* in the number of *problems* being reported by one or a few organizations compared to the number being reported by the large majority of organizations, could be explained by the fact that the under-reporting organization(s) performs simpler tasks or tasks for which *problems* would be below the reporting threshold, or it could be because of some other similar reasons. Otherwise, it could indicate the lack of a *questioning attitude* and *self-assessment* in the under-reporting organization(s).

- Based on benchmarking data, if there is a significant difference in the number of *problems* being reported by the enterprise as a whole, compared to the number being reported by similar enterprises, with the under-reporting enterprise having no apparent advantage in product quality, safety or cost, it's possible that the under-reporting enterprise might not be in a learning mode or may not be learning as rapidly as are the other enterprises.

Leading PIs—Culture (Cont'd)

ORG	# OF PROBLEMS FOR WHICH ORG IS RESP		# & % OF PROBLEMS FOR WHICH ORG IS RESPONSIBLE & WHICH ARE SELF-ID'd			
			# SELF-IDENTIFIED		% SELF-IDENTIFIED	
	This Period	Most Recent N Periods	This Period	Most Recent N Periods	This Period	Most Recent N Periods
A	7	25	2	5	29	20
B	#	#	#	#	#	#
N	#	#	#	#	#	#
Total	#	#	#	#	#	#

- This slide shows the number and percentage of *problems* reported that are self-identified by the organization which owns the *problem*, sorted by organization—for a given single period and for a given number of periods cumulatively.

- Of the seven *problems* reported in the current period for which Organization *A* was responsible, only two, or twenty-nine percent, were self-identified by *A*. Given the absence of any special difficulty with *problem* identification in the processes operated by *A* or in the product produced by *A*, the rate of *A's* self-identification of its own *problems* is unacceptable. On a cumulative basis, it's only twenty percent.

- Again, this would indicate a lack of *questioning attitude* and *self-assessment* or a lack of ability to properly design and assess its processes—or both.

Leading PIs—Culture (Cont'd)

ORGANIZATION	CORRECTIVE ACTION ASSIGNMENT STATUS	NUMBER OF CORRECTIVE ACTION ASSIGNMENTS
A	Open	#
	Open & Overdue	#
N	Open	#
	Open & Overdue	#
Total	Open	#
	Open & Overdue	#

- This slide shows the number of *corrective action* assignments, sorted by status, within each organization, as of the given date.

- In an enterprise with an *EHS&Q culture*, a high number of overdue *corrective actions* is intolerable. Possibly, any number of overdue *corrective actions* is intolerable.

Leading PIs—Culture (Cont'd)

ORG	CORRECTIVE ACTION ASSIGNMENT STATUS	NUMBER	CORRECTIVE ACTION ASSIGNMENT SIGNIFICANCE LEVEL	NUMBER
A	Open	15	SL 1	1
			SL 2	4
			SL 3	10
	Open & Overdue	5	SL 1	1
			SL 2	1
			SL 3	3
N	Open	#	SL 1	#
			SL 2	#
			SL 3	#
	Open & Overdue	#	SL 1	#
			SL 2	#
			SL 3	#

- This slide shows the number of *corrective action* assignments, sorted by *significance level* within each status, within each organization, as of the given date.

- In this case, Organization *A* is in big time trouble with the completion of five of its fifteen *corrective action* assignments overdue. This is especially troublesome because two of the overdue five are for *Significance Level 1* and *2 problems—problems* that would have high adverse impact were their effects to recur.

Leading PIs—Process Performance

TYPE OF THING	# OF PROBLEMS	
	This	Cumulative - Most
Hardware	Period	Recent 12 Periods
System A		
Subsystem 1		
Component a		
Problem Type 1	#	#
Problem Type 2	#	#
Problem Type n	#	#
Component a – Total	**#**	**#**
Component b	Ditto	
Component n	Ditto	
Subsystem 2	Ditto	
Subsystem n	Ditto	
System B	Ditto	
System N	Ditto	
All Systems	Ditto	

- This slide shows the number of occurrences of each *problem* type within each component of a subsystem for each subsystem of each system—system-by-system—for a given single period and for a given number of periods cumulatively.

- When the absolute measure of the frequency of a given *problem* is unacceptable or when the trend of the frequency is unacceptable, the *root cause(s)* of the *problem* should be identified and corrected.

- In the absence of this type of output report, how would one know of the unacceptable frequency or trend?

Leading PIs—Process Performance (Cont'd)

TYPE OF THING	# OF PROBLEMS	
	This	Cumulative - Most
Field Work Packages	**Period**	**Recent 12 Periods**
Electrical		
Work Orders		
Problem Type 1	#	#
Problem Type 2	#	#
Problem Type n	#	#
Work Orders- Total	#	#
Step-By-Step Field Work Plans	Ditto	
Permits	Ditto	
All Electrical Documents – Total	#	#
Instrumentation & Control	Ditto	
Mechanical	Ditto	
Civil - Structural	Ditto	
All Disciplines	Ditto	

- This slide shows the number of occurrences of each type of *problem* within each type of maintenance planning document and for all such documents—for a given single period and for a given number of periods cumulatively.

- The comments on the preceding page apply equally here, except that here the *problems* are with documents, not hardware items.

- As an aside, this presenter is troubled by the ways in which performance metrics are sometimes established and maintained. Sometimes, measurements are made for categories such as the following: *planned outage; planned maintenance; maintenance outage; forced outage; unforced outage.*

- First of all, except for *forced outage* versus *unforced outage*, these categories are not mutually exclusive, which can lead to confounding and misleading data.

- In addition, from the presenter's experience, it seems that for other than *forced outage*, the preceding categories are sometimes viewed as acceptable. Not so. For example, corrective maintenance may be necessary, but it's unacceptable regardless of whether it's performed as part of a forced outage, unforced outage or without an outage, and regardless of whether or not it's planned, as contrasted to performed as *emergent work. Preventive maintenance* is unacceptable if it could have been avoided by better design, regardless of whether it's performed in an outage or non-outage situation or regardless of whether or not it's planned.

- On the following page, there is a presentation of logical categories of maintenance (and modification) work for which measurements should be made.

- For each of the following categories, PIs should exist for man-hour expenditures, safety (in terms of the frequency of various types of accident rates) and quality (in terms of the frequency of *problems* of various *significance*):
  - Forced work
    - Outage work (1)
      - Emergent (2)—*Corrective maintenance* or *corrective modification* (3)
      - Emergent (2)—*Preventive maintenance* (4)
      - Planned—Non-emergency *corrective maintenance* or *corrective modification* (3)
      - Planned—Non-emergency *preventive maintenance* (4)
      - Planned—Refueling
    - Non-outage work
      - Emergent work (2)-*Corrective maintenance* or *corrective modification* (3)
      - Emergent work (2)—*Preventive maintenance* (4) (5)
      - Planned—*Corrective maintenance* or *corrective modification* (3)
      - Planned—*Preventive maintenance* (4)
  - Unforced work—*Modification* that is always a planned upgrade for technical or economic benefit (6)

Notes:

(1) The need for forced outage work, by definition, is undesirable, except possibly for the refueling or restocking portion of the work.

(2) The need for emergent work, not previously planned, by definition, is undesirable. Of course, by performing this work, the situation is improved. But it would be better if this work weren't needed to begin with.

(3) The need for *corrective maintenance* or *corrective modification*, by definition, is undesirable. Again, by performing this work, the situation is improved. But, again, it would be better if this work weren't needed to begin with.

(4) Excessive *preventive maintenance* due to poor design is undesirable.

(5) Any non-outage emergent work for *preventive maintenance* represents a breakdown of a systemic, *administrative preventive maintenance barrier*. The measure for this PI should be "0".

(6) Good.

Leading PIs—Process Performance (Cont'd)

ORG	ROOT CAUSE	# FOR WHICH ORG IS RESPONSIBLE			
		This Period		Cumulative - Most Recent 12 Periods	
		Apparent	Known	Apparent	Known
A	(1)	#	#	#	#
	(2)	#	#	#	#
	(n)	#	#	#	#
A - Total		#	#	#	#
B	(1)	#	#	#	#
	(2)	#	#	#	#
	(n)	#	#	#	#
B - Total		#	#	#	#
N		Ditto			
All Organizations		Ditto			

- This slide shows the number of occurrences of a given *root cause*, either apparent or known, sorted by organization responsible for the *root cause*—for a given single period and for a given number of periods cumulatively.

- Again, if the absolute frequency of a cause or the trend of its frequency is unacceptable, the cause should be corrected.

Leading PIs—Process Performance (Cont'd)

ROOT CAUSE	ORG	# FOR WHICH ORG IS RESPONSIBLE			
		This Period		Cumulative – Most Recent 12 Periods	
		Apparent	Known	Apparent	Known
(1)	A	#	#	#	#
	B	#	#	#	#
	N	#	#	#	#
Total: RC (1), All Orgs		#	#	#	#
(2)	A	#	#	#	#
	B	#	#	#	#
	N	#	#	#	#
Total: RC (2), All Orgs		#	#	#	#
(n),		Ditto			
Total: All RCs, All Orgs		#	#	#	#

• This slide shows the same information as in the previous slide except that the information is sorted in reverse.

Marguglio's Theorems and Principles

Theorems

- A person engaged in creating a characteristic of a process or hardware item may not be accountable for his or her knowledge-based or cognition-based error.
- The higher the organizational level at which a function is performed, proportionate to the opportunities, the greater the significance of error.
- The lesser the specificity of the procedure governing a process, the greater the potential for reflexive-based error.
- The lower the organizational level at which a function is performed, proportionate to the opportunities, the greater the percentage lapse-based error.

- People don't assign themselves to the jobs for which they lack knowledge or cognition.

- Generally, the higher in the enterprise at which a function is performed, the greater the function contributes to the design of the administrative and technical processes or systems. *Errors* in design cause continuously repetitive failure, whereas *errors* in *non-conformance* to design occur sporadically.

- In the absence of procedural specificity, decisions must be made in the field in response to an immediate stimuli. Decisions made reflexively are more frequently incorrect than decisions made with forethought.

- Generally, the lower the level in an enterprise at which a function is being performed, the higher the frequency of repetitive tasks. The higher the frequency of repetitive tasks, the greater the potential for *lapse-based error*.

Principles

- The information received, the way in which it is received, and the way in which it is processed, lead to one's beliefs, in turn to one's values and then to one's attitude—which significantly impact one's behavior.
- Behavior that is desired occurs more consistently when it is encouraged and reinforced by organizational leaders, peers and subordinates.
- Errors are made upstream of the point at which the last error was made.
- Errors are made in the design of administrative processes, technical / conversion processes, and physical hardware, and in the implementation of these designs.
- Errors are caused by the seven causal factors given in Marguglio's *Taxonomy of Human Error Causal Factors*.

Marguglio's Taxonomy of
Human Error Causal Factors

Knowledge-based – Error based on behavior:	Lacking receipt of the knowledge of the requirement, expectation or need
Cognition-based – Error based on behavior:	Lacking ability to process the knowledge (memorize, understand, apply, analyze, synthesize or evaluate the requirement, expectation or need)
Value-based or Belief-based – Error based on behavior:	Lacking acceptance of the requirement, expectation or need
Error-Inducing Condition / Error-Likely Situation-based – Error based on behavior:	Lacking recognition of the error-inducing condition / error-likely situation or lacking appropriate behavior to counteract the condition / situation
Reflexive-based / Reactive-based – Error based on behavior:	Lacking conservative judgment in making an immediate response to a stimulus
Skill based – Error based on behavior:	Lacking manual dexterity
Lapse-based – Error based on behavior:	Lacking attention

Principles (Cont'd)

- Errors can actuate hazards, which if not mitigated or ameliorated, result in undesired effects.
- Errors can occur at four levels:
  1. Failure to establish a barrier(s) to prevent initiating error;
  2. Initiating error;
  3. Failure to establish a barrier(s) to detect initiating error or the hazard activated by initiating error;
  4. Failure to establish a barrier(s) to mitigate /ameliorate the effect of a hazard.

Principles (Cont'd)

- Barriers can be established to prevent error, to detect the error or a hazard actuated by error, and to mitigate and ameliorate the undesired effects of the hazard.
- Error-inducing conditions and error-likely situations can be identified and corrected. Behaviors can be practiced to counteract the error-inducing conditions and error-likely situations that are not corrected.

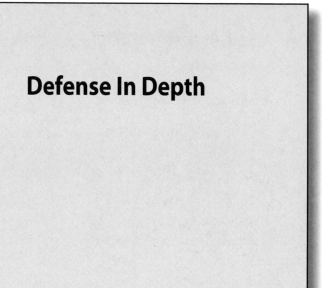

Self-Assessment Defense In Depth
The Six Levels of Opportunity

1. Personal self-assessment—i.e., person initially producing the characteristic of the process or hardware item
2. In-line reviewer assessment—e.g., peer reviewer, first-line supervisor, EHS&Q reviewer or inspector (e.g., Quality Control inspector)
3. Section or department organization self-assessment
4. Independent EHS&Q organization assessment (e.g., Quality Assurance audit / surveillance)
5. Facility independent committee assessment—e.g., Industrial Safety Committee
6. Facility independent organization assessment reporting to the facility's highest level executive

- When the individual creator or producer of a process or hardware item *characteristic* checks his or her own work it's the creator's / producer's personal *self-assessment*. This is the *first level of opportunity* at which to *detect error* and *correct its cause(s)*.

- When a peer reviewer checks the work of his or her co-worker, or a supervisor checks the work of his or her employee, it's a *self-assessment* by the organization in which they work—usually at the lowest organizational level. When the check is performed by the enterprise's *EHS&Q* or similar organization (e.g., Quality Assurance), it's a *self-assessment* for the enterprise as a whole. This is the *second level of opportunity* at which to *detect error* and *correct its cause(s)*.

- In some enterprises, a requirement exists for the sections or departments of the enterprise to perform *self-assessment* in accordance with a process that is very similar to the *quality audit* process, the major difference being that the section / department assessors are not *independent* of the function being assessed. This is the *third level of opportunity* at which to *detect error* and *correct its cause(s)*.

- Most enterprises have a centralized *EHS&Q* Department or Quality Assurance (QA), Safety and Environmental Assurance (EA) Departments. In many enterprises, the quality assurance (and safety) functions have been decentralized and made the responsibility of the so-called line organizations (e.g., Engineering, Manufacturing) with the centralized *EHS&Q*, QA or EA Departments retaining responsibility only for the performance of *audit* and *surveillance*. This is an enterprise level *self-assessment*. This is the *fourth level of opportunity* at which to *detect error* and *correct its cause(s)*.

- Many enterprises have specialized committees, consisting of internal subject matter experts, such as a Safety Committee, responsible for periodically assessing the state of affairs in the given area of interest. Such a committee might report to the chief executive. This, too, is an enterprise self-assessment. This is the fifth level of opportunity at which to detect error and correct its cause(s).

- Some enterprises also employ a specialized committee, consisting of external subject matter experts, meeting periodically, and reporting to the chief executive. For example, such a committee might be established to perform environmental oversight of the enterprise. Given that the committee reports to the chief executive, this is an enterprise self-assessment. This is the sixth level of opportunity at which to detect error and correct its cause(s).

- The functions of these internally and externally staffed committees are usually to assess the:

  - Reasonableness of goals;

  - Progress against goals;

  - Reasonableness of major changes to administrative, technical and hardware systems;

  - Effectiveness of root cause analysis for events and near misses;

  - Effectiveness of preventive corrective actions.

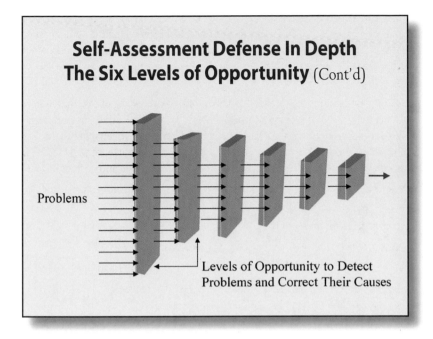

- The model in this slide indicates that there are *problems* and challenges to a worker who is creating the quality or safety *characteristic*. The worker may be of any type—a technician, engineer, administrator, accountant, etc. *Problems* are *detected* at each subsequent *level of opportunity*. Fewer and fewer *problems* should escape *detection* at each subsequent *level of opportunity*.

- In general, the later or higher the level at which a *problem* is *detected*, the greater the *undesired effect* of the *problem*.

- *Problems* that escape *detection* past the *sixth level of opportunity*, as indicated by the red arrow, will be found by or will be *self-revealing* to the customer, client, community or regulator, with the greatest adverse impact.

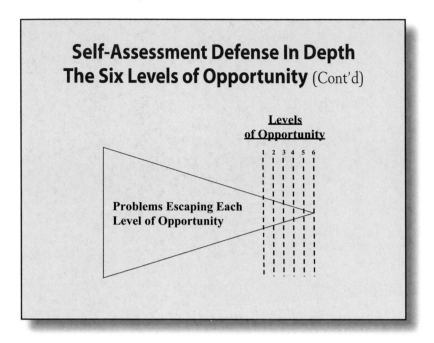

- The model in this slide illustrates the *80/20 rule*. An enterprise should *detect* eighty percent of its *problems* at the *first level of opportunity*. Of course, eighty percent is only an approximation. It could be as low as seventy percent or as high as ninety-five percent or any sharing combination in this range.

- A smaller percentage of *problems* should exist and be available for *detection* at each successive *level of opportunity*.

Marguglio's Four Fields of Focus for Human Error Prevention

Marguglio's **First Field of Focus for Human Error Prevention**

Concern:

Hazards

Response:

- Identify hazards using appropriate techniques for analyzing the design of administrative and technical processes and hardware.
- Eliminate hazards, if practical.
- In administrative and technical processes and hardware, create the three levels of barriers to human error.
- Implement techniques by which to increase the effectiveness of the four types of barriers at each of the three levels—administrative process, technical process, hardware and man.

Marguglio's **Second Field of Focus for Human Error Prevention**

Concern:
Error-inducing conditions and error-likely situations

Response:
- Recognize error-inducing conditions and error-likely situations.
- Eliminate these conditions and situations.
- Use behavioral tools and techniques by which to counteract error-inducing conditions and error-likely situations.

Marguglio's **Third Field of Focus for Human Error Prevention**

Concern:
Inappropriate risk-taking

Response:
- Recognize the thought processes and behaviors that lead to inappropriate risk-taking.
- Practice the thought processes and behaviors that lead to conservative decision-making.

Marguglio's **Fourth Field of Focus for Human Error Prevention**

Concern:

Recurrence of past errors

Response:

- Implement a field observation and coaching system.
- Implement a condition reporting, root cause analysis, corrective action, and performance and status measurement system.
- Identify and correct human error root and contributing causes of problems.

Thank you
and
best wishes for success
in
preventing human error,
detecting it
and
mitigating and ameliorating its effects.

BW (Ben) Marguglio

About the Author

BW (Ben) Marguglio

- Fifty-three years of experience with high technology enterprises. Currently as a management and technical consultant. Formerly a corporate executive, having served at executive and division director levels.

- Originator of the new and unique *taxonomy of human error causal factors*, and presenter of the acclaimed *Human Error Prevention Seminar*.

- Substantially experienced in management systems, tools and techniques, including those for project management; design engineering; procurement; fabrication, assembly, construction and installation; maintenance and operations—with safety, quality and environmental considerations.

- Management team leader for multi-million dollar design and construction projects and management team member for a multi-billion dollar design and construction project.

- Fellow of the American Society for Quality (ASQ) since 1974.

- Certified by ASQ as a Quality Engineer, Reliability Engineer, Quality Auditor, and Manager of Quality / Organizational Excellence.

- Author of over 100 technical and management papers and presentations and two books: *Quality Systems in the Nuclear Industry*; American Society for Testing and Materials; 680 pages; 1977 and *Environmental Management Systems*; Marcel Dekker, Inc; 208 pages; 1991.

- Former adjunct professor at the graduate level.

Bookinar™ Hard Copy Purchase Form

Please download this form and print or type the information for the shipping label at the bottom of the form.

The purchase price per Bookinar™ is as follows:

Quantity Of *Human Error Prevention* Bookinars™ to Be Purchased	Price Per Bookinar™ (U.S. Dollars) (Price Includes Shipping Within the U.S.A.)
1–9	$129.00
10–29	$119.00
30–49	$109.00
50–99	$99.00
100–299	$89.00
300–499	$79.00
500 and greater	$69.00

Add $10.00 USD per Bookinar™ for a shipment outside of the U.S.A.

Payment:

Please send to the address below this completed form and a check or US Postal Service money order made payable to **Bookinars™, Inc.** and made payable in **US dollars**. **Only checks and money orders in US dollars will be accepted. All sales are final. Please allow six weeks for delivery. Thank you for your purchase!**

Bookinars™, Inc.
P. O. Box 100
Cold Spring, NY, USA 10516-0100

Purchaser's e-mail address: _____

Below, please print or type the purchaser's name and address (shipping label):

_____

_____

_____

_____

_____

_____